FIELD OF FIRE

Jeff Connor has been involved in sports journalism for more than 40 years. A former production journalist on the *Daily Express, Daily Star, Daily Mail, Sun* and *Daily Mirror,* and sports editor of three regional newspapers, he is also the author of 12 books, including *Pointless: A Season with Britain's Worst Football Team* (Headline) and *The Lost Babes: Manchester United and the Forgotten Victims of Munich* (HarperSport). His first book was *Wide-Eyed and Legless: Inside the Tour de France,* which is now regarded as a cycling classic and was reprinted by Mainstream in 2011. He has worked as a freelancer in the USA (Orlando) and Ireland (Dublin), and has covered sporting events as diverse as the Tour de France, the Rugby League Challenge Cup final, the World Darts Championship, the World Athletics Championships, two British Lions tours and a Rugby World Cup.

FIELD OF FIRE

The Tour de France of '87 and the
Rise and Fall of ANC-Halfords

JEFF CONNOR

MAINSTREAM
PUBLISHING

EDINBURGH AND LONDON

First published in Great Britain in 2012 by
MAINSTREAM PUBLISHING COMPANY
(EDINBURGH) LTD
7 Albany Street
Edinburgh EH1 3UG

ISBN 9781845961701

A catalogue record for this book is available
from the British Library

Printed in Great Britain by
CPI Group (UK) Ltd, Croydon, CR0 4YY

1 3 5 7 9 10 8 6 4 2

ACKNOWLEDGEMENTS

I AM INDEBTED to all the riders and staff of ANC-Halfords and in particular Malcolm Elliott for his foreword, Geoff Shergold for his photographs and Adrian Timmis, Paul Watson, Graham Jones, Bernard Chesneau, Shane Sutton OBE, Steve Swart, Phil Griffiths and Mick Morrison for agreeing to talk about ANC, the Tour de France of '87 and the details of their lives since then.

It has taken me 25 years to say thank you to Peter Oakes and the late Lloyd Turner of the *Daily Star*, the men who sent me out there, so many, many thanks to both of them. Thanks, too, to Des Cahill of RTÉ, Ian Cleverly of *Rouleur* magazine, Ian Stafford of the *Mail on Sunday*, Mark Stanton (Stan) of Jenny Brown Associates, Bill Campbell and all his staff at Mainstream Publishing in Edinburgh. I am indebted to Claire Rose, Mainstream's senior editor.

Originally, *Field of Fire* was to have been published in 2007, but writing a book is hard work at the best of times and to have to begin life again – starting with what amounted to the mind of a two year old and attempting to take it from there – has been difficult. But it would have been impossible without the help of Lionel Birnie of Peloton Publishing, particularly his interviewing abilities; Tracey Lawson; my mother, Nancy, and my brother,

Richard; Frank Cassidy; Finlay Calder; Monica Dalton of the Stroke Association; Tessa Pemberton of the Association of Speech and Language Therapists; and the staff of Furness General Hospital.

CONTENTS

FOREWORD

by Malcolm Elliott

IT IS ALMOST 25 years since Jeff Connor and I met, just before the start of the 1987 Tour de France. We had been briefly introduced at the end of June, just before the flight from Heathrow to Berlin. The ANC-Halfords management had told the riders a journalist would be accompanying the team for 'several days' and that this journalist was working for the *Daily Star*, which, to put it mildly, took us by surprise. Pressmen do not usually travel with professional cycling teams. But by the time we landed in Berlin we had other things on our mind. We neither knew nor cared about peripheral issues like that, so enclosed were we in our little bubbles. Our thoughts and apprehensions were focused on the monumental task that lay ahead, and fortunately Jeff, initially at least, kept a low profile while we got on with our jobs.

However, I became more aware of Jeff's discreet presence as the race wore on, and we all began to open up to him. In situations like that, you do need someone to talk to from time to time and before long Jeff had also become caught up in the unfolding story of life on the Tour. I think somewhere along the way he, or his sports editor, had changed his plans, and he ended up staying for the whole race.

It was a tough Tour and gradually we lost rider after rider. There were changes among the staff, too, and suddenly Jeff became less a journalist than a part of the ANC team. This unique inside access enabled him to get to the innermost stories of the Tour and its characters, and he went on to produce a startlingly accurate book, which I found out later was his first attempt. *Wide-Eyed and Legless* appeared in 1988 and I know from experience an astonishing number of people have enjoyed *Wide-Eyed*. To this day it is still talked of within cycling in the highest of terms. Jeff and I continued to work together. In 1989, the mutual respect we had built up helped us to write *Sprinter*, an account of my life and career up to that point, and we have stayed in touch since.

Back then, however, when I and three other surviving riders of ANC finally rode up the Champs-Elysées, we had little idea where life would take us, what we had just accomplished and what it would come to mean to us. The intervening years have made me appreciate just what an achievement it was by all of us and how pivotal that moment was to be. It still has a bearing on my life today and it changed the course of my career. I think Jeff would say the same about the '87 Tour's effect on his life in journalism, for it was an unforgettable experience for both of us.

I am extremely glad that Jeff was there to capture his warts-and-all account of life on the 1987 Tour with ANC-Halfords, and 25 years on I wish him luck with this new book, *Field of Fire*.

Malcolm Elliott
Sheffield
September 2011

GLOSSARY

autobus On mountain stages sprinters and non-specialist climbers will work together (in the *autobus*) to help each other to finish inside the cut-off time.

bidon The plastic water bottle clipped to a rider's bike.

bonking or cracking Running out of strength or energy – or both.

broom wagon The vehicle that follows the race and picks up the stragglers.

commissaire Race judge.

criterium A short-distance race with multiple laps.

directeur sportif (**DS**) The man responsible for race strategies and who invariably drives one of two team cars.

domestique Rider there to supply the leader with refreshments, protect him in the pack and generally make his life easier.

Fred An unskilled rider.

green jersey Worn by the leading sprinter.

hors catégorie A climb so hard it is beyond category (the others being rated 1–4).

lanterne rouge The rider placed last.

Milk Race Tour of Britain, Britain's longest-established stage race.

musette Cotton tuck bag used to transfer food to riders on the move.

neutralised zone The few kilometres out of the stage town to the official start.

off the back Getting dropped.

peloton The main group in a road race.

polka-dot jersey Worn by the leading climber.

prime An intermediate sprint within a race, usually with a prize for the winner.

prologue Short individual time trial before the start of the Tour proper.

Radio Tour The short-wave race commentary.

ravitaillement The feed halfway through a stage.

rouleur A rider who performs well on flat roads.

route profile The cardboard cards carried in the jersey pockets which show villages, climbs, sprints, feed area and any difficulties en route.

soft break When riders posing no overall dangers to the leaders are allowed to break away during a stage.

soigneur Masseur who is also responsible for feeding and clothing riders.

time limit Competitors can be eliminated if outside the stage time limit, a percentage of the winner's time depending on the severity of the stage.

time trial A race against the clock, by an individual rider or by a team.

velodrome A cycling track.

white jersey Worn by the best rider under the age of 25.

yellow jersey Worn by the race leader and overall winner.

THE ANC-HALFORDS TEAM

Malcolm Elliott, team leader (English)
Bernard Chesneau, rider (French)
Guy Gallopin, rider (French)
Graham Jones, rider (English)
Kvetoslav Palov, rider (Czech)
Shane Sutton, rider (Australian)
Steve Swart, rider (New Zealander)
Paul Watson, rider (English)
Adrian Timmis, rider (English)
Tony Capper, owner and *directeur sportif* (English)
Edouard 'Ward' Woutters, *directeur sportif* (Belgian)
Phil Griffiths, *directeur sportif* (English)
Donald Fisher, press officer (French/Scottish)
Angus Fraser, *soigneur* (Scottish)
Roger Van der Vloet, *soigneur* (Belgian)
Friedhelm Steinborn, *soigneur* (German)
Sabino Pignatelli, *soigneur* (French)
Steve Snowling, chief mechanic (English)
Steve Taylor, mechanic (English)
Geoff Shergold, mechanic (English)
Nick Rawling, mechanic (English)
Jeff Connor, sports journalist and honorary ANC member
  (English)

INTRODUCTION

WHAT DID YOU do in the Tour, Daddy?

Not a great deal, looking back 25 years. I didn't have to do much at all. I stayed in 21 different hotels over 23 days and, with one notable exception, had a room to myself in each of them. After one week I still hadn't found the time to unpack a suitcase, all those rooms had been booked for me in advance and I didn't pay a Deutschmark or a franc for my food and drink; to this day I don't know who looked after the bills. Some say my employers paid, others claim a cycling team coughed up and there was once a wild rumour that I owe everything to the Société du Tour de France itself.

During the first two weeks, someone else did all the driving while I sat in the back seat and watched what I could of the race. Taking a tour of France for more than three weeks sounded like the best job ever invented, but early on I realised that this was no holiday and if I was going to follow the Tour de France I would not see much of the countryside. On flat stages, we were travelling too fast to take in the beauty of cities and towns like Angers, Poitiers and Toulouse. By the time we reached the Alps, it had been decided that I might have my uses after all and I was driving one of the team vehicles. I was too busy trying to keep a Citroën, or occasionally an Iveco van, in the right direction to admire the surrounding mountains. On the last day, in Paris, everyone was too exhausted to take in the pleasures of the French capital, but at least I could say that I had done my bit – that I did something in the Tour.

As for working for a living, I filed a story on a daily basis to a national red-top newspaper, but since I was a subeditor, and had not done any reporting for more than 20 years, many of the quotes were supplied – within ten minutes of the end of a stage – by the Tour de France *chefs de presse*. They may have been 'flash quotes' (i.e. quotes owing more to what a rider might have said than what a rider actually said) but sports news desks don't care about things like that. Working on sport is different from working on news, for no sportsman in the Tour de France is going to sue a writer for libel for saying he rode badly, even if he thought he rode well. If the worst came to the worst – and with so many journalists there, speaking around ten different languages – there was always the 'lost in translation' ploy. So I got away with that, too.

Everything else was written down with a biro on pieces of A4 paper and in the three weeks I spoke to maybe three 'fellow' journalists out of a total of close to a thousand. There were no esteemed colleagues for me, so helpful for every sportswriter working in a foreign land, in a foreign language and on a foreign sport.

Even in 1987, life had moved on in European journalism while the English tabloids managed to remain motionless. I was staggered to see an American journalist carting about one of the world's first mobiles (a massive Nokia Cityman, as I found out later) and one of the world's first laptops (apparently a Linus Write-Top). I had seen one of the world's first newspaper yuppies.

I knew nothing about cycling and cyclists, and it took me a week to realise that few bike riders, professional or amateur, used fixed gears. Riders could actually coast without having to turn their legs. So I have to admit now that most of the events of 1987 passed me by. I had turned 40 and had worked in journalism for 24 years, but in truth I was the archetypal innocent abroad.

However, it turned into an unforgettable month. There were occasional good times and plenty of bad times. On the first hot night on Berlin's Kurfürstendamm, a prostitute and her pimp – both with hairy German armpits – attempted to mug me, and on the same night a famous Scottish professional cyclist with a large nose suggested that I should 'fuck off'. Not to be left out, when I got in the way at the start of Stage 5 in Strasbourg, a French rider with floppy blond hair and spectacles suggested that I '*cassez-vous*'. Whether in English or French, this was a standard response to an approach from a journalist. I found out later that this was the famous – and now deceased – two-Tour champion Laurent Fignon. Before the start of Stage 12, from Brive to Bordeaux, prompted by another pathetic attempt at an interview, Irishman Sean Kelly went for the hat-trick. He didn't actually say anything – but he made sure I got the message.

In Poitiers, I was treated for third-degree sunburn and in the third week the brakes failed on the ancient Iveco I was driving down the mountains from La Plagne. I was accused of 'cooking the brakes' and told that 'you don't go down mountains with them full on', but one of the mechanics later told me the brakes had failed two days earlier when he was driving – along a flat section of road – through Grenoble. When I climbed aboard at La Plagne, no one had attempted to fix the problem. But I survived.

On the plus side, I did become addicted to Dijon mustard, Café de Colombia coffee, Cabernet Sauvignon wine and Peugeot cars, and I eventually wrote my first book about the Tour de France trials of a British cycling team called ANC-Halfords.

Those three weeks in the summer of 1987 may have been

the most memorable of my life, but it was my first, and last, Tour de France. There were a couple of years after '87 when I watched it every day, and for as long as I could, on television. I even bought myself a bike, but it only took me a few weeks to realise that I would never be a cyclist; car drivers anywhere near me brought out an aggression in me I could not control. I still thought it was the greatest sporting event ever invented and its sportsmen were the bravest anywhere, but I began to lose interest totally when Lance Armstrong arrived and, with his Motorola two-way radio, was able to discuss where, when and who to attack during a stage. The Tour had started sending me to sleep.

Before I flew out to Europe on 29 June 1987, my employers at the *Daily Star*, at the time Britain's newest red-top tabloid, had given me a briefing that lasted all of ten minutes. I was to chronicle the doings of the British team on a daily basis. No problem with that. The *Star* had also decided – and they were deadly serious about this at the time – that I would ride a stage in the Tour alongside the cream of the world's road racers. I was then, said the sports editor, 'to tell our expectant readers what it was like'. It sounded like a tough assignment, but I never batted an eyelid. If they had asked me to ride a killer whale, I'd have been first in the queue. Offered the possibility of three weeks away from the Manchester office and a spell in midsummer Europe, there was only one response: 'I can do that – gizza job.'

Eventually, I was to find that my level of naivety, and that of the *Star* staff, was almost matched by my professional cycling fellow travellers', along with that of their befuddled management.

Not a lot went right for ANC. One teenage French cycling fan had it about right as we drove past him on Stage 6, through the Vosges mountains: '*Les Anglais sont terminés!*' he yelled with a sort of ethereal joy. He was right; in the end we were all terminated.

The first three days in Berlin were a nightmare and I had begun to work out the best way of finding a flight home. On the fourth day, however, as we finally headed for France, it dawned on me that this was no ordinary assignment, that this was no ordinary cycling team and that I was in an extraordinarily privileged position for a journalist. I'd hated Berlin – its history, what appeared to be its troubled future and its heat – but I suddenly began to enjoy myself. The ANC staff, and some of the riders, began to talk to me. Like many sportsmen struggling in a foreign land, they needed a helping hand or at least someone happy to listen to their daily complaints. I suddenly became their best friend and I began to genuinely like and admire all the members of ANC. Like most British tabloid journalists, I had always considered that a sporting disaster could be better, in terms of selling newsprint, than a sporting success, but from then on I was on their side. Later, when I was 'part of the team', I even began to object to the arrival of other outsiders, like the ANC owner's family, the press officer's wife and dog, a number of sponsors from both ANC and Halfords who appeared from nowhere and even journalists who arrived from time to time to get a quote from 'my team'.

I also, surreptitiously, began to keep a diary. At the end of every day's racing (usually around eight to nine hours), I would hide away in whatever hotel room I was billeted to and record some of the extraordinary aspects of the ANC adventure. Some of the events and situations I found myself in seem stranger than fiction even now. The sight of an ANC truck on a motorway today still gives me a thrill of nostalgia. Those Tour diaries eventually begot the book *Wide-Eyed and Legless*, which was published in the summer of 1988 by the Sportspages imprint of Simon & Schuster. *Wide-Eyed* had been out of print for 23 years, Simon & Schuster having decided not to do a reprint, when it was republished in April 2011 by Mainstream of Edinburgh.

But 23 years is a long time. Simon & Schuster had given me a month to finish *Wide-Eyed* when I returned to Cumbria from France in August 1987, and I arrived home to discover that the house had been on fire, which certainly slowed me down. For various reasons, I also missed out quite a lot of detail and, rereading *Wide-Eyed and Legless* in 2011, I felt that, given more time, I could have done a better job (one good reason for never reading your own book). The ANC team leader, Malcolm Elliott, had become a good friend over the years (the look on his face when I proudly showed him my new £60 bike was unforgettable), but of the other riders and staff I knew nothing. I had written a book from inside my own little cocoon. I knew their abilities as sportsmen but little else. I knew their names, their ages and their places of birth, but it was much later that I discovered that in '87 half the team were married with children and had lives outside cycling.

I became determined to find out what had happened to all the main participants – if they would speak to me. As I discovered when I signed on for the first time to Facebook in an effort to find some old acquaintants, people you were friends with years ago often don't want to talk about the past. That was not the case with the riders and staff of ANC-Halfords, and many thanks go to them – again. This is not only a book about them but a book by them.

The result is *Field of Fire*, translated from the French Champ du Feu, the climb to a ski station in those Vosges mountains where things began to unravel for ANC. Our teenage French friend wasn't far wrong in his scornful verdict and never have the words 'field of fire' been more apposite.

Finally, this is a book about ANC-Halfords and the Tour de France of 1987, but some elements of *Field of Fire* include details of the role of a journalist and of the newspaper that originally decided to send him to Europe. I apologise to any reader who has problems with the tabloids.

Having watched on a daily basis the court cases involving some journalists and the battles between Rupert Murdoch and members of parliament, I take their point. However, times have changed for the worse among the red tops and all I can say is that to many people in the '80s a hacker was simply someone who was hopeless at golf and invariably appeared in the works of P.G. Wodehouse.

Jeff Connor
Lytham, Lancashire
February 2012

1

THE FRENCH CONNECTION

You're an errand boy, sent by grocery clerks, to collect a bill.

Kurtz, *Apocalypse Now*

THE LETTER WAS signed by Jacques Goddet, at the time the Mr Big of French sporting journalism and in his last year as the Tour's race director at large. The four staff members of Action Sports, the management company that looked after the ANC-Halfords cycling squad, had been working in the same back-street office in Stoke for just over a year when the postman arrived with the goodies. The two male members of staff were 'over the moon', in the words of one of them now. The two girl secretaries wondered if it meant they would get paid that week.

The Action Sports chairman, Tony Capper, was by then a tax exile on the Isle of Man. He could spend only an annual average of 91 days in the UK, he visited the mainland office rarely, and while there he ran the tightest of ships. Capper's modus operandi was unforgettable. When he first opened his office in Stoke he hired a number of attractive girls from a temp agency to run his little bureau. A lot of the time they were not paid, but at least he had found the cash for some Action Sports business cards. His said 'Tony Capper, Chairman'. Another said 'Mick Morrison, Marketing Manager'.

'The thing was, he wouldn't pay the temp bill so every so often all the girls would go back and he'd go to another temp agency and get a new lot,' says Morrison. 'It was the same with all the office equipment. He had it on lease, but he didn't pay the bills. He'd get vehicles on test and he'd park them outside the office so it looked like we had this beautiful fleet of vans. He barely had a penny to his name, but he had a company, an HQ, all these girls in the office, vans, computers and furniture.'

As it happened the staff – and all the vans and furniture – had another two months in the summer of 1987 before the bailiffs marched in. Before then, Capper was going to send a British team to the Tour de France, and whether this team would live or die was irrelevant to Goddet once they had paid him their £37,000 joining fee. The riders of teams, the names of teams and the sponsors of teams changed by the year, and Goddet knew that. For now, the 81-year-old Frenchman, educated in a private school near Oxford and claiming a deep love of England and the English, was delighted 'to invite the team of ANC-Halfords to take part in the Tour de France of 1987'.

Why ANC? There were better and more established cycling teams in Europe. No one from Goddet downwards has been prepared to offer an explanation, except that they had been chosen as a wild card. But Goddet and the Société du Tour de France had always been quite clever in their choice of stages and teams: 1987 happened to be the 20th anniversary of the death of the British rider Tommy Simpson on the vicious climb up Mont Ventoux in the south of France, and the Tour of '87 happened to include Mont Ventoux. A famous posed photograph, taken just before the start of the stage the day after Simpson's death on 13 July 1967, shows the devastated teammates of the Englishman alongside the yellow jersey holder . . . along with a suitably sombre Goddet and his fellow Tour organiser Félix Lévitan. The Société and Goddet had always liked their little dramas, with stages, towns and cities regarded by them as others look on wedding anniversaries. Ventoux and Simpson apart, the '87 Tour also coincided with the 750th birthday of Berlin – hence the prologue and the first two stages there.

The city – no longer divided – will be hosting the Tour again in 2017 . . . for the first time in 30 years.

'We got the news in late May or early June in '87,' says Phil Griffiths, who at the time was working with ANC, among other companies. 'We got the invitation and we had the £37,000 to pay and a contract to sign. No one was willing to sign it and send off the cheque. Our hands were shaking. We had the money in the bank and not many, if any, British teams would have had that sort of money just sitting in the bank, but it was a few days before we took the leap and I eventually signed it, wrote the cheque and sent it off. Hey presto, we're in the Tour.'

The celebrations began at once in the Action Sports office, until it occurred to someone that they should tell their riders that nine of them would soon be taking part in the world's greatest cycling event, that they would be leaving from Heathrow for West Berlin on 29 June and that they would be away for up to 27 days. Then someone else had a brainwave: most of the boys were appearing on *Blue Peter* on the BBC the same day and this was the best timing imaginable. It could be useful publicity for ANC-Halfords, Action Sports and the city of Stoke-on-Trent itself. It was also a coup for the BBC and *Blue Peter*. The riders saw it differently, as Paul Watson, one of the chosen ones, recalls: 'We were in the *Blue Peter* studio, doing a piece on the show, when Caron Keating, the presenter, came running in and said, "You're in, you're in!" And we just put our heads in our hands. She couldn't understand it. She was expecting we'd be "Wahey, we've just won the lottery", but we were thinking, "Oh, fuck."'

* * *

The Action Sports locals – Capper, Griffiths and Morrison among them – would argue with much of this, but did you ever visit Stoke-on-Trent in the mid-'80s? The city was blackened by the dust from factory chimneys and surrounded by coal pits, the remains of steelworks and terraced houses that all looked the same. To most outsiders the city was famous for Wedgwood and Royal Doulton potteries – before they moved to China and Indonesia – the Michelin tyre factory, a football club with players that had once included Sir Stanley Matthews and Gordon Banks and a memorable nightclub called Jollies, once home of the World Darts Championship. For a short time, between 1985 and 1987, the town was also recognised as the residence of a professional cycling team that regularly cleaned up around the British circuits, made its mark in Europe and – famously or infamously, whichever way you want to see it – took part in the Tour de France. The staff and riders who between them managed to get themselves into the race certainly knew where they came from and where they were going to, but little else.

Griffiths, a former amateur rider good enough to compete in an Olympics and a Commonwealth Games, is the only person I have ever met who instead of greeting telephone callers with 'hello' prefers a burst of laughter. He has always reminded me of the US golfer Phil Mickelson, a big man with an aw-shucks smile, even when things were not going too well. Unlike Mickelson, Griffiths could be frighteningly indiscreet and was known as a man happy to call a spade a spade. After the Milk Race of 1987, some of the ANC riders, led by Watson and the talented Liverpudlian Joey McLoughlin, had basically mutinied, producing a petition in an effort to oust Griffiths as team manager. 'I told them to destroy it,' says Malcolm Elliott, 'and that appeared to be the end of that.'

With his staccato speech, Griffiths is a gifted salesman (well past his first million by now and, it is said, with as many super-cars as Nick Mason of Pink Floyd). He had worked for British Telecom for 17 years when I met him in Stoke en route to Berlin and the start of the Tour.

'I got a silver medal in the Commonwealths in 1974. So when BT asked what I was doing next, I would say, "Well, I'm training for Montreal." And by the time you'd done an Olympics, you had credibility, so you could say you were training for Moscow. But by the early 1980s, my time was running out. I said I was training for Los Angeles, but that was stretching it a bit far. I never worked for BT in the conventional sense. I started with them in 1969, but I was never, ever going to be a BT employee for the rest of my life. I still get a pension from it today, which went on a Porsche for my 60th – I'm into cars – and it was also a nice down payment on a GT3.'

By 1986, Griffiths was a one-man band importing Swiss Assos cycling clothing to the UK, was still being paid as a telephone engineer and was managing the ANC-Halfords cycling team, in nomenclature a mixture of Associated National Couriers and Halfords, the UK's leading retailer of car parts and bicycles. He had met Tony Capper, who had just started an implausible new career as a cycling team manager, at Aintree in 1985; both were there for the classic Eddie Soens Memorial race.

'I knew Micky Morrison, who was a local rider in Stoke, and he introduced me,' says Griffiths. 'Capper asked me what was going to happen in the Soens race. Dudley Hayton, who was in his 30s at the time, was in the break and Phil Thomas of ANC was in the bunch. I accurately predicted that Hayton would come fifth out of five in the break and that Thomas would win the bunch sprint. I pointed out that Capper's team tactics were not the best and he was amazed that I got it spot-on. A few months later, ANC had been let down by someone for the Sealink International and I got a call from Capper asking if I'd take the team. Even with good riders like Joey McLoughlin and

Phil Thomas, ANC weren't winning too much, but we immediately went out and won two stages, one for Thomas and one for McLoughlin, and McLoughlin won overall.

'I said to Tony, "Look, let's give the riders two-year contracts so we can avoid the Aintree issue," which was that people like Dudley were having to race for their crust instead of being able to take a team role and help the team to win. So, instead of them being a collection of individuals in the same jersey, we tried to make them a team. I'd always been a team player – I was brought up on team sports – so I could see the strength of it.'

Those meeting Capper for the first time tended to decide, as Griffiths did, that he was what the sociologist Max Weber defined as a 'charismatic authority figure' and what others would describe as 'a good person, but one with uncouth manners and dress'.

'Yeah, I thought Capper was a rough diamond,' says Griffiths. 'He couldn't walk past a fruit machine without stopping and having a little spin, and he couldn't wear a tie. Whatever he'd been in life, he had a weakness for things. But he had an energy, an intoxicating quality, which attracted people. You were drawn to him. People were either sucked in by the energy or they weren't.'

Capper had no ambitions to send an ANC team to the Tour de France in 1985 or '86. It was an event he hadn't even seen. But, says Griffiths, Capper 'had these massive targets, like, "Could we win the Milk Race?" People need to realise it was a step-by-step progression. I don't know if Capper knew what the Tour was about in 1985, but this guy learned quickly. If he'd known what the Tour was in '85, we'd have gone in '86.

'He was something special. He set up a company that is very, very successful. He was a taxi driver who in the end was delivering more parcels than he was people, and he was a team player like me. When he was running his taxi company, he got all these other Stoke taxi drivers to come under the banner of City Radio Cabs so they were a stronger business. They had a centralised number, they never needed to turn down a job and they shared it. So when he did the parcel business, he set it up as a franchise system. He got all these family companies to give up their name to come under the same umbrella. He was an amazing guy with the other franchisees. He was a people person. He talked to people individually and tried to get inside your mind and find out what made you work and what you were good at.

'And he could draw you in. If he took a passion, he'd put some money in. Straight away, Joey and Phil got a nice car each and the team car was a Granada Ghia 2.8, the best you could get. We had a small bus, when no other team had one at all. From the start, there was some vision about him and there was some glitz to make you want to be part of it.

'Capper was talking to a lot of people all the time, people like Mick Bennett and Alan Rushton, the men running the TV criteriums, and there was a lot on offer. It was perfect timing for someone to be coming in, because the TV was very attractive to Capper. He was running his franchise and by then that was a nationwide business, and he knew the publicity would be good for ANC.'

The problem, says Griffiths, was that Capper had a yearly budget from the franchisees of ANC, and he tended to spend it. 'By the middle of 1985, he'd spent the lot. He wasn't slow in spending money. He'd have to go to his board for more – and *then* he'd spend that. He didn't budget or plan and meter it out. He would win the races, collect the cuttings and say to the board of franchisees, "What do you think of that then, lads?" and they'd double the money available for the team. This happened in '85, '86 and '87. This was how he operated. He thought, if we deliver, we deserve more money. "Let's win the races and then get more money," he would say. In 1987, he needed a big company from British industry to come in.

'Three years before that, I'd started importing Assos.

The team was in Assos kit for 1986 and 1987, and I was employing people to sell Assos for me. Capper would ask me how my business was going and what my turnover was. He recognised that this clothing was something special, and he said to me, "In four years' time, you'll do your first million-pound year in terms of sales." He said I'd be selling millions of it in the future. To me, it was such a silly thing to say, a silly statement to make, but I've never forgotten him saying that, and today my company sells £10 million worth. I've stuck with it.'

Griffiths and Capper, both capable of being swept away by enthusiasm for almost anything, got on well together from the start. Capper was still living in Stoke when they met and Griffiths went to his house most days to plan the race programme and how to look after the staff. 'I wasn't stepping into an existing job, I was building a job. And he took ANC-Halfords on personally. To him, it was his team, and he loved it. I even had a photo of Malcolm Elliott and Joey in Assos winter jackets, alongside Tony's shotguns and an ANC Land Rover. The team was his passion.

'You go into great depth with every race and every event. After Joey won the Milk Race in 1986, Capper said to me, "Right, take me to *the* stage of the Tour de France." He didn't say, "Let's go to Dunkirk to watch the Tour," or whatever, he wanted to go to *the* stage. I didn't need to look at a map to find the right one. I said, "Tony, there's only one stage. It's Alpe d'Huez."'

Griffiths could hardly have picked a better stage or a better year. The mountain, located at 1,869 metres in the Oisan Alps, with its famous 21 hairpin bends and an average gradient of 8 per cent, had been the most dramatic stage in the Tour since 1952, when it was won by the legendary Italian Fausto Coppi. That year, Jacques Goddet had signed a contract worth the equivalent of 3,250 euros to include the race in the Tour. Coppi's win turned the Alpe into an instant legend, and one French journalist has even written a book about the climb (*The Tour Is Won on the Alpe* by Jean-Paul Vespini). Every rider wanted to win an Alpe d'Huez stage and every fan wanted to watch it, Capper soon among them. Griffiths didn't even need to sell it to him; driving up the mountain to find the best views, they were just in time to see Californian Greg LeMond striding up the hairpins with five-time winner Bernard Hinault hot on his heels. Griffiths couldn't have done better if he had taken Capper to see Sugar Ray Leonard taking on Marvin Hagler or Argentina beating Germany in the football World Cup.

And it turned out Griffiths had found a Stoke version of Mr Toad of Toad Hall, the rich village squire able to indulge his impulses. Toad moved from punting to houseboating to hot-air ballooning to cars all within a couple of years; Capper of Stoke Hall had found his own new plaything. Griffiths says: 'Capper was an excitable chap and his biggest problem – well, limiting factor – was the amount of funds he could pull in. I have said that if Tony had had more money, he'd have been dangerous! But it wasn't his money. It was a franchised operation, so he couldn't just spend whatever he wanted on the team and on getting to the Tour. But I knew the atmosphere and crowds of Alpe d'Huez would impress him. Well, it totally blew his mind, and he said, "We'll come back next year." He gave himself 12 months to get the team to the Tour.

'We were doing bigger races. Joey was fourth at the Amstel Gold, Holland's top race, in 1986 and people were starting to listen to us. Capper was a salesman and he would be on the phone while I looked after the race side. Capper and Micky were speaking to sponsors, bringing people in. The two of them were fuelling each other. Then I came along and it was an amazing partnership, it really was.

'We got a letter saying they were interested in having a British team in the Tour. They said they'd seen our results, but we would have to go to France and do some of the events there.'

The Tour wanted ANC to put a team in for Bordeaux–Paris – the 600-km epic part-motor-paced one-day race – and for classics like the Midi Libre and the Dauphiné. Capper and Griffiths also cleverly found a token Frenchman or two to ride with ANC, for the sake of Goddet and his fellow directors.

'All those races,' says Griffiths. 'But we were thinking, "What the hell has Bordeaux–Paris got to do with the Tour?" Fortunately, we had a guy [Guy Gallopin] who was rock solid, who wanted to win Bordeaux–Paris. But we also had to send Nigel Bloor, who had not been able to do the preparation for it. He'd not done the races, not done the kilometres behind the motorbike. But we had Guy, who could have won the Bordeaux–Paris [he was second in 1986 and third in 1987], and we had other guys who were just there so we had a presence.'

As suggested by Goddet, ANC also went to the multi-stage Midi Libre, where they suddenly hit pay-dirt. Adrian Timmis, a desperately shy 23 year old from Stoke, was to shock European cycling and even his own teammates. Malcolm Elliott, by then the ANC superstar, remembers thinking, 'Hey, little Adrian's won a stage. How did he manage that?'

'Adrian was a great rider, he really was,' says Paul Watson. 'He was phenomenal. It'd be lined out and we'd be in the gutter, and I'd look up to the front thinking, "Who the hell is on the front setting this pace?" and it'd be little Adrian. I think if people like Adrian, Malc, Joey and me were coming through today, looking at how the races and the teams everywhere have changed, it would be a lot different.'

Timmis recalls: 'I heard some time after the Milk Race that I would be going on the Tour, and me winning a stage at Midi Libre may well have been the final confirmation and one of the reasons we got the ride. The plan was to aim for the Tour, but it was a bit last-minute. It wasn't as if we knew in December that we were doing it and we could prepare for it. But we had to do as many races as we could to get selected. We did a season half at home, half in Europe. At Étoile de Bessèges, the early-season stage race in the south of France, I got in the break on the first day and I was second overall going into the last day, but I cramped up and lost that. I had had a bit of a knee problem in the winter and had missed a bit of training. We did Paris–Nice, too, so we were progressing towards the Tour, but I don't think anyone really thought we'd get in. Not that year. I think the riders were taking each race and learning as they went along, maybe thinking that 1988 might be the best time to go to the Tour.

'We did the Belgian and Dutch classics – Gent–Wevelgem, Flèche Wallonne and Amstel Gold – so we were racing with the top teams. But we'd done a fair bit in 1986, too. My first race for ANC was the Ruta del Sol in the south of Spain. We won the Milk Race in 1986 with Joey, and then with Malcolm in 1987. In 1986, I missed a bit of the summer with tonsillitis, then I trained like mad for the Nissan Classic in Ireland and got a good result, fifth. So I was coming into 1987 feeling good. I was getting stronger and stronger.

'I've got a picture on the wall here of my win in the Midi Libre, ahead of the top ten riders. It was a select group of maybe 20 riders that got away over some small mountains into Béziers. Luc Leblanc, who was world champion in 1994, attacked with three kilometres to go. We hit Béziers and there was a ramp up into the town. I had a bit of cramp, but it went away. Leblanc was just hanging off the front there and I saw the opportunity to attack with a kilometre to go. The finish was down a boulevard and then up the other side, and I caught Leblanc at the turn and got to the line.

'I remember slapping someone's hand as I crossed the line, a high five, and, yeah, it was a big win. Second was Leblanc. Claude Criquielion, a former world champion, and Sean Kelly were in the group. I knew it was a big win. Phil Griffiths was really happy. He was managing the team really well. If you were going well, you had a chance to do what you could. I had spent the Milk Race working for Malc, but in the Midi Libre I could do something for myself.

'It wasn't like, "Right, Adrian, you're the leader, you'd better get up there." There was no pressure or anything, but we were encouraged to get stuck in and have a go. I was the only ANC rider to make it over the climbs in the lead group that day, so I saw my chance and took it. My time had come. It was what I'd been working for. I had a second place at Midi Libre, too. I attacked on a descent and got away with a Belgian, Luc Roosen, and we went away. So my confidence was full-on heading to the Tour.'

Of the nine ANC riders chosen for the Tour, only the Frenchman Gallopin and the Englishman Graham Jones knew what to expect. Timmis hadn't even seen a map of the Tour. He says: 'I hadn't even been out there. I knew nothing other than what I'd read in cycling magazines. I'd seen the odd bit of the mountains on the TV. That was it, really. Midi Libre is a hilly race, but it's not in the high mountains, it's in the foothills. It's a different story from the Alps, it really is. People said I was a climber, but I wasn't used to climbing for 45 minutes to an hour at a time, which was what you needed for the likes of Alpe d'Huez and Ventoux.'

Griffiths says: 'In the Midi Libre, Adrian had passed Luc Leblanc in the final kilometre like he was standing still, and if you looked at Malc, Adrian and Paul Watson's results, you could say, "Yeah, we were as good as the rest." Maybe we were naive in certain areas, but that team today would ride unbelievably well on the more level playing field that we have now. I mean, you have to bring drugs into the discussion, sadly, and we were riding on bread and water.

'Anyone who thinks we just turned up doesn't know

what they're talking about. There's so much distortion. Recently, a film producer phoned us up and he said, "I'd like to congratulate you on your efforts in the 1987 Tour. We'd like to make a film. To turn up in Paris, borrow bicycles, start the Tour with the money in your pockets and then have four riders finish is absolutely unbelievable."

'I said, "What do you mean, turn up and borrow bikes?" Borrow bikes? That's the biggest distortion ever. We had the best kit available. We were sponsored by Campagnolo, by Wolber and by Peugeot. We had the finest we could find.'

Money, says Griffiths, was not a problem for ANC when they first applied for the Tour. 'It was strong enough riders we needed. That was where the shortcomings were. We did want a big British presence in the team and we regarded ourselves as British – there was a Union Jack on the jersey, the colours were red, white and blue – but the difficulty was finding British riders who were ready. Then there were the preparation races, Paris–Nice and the rest. The idea was to be building up races, not wearing people down. We'd come from England, racing a fairly light programme compared with what the top riders heading to the Tour would do, but then everyone had to ride everything all of a sudden, because we were trying to get this invite. We needed to go to those races, but it was a catch-22. We weren't trying to wear people out, but they had to do those races and that made us vulnerable.'

Griffiths also spotted problems with Capper even before the 1987 Tour. 'We turned up at Paris–Nice in March and I saw our mechanic, a French guy who had worked the Tour of the Mediterranean the previous month and was supposed to be with us for the race. But he was immaculate in his Sunday-best suit, and I thought, "Uh-oh, what's going on here?" He came over to Capper and said, "You didn't pay me for last month." Capper said, "No problem," and paid him the cash immediately. And the guy said,

"Thank you very much. Now I go home." And this was our mechanic for Paris–Nice.

'But that was what we were dealing with. Capper never saw it as a problem that he had to be asked to pay people. He thought once a guy had been paid he'd get back to work. But not this time. So I was driving the team car all day, trying to manage the team and washing the bikes at night, until I could get my friend Phil Corley, a former rider – he now owns a bike shop in Milton Keynes – to come out and take over as mechanic for the rest of the race. Fortunately, we had already prepped the bikes, glued on the tyres, before we went to France. That was Capper's problem. He paid, but he was trying to look after his cash flow.

'His ways did make my job a lot harder at times. I really was piggy-in-the-middle, with the riders on one side and Capper on the other. You had a team manager, me, taking riders on, then Capper signing people, too. He'd sign someone and then three days later say, "Shit, I didn't realise he was that old." He was a dabbler. He loved playing, but what could you do? He was the money man, he was buying and selling. But as the game got more serious, the stress was on me. I was having big trouble with Capper. But he taught me something. He recognised people's strengths, and he took notice of those far more than their weaknesses. He'd say, "You see that guy over there? That is the best diesel fitter in the Potteries, but don't expect him to turn up at eight o'clock in the morning."

'He had a mate called Donald Fisher who went on the Tour as Capper's press officer. He lived in Paris and understood how big the Tour was. Fisher and Capper wanted to go Europe-wide. The hub of ANC was Stoke-on-Trent, but they wanted to go into Europe and have a hub in Luxembourg, which appealed because it was a tax haven. He wanted to take Italian freight, French, Spanish, German, Austrian, Scandinavian – this was before the Euro – and

Capper and Fisher were doing feasibility studies on all this. But that wasn't good enough for them and one day Fisher said, "We need to *win* the Tour de France.'"

Capper knew that ANC were not going to win it, or even a stage, on the strength of his British cyclists, and he went looking elsewhere. There were meetings with superstars such as the Irishmen Sean Kelly and Stephen Roche and the Australian Phil Anderson.

'We met Anderson at the Holiday Inn in Ghent and we talked,' says Griffiths. 'I am not knocking them, but you couldn't have expected Paul Watson or even Malcolm Elliott to have realised what the longer-term plan was, because they were just there to ride their bikes. You had to be with Micky, Tony or myself to see the work that was going into building it. And bear in mind that at the time Capper was being offered millions for his company. He said, "You have to work out whether you want to be the sole owner or whether you want to have a slice of a much bigger cake." He issued shares and took in money to grow the business. But he was getting these offers for ANC, which was this young, trendy, fresh company that was growing at such a huge rate. Capper didn't want small. He wanted to go bigger and bigger. He loved the numbers involved and he loved the size and scale, and the cycling team was part of a bigger plan to make ANC a Europe-wide business.

'Capper found pro cycling fascinating because he couldn't believe that even the best riders did not have long-term contracts. So he thought, "Well, if we have the money, we can get whoever we want." He loved the fact he could go up to Sean Kelly and have a chat and then say, "How much do you want for next year?" I am sure Capper's frustration was that he had this vision and he knew he could get the riders – but could he get the money?

'Right from the start, we were getting interest. We had a major sports promotion company come to us and say that a big car company wanted to sponsor the team but that we needed to win the Tour de France. I was saying, "Well, that's the easy bit," because if you had the money, you could hire Stephen Roche or whoever you needed. Good riders were looking at us, casing us, interested to see what we were up to. We had a lot of top riders tap on the team car window during races to stop and have a chat.

'When we first turned up, people did think, "Who the fuck are these?" but we established ourselves quickly. In the Tour of the Mediterranean, Paul Watson punctured and we couldn't get up to him because the other cars were in the way. Roger Legeay, a respected French former pro, was driving and we just cut across him and took the front wing mirror off his car. We didn't have any problems after that – people had to take ANC seriously.'

Capper's Stoke-on-Trent office, at Uttoxeter Road, Longton, was run by Mick Morrison, a former professional cyclist who, according to many, should have been a professional comedian. 'Capper appeared on the scene in 1984, when he met Micky,' says Malcolm Elliott. 'Micky was a likeable and humorous chatterbox, and Capper had apparently taken him on one side, as was his wont, and said something like: "Son, I can make you a star." Micky was hilarious. In 1986, we were out training, longish rides, for the Ruta del Sol in Spain in February and Micky, who was by then part-time and near the end of his career, got dropped. He arrived back three-quarters of an hour after us and we had all showered and changed when he staggered in, hair all over the place, tongue on the floor and eyes on stalks. "What a stupid training ride," he said. "One in four for fifty miles. I'm not doing that again, I'm finished." And he was. He used to keep us in stitches.'

Morrison may have been a comedian then, but now he is a semi-pro magician – and he is quite serious about this – in Turkey. He says: 'At ANC in Stoke, there was a guy called Ray Barnett that Capper appointed as marketing director, and managing director, too! There was a girl called Julie Howells, who was great. Tony, of course, was chairman. I was still getting paid by ANC but working for Action Sports. Tony had started up the parcel company on a franchise basis, but before that he'd been a policeman and he got fired. Rumour has it, unconfirmed by Capper, that he was using the police van at weekends to go market trading, selling jackets and jeans, and he got caught. Then he ran a taxi firm in Stoke. He started up ANC with a van. He realised that if he got a delivery in Birmingham, by the time he'd paid his petrol and the time, there wasn't very much money in it. There had to be a better way, so he'd arrange with a Birmingham courier firm to meet halfway. And if they had a parcel for Stoke or nearby, he'd take that. That's basically how it started. It was revolutionary at the time. This lad had no money, but he had a vision.

'Capper needed premises for his hub. He'd made an agreement and signed, but one day he said, "Can I borrow the keys so I can go in and measure up for furniture?" Well, he went and changed all the locks and used squatters' rights for about a year so he didn't have to pay any rent. He didn't even have the deposit for the vehicles he needed. A mate assisted him in getting a fleet of vans. So he was starting it all off on a wing and a prayer.'

Morrison was born in December 1954 in Kaduna, Nigeria, where his father worked for the Government Ground Nut Scheme before the family moved to Stone, Staffordshire. He was shortlisted for the 1980 Olympics in Moscow but didn't make the cut. His Olympic dream was over, but by then he had other things on his mind: 'I just wanted to turn professional. My father had worked for a big engineering company and knew the chairman, a man called Michael Howe. When he retired, he set up a little company called Moducel, which did air-conditioning units for supermarkets like Sainsbury's. His business partner was John Wilshaw. When my father died, Michael Howe contacted me. I'd been thinking about sponsorship and so I suggested that I could be a rep on the road for Moducel.

'I got that sponsorship through a family connection and it was really like a gift. But John Wilshaw saw the potential. I was racing and getting into *Cycling Weekly*, and the thing about cycling was you could name your team after the sponsor, which is pretty much unique in sport. Perhaps Formula One is the only other one. I was pretty good at getting my name about, but I didn't just want to get the firm's name in the cycling magazines, so I contacted the Staffordshire papers and got on BBC radio talking about cycling. This was the early 1980s and cycling was just starting to take off.

'Wilshaw got some better riders in. At first, it was just me, but we got Dudley Hayton, Phil Corley and Steve Joughin. We were getting more exposure and more riders, but my salary wasn't getting any bigger. I was like a one-man band banging a dozen drums. I was getting the coverage and was helping to grow the team, but there was little in the way of money to show for it. A friend of mine had a PR company and I used to keep all the cuttings, and it dawned on me that the coverage I was generating was worth more. I was getting £2,000 and my neighbour next door, who was a plumber, was getting £9,000.

'I thought, "Hang on a moment." When I went to get a mortgage, the bank manager asked me what I did for a living and I puffed my chest out and said I was a professional cyclist, a sportsman. The guy asked me how much I was on and I said, "£2,000." He said, "A month?" I said, "No, a year." I was declined. I loved my sport, but it wasn't a real living.'

Morrison came up with a plan to get three sponsors to contribute £3,000 worth each. Peugeot agreed to supply bikes, and Bean Bag, the clothing company, sorted out the cycling kit. He needed a third. 'I went to see a friend of mine who ran a Ford dealership, the Chatfields garage, and I asked if I could do a presentation to see if they'd sponsor me. He said he could do better than that. That was when I came across Capper.'

Their first meeting was set up for Capper's office in late 1983. 'He had said, "That guy's a good lad and he's always getting in the papers. Tell him to come and see me." Off I go, with a little portable TV set with a video player in it, and press cuttings with all the pictures of me. The key point was that this team could be named after your business. I had it all planned, and what I was going to say. I put the video on and after a couple of minutes he said, "Right, switch that off." He flicked through the book, but he didn't seem interested. I thought, "I've blown it."

'Then he said, "How much do you want?"

'"Well, can I tell you a bit more about the sport?"

'"No, not really. Just tell me what you want."

'"Well, don't you want to know more about it?"

'"No. You're a people person and I want to sponsor you."

'I explained I wanted three sponsors to each put in £3,000. He said, "I'll give you £7,000 as your main sponsor and I'll give you a car. We'll come up with a bonus system, £100 for a win, £75 for second, £50 for third. But I want you to come into the office for two afternoons a week to be my marketing and promotions manager."

'I was never going to win the Tour de France, but now I had a chance to learn a new industry. I was going out the door with £7K and a brand-new Ford Orion, and I had my feet under the table in the marketing world. When your career in cycling finishes, it finishes. You're only as good as your last race. So I was made up.

'Before I left Tony's office, he said, "Well, we haven't really talked about cycling. What are the most important races?" Tony was a big, fat guy. Huge. His shirt buttons were always straining and his shirt was always coming untucked. He'd have one cigarette in his mouth and another already lit in the ashtray. I said, "There's the Kellogg's series of city-centre races and the Milk Race. The big races are the classics in Europe, and the biggest of all is the Tour de France."

'Tony said, "Right, we need a three-year plan. We'll win the Kellogg's series, then we'll win the Milk Race and then we'll have a man on the podium in a classic. After that we'll have a team in the Tour de France."

'It sounds incredible, but he really did think like that. As I left, I said under my breath, "This guy is crazy." But of course it did happen. By 1986, we'd won the Milk Race and Joey McLoughlin had come fourth in the Amstel Gold. Malcolm was third in the same race in 1987 and we did get a team to the Tour.

'Tony fell in love with the sport immediately. In 1984, I rode the Michelin Classic on the Isle of Wight and ANC started with just me. Then two months into the season we took on Simon Day. Mick Bennett came to me and said that Shane Sutton, the Aussie rider with Ever Ready, had brought over another Aussie, Neil Stephens, and could we find a place for him. So we tried Neil for a time and the three of us rode in the Isle of Wight with Tony driving the team car. The race was held on closed roads, so as "a former rally driver" (he had also played rugby at some point, he said), Tony was loving it. He could go through red lights and drive on the wrong side of the road, and the bug had really got him. The enthusiasm he had was remarkable.

'Joey McLoughlin was relegated from the win at the National Amateur Road Race in 1984 for switching Neil Martin in the sprint. He took Neil all across the road, there's no doubt about it, but Joey was a talent and Capper knew it. Phil Thomas had come to us and he was related to Joey, so we took Joey and then took Phil on. I was due to get £9K in 1985, but I gave a bit of money back so we could grow the team. It seems all I ever did was give back my pay rise.

'Tony couldn't be stopped. If it had been left to him, he'd have signed every rider he saw. In 1985, Joey was riding well, Phil was riding well, but Tony wanted to expand the team. The rule in Britain at the time was that you could only have six riders and he worked out how to get round that right away. I was number seven, but for 1986 I managed to get another sponsor. Interent, who supplied most of the cars to the ANC team, came in, and we got Nigel Bloor, John Wainwright, Dave Rayner and Stuart Coles. So that was the way we could run two teams.

'We got a call in 1986 from a lady who was very polite and I thought, "Well, this has got to be the CID or the taxman if she's calling me Mr Morrison." She was from a company called Lycra. We knew Lycra, being cyclists, but we didn't realise that the parent company, DuPont, was one of the biggest in the world. She said they were having a fashion show at the Grosvenor Hotel in London and they'd like a cyclist there. They'd heard, she said, that Malcolm Elliott was "very presentable", so the obvious idea was to take him. She asked what the fee would be and I had to admit that we'd not done anything like this for an outside company. She said we'd have first-class travel and stay in the hotel the night before. "It'll only be 15 minutes and we'll pay £500," she told me. Great. So I rang Malcolm and told him he'd be getting £100 for 15 minutes' work. I've never been good with the calculator!

'We were building this pool of riders and of course we needed another team with closer links to ANC. Halfords had come on board by then and so we had a bit more money to play with. With two teams, we weren't allowed to call them both ANC-Halfords but we could use Halfords as co-sponsor for both, which offered them a bit more value. We needed another name to put on the jersey and we needed about £30,000 for the second team. I rang the lady at Lycra and she said she would put a proposal together for a guy called Peter Adcock, who used to ride for a club in Leicestershire and was really into his cycling. He was European marketing director for DuPont. We met and suddenly we had the £30,000 and they were getting a good deal for all of us. We had ANC-Halfords and Lycra-Halfords, and I was still riding with Interent.

'We saw Peter Adcock in a fancy hotel in London. Tony, then the chairman of Action Sports, waited until the end of the meeting before telling me, "Give him one of your cards, Micky." Afterwards I said, "Why did you ask me to give him my card? Yours says 'Chairman' on it – that's surely more impressive." He pulled open his jacket and in his inside pocket he had the silver salt and pepper pots he'd pinched!

'It was Adcock who came up with £30,000 for the Tour, not Capper. We had done all the races – Midi Libre, Dauphiné Libéré, the classics – and we'd won the Milk Race. Capper was paying the wages on time and he hadn't had to use the riders' money to enter the Tour. It sounded great, but the balance was way off. Then he started taking his family to races, and lots of guests. He thought his enthusiasm and success would spill over and the sponsors would be happy to pay more. He thought that he could keep going back to get more money. But if a sponsor has agreed to pay £200,000 for a year, they're not going to keep paying on top of that.

'In early 1987, he sold ANC to British and Commonwealth Shipping. He got just short of £1 million for himself, and an agreement to continue with the cycling team. ANC were happy with that and it was good publicity for them, but Tony wasn't in a position to go back to his little pot for more cash any more. He wasn't in charge of the team's budget and it was already in a mess.

'Think about it, though: he built a business from nothing to nearly a million pounds in three years, and he had started with not a penny in his pocket. The problem for Tony was that if he had two million, he would spend three. I'd have loved the Sky budget of today, but Tony would have blown that in a month.

'When we started, the company name, Associated Nationwide Couriers, was on the logo, which was a big dart. The problem was when Bean Bag came to do the first jersey the logo went from one arm to the other. Back then, I was thin; these days, the size of me, you could print the Bible on there! Bean Bag came up with a new logo. It was the three letters with the "A" slightly on a slant and the Union Flag in front of it. ANC adopted it and kept it for years, but it was designed specifically to fit on *my* chest.

'Griffo will confirm that once money arrived with Tony, he saw it as his. He thought possession was 99 per cent of the law. Getting money out of him was like drawing teeth. He would think, "Right, I'll have a nice Range Rover." As we were getting towards the Tour, he said, "I've signed two more French riders, a couple of mechanics, the Czech Palov and a manager from Belgium." He couldn't see the finances were wrong. Griffo, who was trying to keep track of things, would tell him, "We don't need another rider. It's not like we've signed Bernard Hinault. This guy isn't any better than the ones we've got." Or, "We don't need any more mechanics." If Tony was at a race and he saw you, a journalist, and he spoke to you and he liked you, he'd say, "Right, I want you as my press officer." At the next race, he'd see some other journalist and say, "Come and be my assistant press officer."'

After the wins at the Midi Libre and the Milk Race, and near misses all over Europe, came the letter from Jacques Goddet. There were celebrations in the Stoke office, a page lead in the local paper and a little scoop for *Blue Peter* and the BBC. A British team was going to take part in the world's greatest cycling race, and the ANC and Halfords names would be seen by millions all over the world.

'As always, though,' says Morrison, 'Tony got a bit carried away.'

He and McCann-Erickson, his PR company, wanted a national newspaper reporter to travel with the ANC team for what amounted to a month of the Tour de France. Worse still, the journalist worked for a red-top tabloid and would eat with, sleep in the same hotel as and interview most members of the team throughout. It didn't go down too well with Griffiths and most of the riders. It hadn't gone down too well, either, with the *Star*'s chosen reporter.

Morrison, plainly an expert people watcher, had it spot-on from the start: 'Jeff Connor came to Stoke to meet the team and he looked about as interested in it as a goldfish in a bowl. I think someone must have twisted his arm. But then, as far as I know, he came along, saw there was a story and used up his holiday to stay. I am pretty sure the *Star* wasn't going to pay him to stay on the Tour de France for four weeks.'

2

PAPER TIGER

When you find the colonel, infiltrate his team by whatever means available, and terminate the colonel's command.

Colonel Lucas, *Apocalypse Now*

'**DO YOU FANCY** a month in Europe this summer? We're looking for a reporter for a couple of days in Berlin, a day or so in France and as much food and drink as you fancy. Britain has a team in the Tour de France and it's being run by a man called Tony Capper. By the way, do you know anything about the Tour de France – and have you ever done any cycling?'

That sounded fine, with two exceptions: I had never heard of Tony Capper and I was a subeditor, not a reporter. That to me was the difference between a bus driver carrying Mancunians around Chorlton Street and a train driver taking the *Flying Scotsman* from King's Cross to Edinburgh. Looking for a reporter? I was a sub; what was more, I was one of the paper's two splash subs, one of whom looked after sport and the other news. Most splash subs – myself included – felt they were so good at their jobs that they would throw tantrums if asked to look after anything down page; they had to beg us to get some help with any story with a headline under 48 point.

49

It was a great job. When I joined the sports desk of the Northern version of the *Daily Mirror* in the mid-'60s, the splash sub there spent every night looking after the Frank McGhee column – and little else. As the McGhee words – even his semi-colons – were untouchable, my colleague didn't have a lot to do. That was definitely a job for me.

By the time I joined the *Star* in 1978, I had landed the dream and I, too, sat there on the sports desk back bench for most of the night with little to do. But I did believe I produced what I considered were good headlines, always made sure that stories were grammatically and factually correct and produced the swiftest of rewrites of reporters' words.

A sub was an artist; a tabloid reporter was someone who was sent out for door knocks and to find nanny goats (quotes), which were passed on to the subs, who would then make sense of them. Subs at the *Star* even had their own monthly exes (expenses), and we never even left the office. We got exes for our home phone calls and even our own supply of daily newspapers; in our view, most reporters made their exes up. No wonder the *Star* eventually went down the pan. If the management had done their jobs properly, some of the reporters would have been in court and charged with fiddling expenses long before all those naughty MPs were caught.

Tabloid sports reporters had a lot to answer for for what I called the Decade of Dumbing Down, beginning in the late '80s, when they managed to change the tone and presentation of sports journalism for ever. Their words were growing increasingly formulaic, and they had begun to repeat descriptions of sportsmen and women that became cliches. 'A model professional' in tabloidese was what a reporter considered a boring bastard who didn't drink and went to bed before midnight. An 'insider/ source' meant that no one would go on the record, so the reporter was making the quotes up. For 'the worst-kept secret in the game', read 'I missed the story but knew about it all along', and 'one of the nicest men in the game' was a sportsman who had once said good morning to a reporter in a hotel corridor. 'Too little, too late' (usually in a match report) was the stand-by last paragraph when a deadline was due, and departed football managers were always, in the words of sports reporters, 'the late, great' (Bill Shankly, Jock Stein, etc.). Never just late – or just great – but always late and great. And finally, the one I disliked above all: 'Land of the White Cloud', served up by rugby reporters who had already used 'New Zealand', 'Kiwi' and 'All Blacks'.

It was in the 1980s, too, that sports journalism's 800-lb gorillas – the heavyweight, heavy-duty columnists who appeared on the grandest of sporting occasions to add their wit and wisdom to proceedings – were vanishing slowly from the scene. A big hitter such as Martin Samuel – and he is a heavyweight in the strictest sense of that word – would disagree, but the sports columnists of today are not in the class of Peter Wilson and Frank McGhee (*Daily Mirror*), Ian Woolridge (*Daily Mail*) and, the last of the breed, Frank Keating (*The Guardian*). Between 1950 and 1980, the 800-lb gorillas, of whom Walter Cronkite was among the first, were, justifiably, megastars in their own right. Their names would appear on billboards outside Wimbledon, Wembley or Twickenham (PETER WILSON IS HERE TODAY) and they would be recognised and stopped in the street. In the case of the broadsheets, they were one of the main reasons for the massive circulation figures of those days. Their armoury in every case was a deep knowledge of sport and an awareness that the essence of the business was simple: young people performing to the best of their ability at something they loved. They were journalists who believed that hard fact was far more important than opinion. Nowadays, the columnists come armed with nothing save a *Roget's Thesaurus*, a dictionary of quotations and a belief that the most important part of any event is themselves.

For all the supposed bombast of writers like Peter Wilson, they never denigrated sportsmen, preferring to let facts speak for themselves. Readers could also believe everything they wrote. How things changed, and how quickly they changed. Once, during a random search through 50 tabloid soccer 'exclusives', I found that 75 per cent of them proved to be untrue. They are simply figments of a reporter's imagination or, possibly, an agent's imagination. If you see a headline above an 'exclusive' tag saying something like 'Gerrard Considers Chelsea Shift', with the words below telling you that 'a friend of the player told the *Sun*', someone is telling porkies.

Nor were many sports reporters able, or more often willing, to recognise a story even if it introduced itself and sharpened a pencil for them. Going back to 1970, those sportswriters who covered the football World Cup in South America and who were on the plane transporting the England football team from Bogotá to Mexico City were guilty of a gross dereliction of duty. None chose to question the absence of the blond-haired captain of the then world champions, who apparently had missed the plane, and none attempted to leave the aircraft and reach a telephone when the plane made a stop at Panama. By the time they reached Mexico City, the news that Bobby Moore had been arrested back in Bogotá, on suspicion of stealing a bracelet, had reached London. There were some fearful bollockings, but most football writers considered it none of their business. They were there to cover the football. One of them summed up their modus operandi rather well: 'Whatever a player does off the field of play is nothing to do with me.'

Finally, I could put up with the booze culture in journalism, but not the hypocrisy of sportswriters who could condemn the likes of George Best with one hand while sipping a treble Scotch with the other.

I had once been one of the lowest of the low, but I had gone off reporting for good as far back as 1964, when my sports editor at D.C. Thomson's legendary *Weekly News* – a starting point for many adolescent journalists in those days – had presented me with a rail voucher for the journey from Manchester Piccadilly to Fitzwilliam in the West Riding of Yorkshire. I was to door-knock a cricketer called Geoffrey Boycott and ask him if he would tell our readers about his career to date. It was felt (correctly, as it turned out) that he would be selected for England at some stage that summer.

Mr Boycott, or rather his mother, with whom he lived, was not on the telephone and the journey was undertaken in the knowledge that he might not be home. But travelling hopefully was standard operating procedure for journalists then. I had never heard of Geoffrey Boycott, but I believed, with the naivety of a 17 year old, that cricketers would be just as compliant and cooperative as most other sportsmen.

The train journey to Fitzwilliam involved changes at Leeds and Wakefield, and after around three and a half hours of travel through a landscape of back-to-back terraced houses and coal tips, I arrived at the birthplace of my prey. Mrs Boycott and her son lived at the end of a vast line of identical homes on Railway Terrace. She opened the door in person and seemed pleasant enough but stiffened perceptibly when I announced my profession. There was no invitation to step inside and when I asked if Geoffrey was home she braced herself in the doorway like a nightclub bouncer. 'I'll ask,' she said, without enthusiasm. There followed the sort of three-way conversation familiar to anyone who has seen the shop sketch on *Little Britain*.

'Geoffrey!' shouted Mrs Boycott over her shoulder. 'There's a journalist here to see you.'

'From Manchester,' I said.

''E's from Manchester,' said Mrs Boycott.

'What does 'e want?' demanded a voice from within.

'Geoffrey says what do you want?'

'I just want to ask him about his career and whether he thinks he will play for England soon.'

'How much?' said the voice.

'Pardon?'

'Geoffrey says how much?'

'Well, I don't think we usually pay for interviews, but I could go and ask my sports editor,' I said.

'No brass, no interview,' said the voice.

I trudged back to the nearest telephone – at Fitzwilliam station – and made the 2p call to my sports editor. There was silence for a few seconds and then: 'Tell Mr Boycott to fuck off.'

There were two lessons from this misadventure. The first, which turned out to be awfully prescient in the light of what was to happen later in the business of sport and its relations with the media, was that some personalities want paying for their time. Some also prefer to negotiate through a third party. Mrs Boycott, although no doubt she and her son would see it differently, was my first encounter with a sporting agent. Later, when I put in a claim for the cup of tea and ham sandwich bought at Leeds station, the *Weekly News* sports editor, a dour Scot from Dundee, refused to sign it off. 'No receipt, no dosh,' he said.

That was the end of my reporting career, but now, in the spring of 1987, I was being asked to hit the road again. They had picked me, they said, because they had wanted someone 'quite fit', which was where the sports editor's question about whether I cycled came in. But I definitely didn't look forward to having to watch 200 men on bicycles chasing each other for 100 miles a day and then write a story about a game I knew nothing about.

Compared with the other staff at the *Star*, I was indeed 'quite fit', although too often I sank into the boozy cesspit of Express Newspapers. The *Star* staff might have been younger, but this 'one for the road' gang could hold their own with the old campaigners across the floor at the *Daily*

Express. When I'd stopped climbing in the mid-70s, after my colleague fell to his death on Mont Blanc's Route Major and I decided that wives and families should never suffer something like that, I'd gone looking for another sport. I began to run on a daily basis – and if I got bored with that, I would play three rounds of golf a day before my regular 6 p.m. start at the *Star* – but six miles a day was invariably followed by six pints a night.

The running sessions were over the hills of Lakeland from my home in Eskdale at weekends and round the back roads of Ancoats during breaks at work. If in the mood, there were 10 or 11 pubs within a radius of 200 yards, and after work, if the night owls felt like it – and most of us did – there was the notorious all-nighter, the Express Club, right outside the office back door. I was, as my wife would say, a bit of an extremist.

It was difficult to work out which was worse when going for a run around Ancoats: the shouts of 'get those knees up' from the good citizens of Manchester M4 (recreational running was still in its infancy in those days) or the smell of beer and fags wafting out from the numerous pubs I passed. Like a slap in the face. In the depths of one winter, I helped a local bobby bring down a fleeing drink-driver on Hyde Road. The station inspector, by way of gratitude, issued me with a warning about antisocial behaviour. Two nights later, the driver, this time on foot, was waiting in the same spot with three mates. They couldn't catch me; I was fit all right.

But as I had to tell Peter Oakes, the *Star* sports editor at the time, I hadn't been on a bike for 30 years. And I had already worked out that while a month in France sounded fine, there had to be a catch somewhere along the line between Ancoats Street, Manchester, and the Champs-Elysées, Paris. After 25 years in journalism, I knew the whys and wherefores of the business and, in particular, the foibles of the Super *Star*. You never got anything for nothing on a national tabloid.

'We were,' says Oakes today – and I take this as a compliment of sorts – 'looking for someone a bit crazy. We wanted someone to ride a stage of the Tour de France.'

The minutiae of the *Star*'s operation were straightforward to Oakes: 'When I was a freelance in Devon, I did a cycling column, and as a kid I was always a cyclist. The well-known Eddie Soens shop was 300 yards from where I lived in Liverpool. The *Star* embraced a lot of sports. If you wanted to read about minor sport, it was the *Star* you bought, and it is fair enough to say that the *Star* was the tabloid version of the *Telegraph*. We gave the Milk Race big shows. We had the *Daily Star* logo on all the banners. We even had *Star* girls just like the podium girls in the Tour de France. But the best thing we had was an editor who was interested in sport. When I went into morning conference, Lloyd Turner was as interested in sports as news and features – a rarity in an editor. And no one could ever pull the wool over his eyes.

'Basically we picked on you because you were a bit crazy. It was hard to get you out of the office and you were good at quirky stuff. We couldn't afford to send someone like one of the reporters, who strictly speaking should have gone, but they wouldn't have had a chance riding a stage. It was the combination of cutting costs and your fell-running that got you through.'

Our place of work was a huge office building, known as the Black Lubyanka, in Great Ancoats Street. The Lubyanka (as in the KGB building) had twins in Fleet Street and Glasgow, and all three were hardbitten worlds of boozers, brawlers and oddballs. Many of the staff were indeed crazy; too many of them were alcoholics. I was to spend 11 years at the *Daily Star* – from its birth in 1978 to 1989, when it moved its operation, lock, stock and smoking typewriters, from Manchester to London. It was a sort of downmarket adjunct to the *Daily Express*, with which it shared a building. The *Express* had arrived in Manchester in 1927, when Lord

Beaverbrook bought a former corset warehouse at Ancoats for his new newspaper. Within ten years, a sister to the Black Lubyanka of Fleet Street had been built on the site, and for more than fifty years the *Express*, the *Mirror* and the *Mail* – just half a mile away across the city centre – went at it hammer and tongs.

By the time I went to the Tour de France, the *Mail* had given up the ghost, closed its Deansgate office, and in May 1988 Withy Grove, once Europe's largest printing centre, followed suit. The *People*, *Mirror* and *Sunday Mirror* staff lost their Northern jobs. The *Express*es and the *Star* wobbled on for another 12 months, after which we were told we could move to London or take redundancy.

The *Star*'s owners at the time, United Newspapers, had originally seen the paper as a rival to the red-top domination of the *Mirror* and more particularly the super soaraway *Sun*. Things had never quite worked out that way. We published solely in Manchester (with a small office in Fleet Street) and were regarded as country hicks by our rivals, many potential readers and even too many of our so-called colleagues in London. But by dint of some dedication, a little talent and a groundbreaking bingo promotion (about the only thing ever copied by *The Sun*, which for the most part totally ignored the Manchester upstart), the *Star* had built up a healthy circulation of around 1.9 million. Turner, the editor, was a brash Australian given to genuine moments of inspiration. While most of us had moved from the *Express* offices a few yards away, Turner had brought in, and occasionally bought in, staff from all over Britain, some of whom were to become quite famous in later years.

At the time, they were nobodies. Roy Greenslade, later to become managing editor of the *Sunday Times*, editor of the *Daily Mirror* and eventually the guru of media commentators on *The Guardian*, was a features editor on the *Star*. Neil Wallis, arrested by the Metropolitan Police in 2011 over the *News of the World* phone-hacking scandal, and known in his days on the *Star* as 'the Wolfman' because of his lupine appearance, was then just a humble hack, so to speak. Tom Stoddart was plainly a gifted photographer even then, while his fellow Geordie, Carole Malone, later better known as a celebrity on *Big Brother*, started her national career as a columnist on the *Star*. Nicknamed 'Piggy', her main claim to fame remains even now for many of us who worked on the *Star* at the time an unforgettable interview with George Best's then wife, Angie, and her description of George's demands for a regular blow job. Not quite in the class of the Prince of Wales/Camilla tampon tapes, but pretty good for the '80s. It didn't get in the *Star*, but it could be said Carole Malone rose swiftly through the ranks from then on. Our royal correspondent was James Whitaker, a reporter *à la* Lois Lane, determined to unmask the supermen and women of Buckingham Palace. Whitaker was a man who never sat down to write a feature without a plate of smoked-salmon sandwiches and a bottle of champagne. A *Star* news sub called Andrew Morton (whom most of us considered none too bright) thought he could do better – and eventually he did.

The sports staff had its own 800-lb gorilla in Peter Batt, a Londoner whose joke when he joined the *Star* at its launch in 1978 was: 'I've been sacked from every other newspaper in the land, so they had to start a new one for me.' In 1985, Batt could add the *Star* to his list of dismissals – and getting sacked took some doing on the tabloids back then.

For all his originality, brilliant writing skills and ability to communicate with the sports stars of the day (he broke the news that Ali was suffering from what turned out to be the early stages of Parkinson's disease after a one-on-one with the retired heavyweight in 1983), Batt, like many alcoholics – and not just in journalism – tended to counter a flash of genius with an act of madness in an effort to balance the books. The Ali exclusive was followed by a two-week bender, which earned him a warning from his editor. By early 1984, though, he had earned back enough brownie points to be trusted to go to the Los Angeles Olympics.

Batty's performances there have become enshrined in journalistic legend. One story has it that he never actually attended a single event in person (although he definitely was in LA). I was on the dog shift – the late-night stretch, usually from 6 p.m. to 3 a.m. – when he telephoned the sports desk in Manchester two weeks into the Games. His copy until then had been exemplary, but here were signs that things were coming apart at the seams.

'Batty here, what time's this facking swimming race start?'

'What race is that, Batty?'

'The facking 400 metres, mate.'

'Well, you're there, Batty, don't you have a programme?'

'Nah, no one's given us one, mate.'

At that moment, there was an interruption – a cry of 'room service', the sound of a door opening, the clink of coins changing hands and bottle against glass – before Batty returned to the phone. Then: 'I don't suppose you know what facking TV channel it's on then, mate, do you?'

Even with Batt in full flow, the *Star* sports section was tiny by *Sun* and *Mirror* standards, and we could never compete in terms of 'exclusives' and blanket sports coverage, but by concentrating on minority sports – we carried basketball, stock cars and non-league football columns – we managed to hold our own. The production of a sports page wasn't quite as dubious then as it is now; the *Star* did like its 'exclusives', but they were seldom as manufactured as they are now. Subs wrote headlines that were fairly straightforward and not the over-the-top efforts of today. We did not, for example, call every Scottish sportsman 'Braveheart', write 'Kop That' whenever Liverpool won at home, use 'I'm Gunner Do the Trick' for every Arsenal striker's pre-match boast or call any team with a home ground a mile from the sea 'the Seasiders'. Nor was it a requirement that the *Star*'s sports experts had to make predictions about every major sporting event. In other words, Woods will win the Open, Federer will win Wimbledon, New Zealand the Rugby World Cup and Andy Murray will . . . well, we'll leave that one for now. It goes without saying that I wasn't expected to come up with the winner of the 1987 Tour de France.

Then, as now, the *Star* was drastically underfunded, but it had latched on to cycling in a big way, with monumental (for the media at the time) coverage of the Milk Race, the original and long-standing Tour of Britain sponsored by the Milk Marketing Board. We had *Star* girls to plant kisses on the cheeks of the stage winners, and a reporter and photographer to follow the event on a daily basis. Not surprisingly, this had won almost universal approval within the publicity-starved cycling fraternity, and the dominant team of that tour, and indeed of British professional cycling, ANC-Halfords, had garnered unprecedented newsprint.

Now they, or rather Tony Capper, wanted to return the favour. By way of a quid pro quo, a representative of the *Daily Star*, Capper had said in his moment of madness, was welcome to travel with ANC-Halfords on the Tour de France, starting in July.

Great Ancoats Street and the *Star* were ideal places to get away from for three or four weeks, but outsprinting vengeful Mancunian drunks on icy pavements was somewhat different from turning a wheel for 100 miles or more in midsummer France. I didn't own a bike and couldn't tell a *bidon* from a *bidet*, but I was to travel to France in early July, said Oakes, 'infiltrate the Tour de France, ride a stage and describe it all to our readers'.

I had around six weeks before the Tour was due to start in Berlin, and I began to do some homework on cycling, the Tour de France and my unwilling travelling companions. I would also have to go and meet them in Stoke, acquire a bike, begin to ride on a regular basis and, worst of all, stop smoking and drinking. Much later, the wise words of BBC sports guru Des Lynam came back to me. Sports journalism, he has said, 'requires knowledge of the subject, fluency of language and respect from whichever experts are put in front of you'. On that basis, I scored maybe one out of ten, with the one owed to my knowledge of how to say 'hello' and 'goodbye' – and how to ask for *vin rouge* – in French. The *Star* sports desk may have been living in a fantasy world, but I don't think now that ANC envisaged a reporter sitting on the starting line with the world's greatest cyclists. They played along with it for a time and while I was with them in France my inexperience became a standing joke, with the riders asking me questions along the lines of: 'Do you know what's the hardest part of learning to ride a bike? The pavement.' That sort of thing. But there certainly was a notion inside the fevered minds of the men who ran the *Star* sports desk. They had mistakenly envisaged me as the George Plimpton of Great Ancoats Street, and I was to attempt to slip into other people's high-profile careers – a hapless adventurer who was pretty poor at most sports but keen to give it a go. Plimpton had been beaten up by the world light heavyweight champion Archie Moore in 1959, had pitched in the baseball leagues and had also lost badly to Arnold Palmer and Jack Nicklaus at golf. As far as I knew, Plimpton had never cycled a stage of the Tour de France.

The *Star* had long specialised in the sort of subjective gonzo sports journalism pioneered by the likes of Plimpton and John 'Get Down, Shep' Noakes, the *Blue Peter* action man. One of the subs, a useful club cricketer, had faced an over from West Indian pace bowler Michael 'Whispering Death' Holding, when he was in his prime; this was the man who almost battered to death the aged England batsman Brian Close during an England v. West Indies Test in 1967. Another writer had cajoled a ride in an F1 car, and I had played in a game alongside Alton Byrd, at that time

61

the superstar of British basketball. These were stories that cost nothing save a bit of sweat and fear. Personally, I thought I would rather cycle a few miles of the Tour de France than get my nose broken by Michael Holding or be made a fool of by Alton Byrd again.

There were a couple of drawbacks: Plimpton, Oakes and others had always asked permission of the relevant sportsperson (or his manager) to make fools of themselves. I might have been naive about cycling, but I would have bet a million pounds that whoever ran the Tour de France wasn't going to stand by and watch a journalist line up at one of their starts. It had never happened in the past and they had even refused permission to a cancer-stricken cycling fan who had a week to live and wanted to go out in style. The only way of getting onto a Tour stage would be to sneak in and hope for the best. But I was 41, knew nothing about cycling and stood a good chance of doing myself some serious damage in France that summer.

'We thought you were a professional sportsman,' says Oakes. 'We thought a professional fell runner would be fit enough to ride a bike for a distance.'

Some people indeed liked to call me a 'professional fell runner', but initially that had not been my choice. I was a 'pro' simply because the Amateur Athletic Association had famously (it marked the one and only time I was to appear in *Athletics Weekly*) banned me from amateur athletics for winning a quid at a local hill race in Cumbria. As far as I know, I am still *persona non grata* with the AAA, and I am in my 60s as I write this now.

My main claim to fame was that I could call myself 'British Over-40s Hill-Running Champion', which sounded marvellous. I was happy to tell people all about that, but I never pointed out that there were only five runners involved as Over-40s. One of them was in his 60s, two brothers from Doncaster smoked and drank more than me and the other was a mother of four from Sheffield. Compared with the soaks, chain-smokers and general layabouts who made up the staff of Express Newspapers, I was up there with Björn Borg and Daley Thompson, but cycling was a different matter altogether.

As promised, however, on 29 June 1987, I drove down to Stoke-on-Trent, met the ANC staff and some of the riders, had my picture taken (complete with an ANC cap) with Malcolm Elliott by a *Star* snapper and duly climbed aboard flight BA744 from Heathrow to West Berlin.

Even I could sense the irony of this: Capper and the *Star* had chosen a 40-something subeditor whose life revolved around the hedonism of tabloid journalism. He was to spend three weeks living with some of the fittest men in sport, write a daily report about them and, somewhere along the way, ride a stage of the Tour de France. The professional cyclists of ANC-Halfords and I may have lived and worked in the same country, but that apart we resided in parallel universes.

3

HEART OF DARKNESS

*I was going to the worst place in the world, and I
didn't even know it yet.*

Willard, *Apocalypse Now*

BERLIN . . . SHIT. I'm still only in Berlin. Every time, I
think I'm gonna wake up back in England.

Even in 1987, I'd seen *Apocalypse Now* a dozen times,
and the opening words of special operations officer Willard
came back to me every time I woke up alone in a strange
bedroom, mildly pissed, sweating and in a city I had hated
from the start. I was a long way from home.

Willard, sent into the middle of nowhere by his superiors,
was travelling with a sombre navigator called Chief, a
second in command prone to emotional outbursts, a GI
surfer addicted to suntanning and a kid drafted into a war
he knew little about. Somewhere along the way were
Willard's target, the evil genius Colonel Walter E. Kurtz,
and the badass Lieutenant Colonel Bill Kilgore, a man with
a screw loose and a ludicrous battle strategy. Francis Ford
Coppola, the director of *Apocalypse Now*, could have
written this for ANC.

It was 6.30 a.m. and I was on the third floor of the
Novotel, Berlin Airport. Down the corridors were the ANC
staff: two *directeurs sportifs* (with another on his way from

65

Stoke-on-Trent), a press officer, three *soigneurs* (and another on his way from Scotland) and eight riders. The ninth, the Czech Kvetoslav Palov, was already out and about, I discovered later. As were the three mechanics. All had got up early for different reasons and all were representative of the first, and arguably the best, British cycling team since 1967 to take part in the Tour de France.

I was yet to be impressed and I still hadn't worked out where my newspaper's daily stories, and the Tour's newsworthiness in general, were going to come from. But I knew they would come from somewhere eventually. A look back at the history of this race had told me so. Two decades previously, a Briton had died during the Tour, on Mont Ventoux in the Provence region of southern France, and we were heading in the same direction. I was looking forward to that.

It doesn't take you long to lose your fresh-faced acuity and sensitivity in tabloid journalism. If you are lucky, the scepticism doesn't set in for a couple of years, but by the summer of 1987 I had been at it for more than two decades. The contempt for accepted standards of morality was part of my life, and being asked to follow the Tour de France and report on what could be the foibles and failures of a British team taking part in it was par for the course for me. Like many of the staff at the *Star*, I was happy to follow the principles of Charles Tatum, the hardbitten news hound in *Ace in the Hole*: 'I can handle big news and little news. And if there's no news, I'll go out and bite a dog.' An Express Newspapers friend of mine, Peter Thomas, who had died three years before the 1987 Tour, had his own favourite: 'If you saw a man drowning and you could either save him or interview him . . . do you use shorthand or a recorder?' He was joking, but he was also fond of quoting the word of Orson Welles: 'A reporter makes a statement and then asks of the subject, "Is it true?"' In other words, a reporter makes his mind up in advance and then asks a sportsman,

'How happy are you that you won today and that you took that great pass from Bobby, got past the full-back and then fired an unstoppable ball into the back of the net?' The subject has only one answer to that; it's a fair bet that he's very happy, which is precisely what the reporter was looking for in the first place.

Tabloid subeditors were not much better at times, working on the basis that you take a news item, have a guess at what your readership's attitude towards it will be, then write a headline and story that reinforce that attitude. So my first thought was that if someone from ANC were to die on Ventoux in 1987 at least I would get a story out of it, and once I had filed the story someone back in Manchester would write the ideal headline, something on the lines: 'Another Brit Cyclist Dies on Death Mountain'. I was cynical about the world in general back then; now I'm just cynical about journalism.

In Berlin, I hadn't a clue what the pro riders and the ANC staff were all about and didn't know half their names. But I was getting there. All of them had the sort of nicknames we had used at school. We had 'Swarty', 'Ches', 'Watto', 'Malc' and 'Muddy' (as in Waters, although obviously Ward Woutters, the dour Belgian *directeur sportif*, was never called that to his face). Palov answered to 'Omar', a nickname that remains a mystery to me today. The only Omar I knew was the man who had starred in *Lawrence of Arabia*. I'm pretty sure they called me 'Pig', as in 'Tabloid Pig'.

Elliott was the good-looking Yorkshireman with the permatan, Shane the Aussie joker who talked a lot and liked to take the piss out of anyone, particularly me. Three of the other riders, Steve Swart, Adrian Timmis and Palov, said hardly a word to anyone, each seemingly determined to do the best impersonation of Harpo Marx. It was a toss-up between the Mancunian, Graham Jones, and one of the two Frenchmen, Bernard Chesneau, as to who looked the more ill. The guy from High Wycombe, Watson, with bleached blond hair and an earring, seemed to be in permanent expectation of the arrival of a guest, and I had bet myself within an hour of meeting him that he thought a lot of women, and vice versa. Within another hour, on the first day in Berlin, I had won my own little wager when a girl turned up at dinner asking if she 'could see Paul'. That upset one or two of the staff, but it was fairly easy to upset them.

Woutters spent most of his days criticising his riders and Tony Capper, the big fat guy who had told me from the start that he was The Boss, seemed to have a permanent monk on, as they say in North Yorkshire.

After our arrival in the Novotel, Capper had shown his mettle in the command of troops with a fair impersonation of George C. Scott in *Patton*: 'When a rider looks up from his dinner, all I want him to see is a teammate. I know we're in the dark about this Tour, and every day is going to be different. We're going to be pissed around – a lot. But this team's going to do things right.'

Capper's first, and what turned out to be his last, pep talk was over, and in the words of the BBC on budget days 'the Chancellor sat down at 5.34 p.m.'. It was an impressive speech, but he had lost his audience from the start. Three of the riders had little or no English and most of the others hadn't listened to a word he had said. Sutton, the Aussie, and his joker in crime Watson smirked and laughed all the way through. Capper was furious, but instead of bollocking his riders he took it out on me – for mistakenly giving him a round of applause. 'You are only here as a guest,' he said. 'I don't like people trying to take the piss.'

I'd met him and the rest of his brigade for the first time on the Heathrow flight, and Capper, who hated flying (because, as he told anyone who would listen, 'I can't have a tab in here'), didn't seem to think much of journalists, either.

'Newspaper, what newspaper?' he had asked.

'The *Star*, we invited them,' he was told.

'Yes, but who the bloody hell is paying? I'm buggered if I'm forking out for a bloody journalist.'

This, I discovered later, was what passed for Capper's sense of humour, and, like many journalists, I found it harder to take a joke than to make one. I put on a worried pout until Capper said to me, 'Don't worry, son, only joking.'

I thought he was a chancer, and he had formed an early opinion of me, too. He told me he liked people to respond to everything he said or did and that 'really, you are a listener rather than a talker, and that drives me mad in folk'. I got the message and made an effort to speak to him, and even smile at him, every single day. From then on, we got on fine.

Even when we first arrived in Berlin – and before the Tour had even started – it didn't take a genius to recognise the problems he faced in attempting to keep a disparate bunch of people from different parts of Europe together for close to a month. It was to prove too much for him in the end. The Tour de France of 1987 was to make him one of the most controversial sports owners of all time, and there have been quite a few of them. To Malcolm Glazer of Manchester United and George Steinbrenner of the New York Yankees add Tony Capper of ANC-Halfords. If British cycling fans talk about the Tour of '87 now, they invariably mention the name of Capper ahead of those of Jacques Goddet (in his last Tour), Laurent Fignon and even the eventual winner, Stephen Roche. The Capper Tour, they call it.

Capper's team, and the man from the *Star*, also seemed to have collected a troublesome poltergeist somewhere along the way from England. Two of the mechanics, Geoff Shergold and the chief mechanic Steve Snowling, had had a problematic start before they'd even landed in Europe. Having been asked to pick up one of the Tour cars in

Belgium, they were heading for Dover to find a ferry to Calais. Shergold, who was eventually to work on 28 Cyclo-Cross World Championships and 'found those more rewarding than the Tour de France', recalls: 'No problems getting to Dover, and we were bantering with the check-in girls at Calais, but they wouldn't let us in because we didn't have a signed *carnet*. Fortunately, we got back on the ferry for nothing and headed back to Dover, where they signed the *carnet*. When we got back to Calais, the guy there never even looked at the *carnet* and just signed it. Three trips on the same boat with one payment, but we had lost four to five hours already and we had to head to Belgium to pick up the car.'

The Tour had also almost ended for us on the first night in Berlin, when, to the riders' annoyance, having trained, eaten and had massage, they had to put on their ANC cycling clothing, complete with Union Jacks on the jerseys and in the colours of red, white and blue. After a brief interview with Phil Liggett of Channel 4 they were to do their bits for German TV at an opening night show in front of an invited audience of personalities, local politicians and past Tour winners – Eddy Merckx, Bernard Hinault and Jacques Anquetil, along with some I didn't recognise – who all rode into the hall on a bizarre 11-man tandem. The Tour de France, when in France, has its own little regiment of police motorcyclists, mostly from the country's elite Garde républicaine, but their German counterparts were not in the same league. As far as the Tour de France went, they had a lot to learn. With two of the ANC riders in one of the team cars, and with the bicycles stacked on top, the cop taking us to the show told us to follow him down an underpass just eight feet high, and only a remarkable piece of braking by Woutters prevented us from wiping out several thousand pounds' worth of racing gear. The Polizei man never batted an eyelid.

Then there was poor Palov. Even at 6.30 a.m., he would

be wandering around the hotel corridors or hiding somewhere. Capper regularly complained about the rider's inability to rest on his bed between races – a necessity for every pro cyclist when he is not actually on a bike. 'Go to bed and read a book or something,' ordered Capper. 'You don't have to sleep, just lie down for a bit. Guys like Sean Kelly will just lie there and do nothing. I'll even lend you a book if you like.' Palov had other things on his mind. He certainly didn't want to sit in a Berlin bedroom and read a Zane Gray and he told me later, as we argued about who was the more terminally sleepless person on board, that he had only managed a couple of hours a night. Even I couldn't get close to that measure of insomnia.

Palov didn't like to talk about his past, but all of us knew that the 24-year-old Czech had defected from the East before joining ANC. A few weeks later, he was told he had been selected for the Tour and that he and ANC would spend the first three days in Berlin. The fall of the Wall was still two years away and Palov didn't need to be told that the headquarters of the Stasi, the East German state police, was in Normannenstrasse, less than ten miles from our hotel. And it got worse for him. The official Stage 1 of the Tour started by the Brandenburg Gate, and Palov had a bird's-eye view of the grim lookout towers and machine guns over the Wall. Most of the other riders were sympathetic towards Palov and his difficulties; at least one of them had no sympathy for him at all.

Like the Czech, I thought I could live without the Tour de France. I already missed my wife and my dog and my cottage in Eskdale. I even missed the *Daily Star* and dirty old Ancoats Street and its dirty old pubs. At least the newspaper staff there spoke to each other, albeit sticking to conversations about the possibility of a pay rise, the character flaws of the paper's back bench and which drinking den they would head for after work. It seemed I had nothing in common with anyone in ANC. What was worse, most of the staff and riders felt the same way.

The only person I had got reasonably close to in Berlin was a young Irish radio journalist – hence the hangover. We had met in the huge entrance hall of the city's Palais am Funkturm, which the *soigneur* Friedhelm Steinborn, a large, shambling German with a crushing handshake, had described as 'the biggest ballroom in Europe, bigger even than your Blackpool!' For Des Cahill and myself, it turned swiftly into the biggest balls-up in Europe. After we'd spent twenty minutes sweating in one line in an attempt to get our press passes, the older of the two media officers charged with handing them out ordered us into the second line. We had a laugh at that and, as is usual when two strangers meet in a foreign land, Cahill and I agreed to have a pint, 'as long as we can find a pub that sells Guinness'. He had joined RTÉ in 1984 as a TV news reporter and by the time the Tour arrived in 1987 he had taken over the RTÉ *Sunday Sport* programme on Radio 1. His cycling debut had been on the Giro d'Italia in May and June the same year. Compared with me, he was an expert. Cahill was later famous as the founder of the ABU (Anyone But [Manchester] United) Club in Ireland. He never mentioned his feelings about United in Berlin, so I was happy, nay desperate, to find an Irish pub. After much searching, we came across one in the basement of a huge shopping centre. We got on fine and, despite the turmoil of the city and 'that Tour bollocks who kept us waiting', we even had the odd laugh – particularly when an Irish barman, supplying us with our sixth Guinness, decided Des was actually Stephen Roche and that he had 'better leave the pub soon as you have a busy day tomorrow, Stephen'. But that was the last I would see of Cahill until I was giving him a lift down from La Plagne after Stage 21 and the brakes failed on the ANC Iveco.

There were four Irish riders on the 1987 Tour, which must have made life easier for Des Cahill. Roche was to win the Tour; Sean Kelly crashed out on the road to Bordeaux during Stage 12 and had the dreaded DNF (did not finish) on his name. In radio or newspaper terms, that was almost as good as an Irishman winning it. Of the other two Irish rovers, Cahill introduced me to another Dubliner called Paul Kimmage, who seemed to have the weight of the world on his shoulders. I worked out a couple of years later that if you are trying to stay in the Tour and write a book at the same time, you will indeed have things on your mind. Half-heartedly, I asked him if I could meet him at his hotel for an interview and, even more half-heartedly, he agreed. It didn't come about, though, and I gave up on that idea, assuming he had little time for journalists. But by 1990, I was astonished to find that Kimmage had moved on from his days as a cycling *domestique*, and was now a highly regarded writer. His life had definitely changed for the better, as was clear in a 2008 *Sunday Times* article on the Russian tennis princess Maria Sharapova:

> And that's when it happens. Suddenly, inexplicably, I start to envy her dog. *I want to be Dolce.* I want to die and come back as that fluffy Pomeranian pooch and for the next five minutes I completely derail. It's like that scene from *American Beauty* when Lester Burnham (Kevin Spacey) is watching his daughter's cheerleading rally and is mesmerised by her cute, blonde friend. I gazed at Sharapova with eyes as big as dinner plates and was suddenly skiing off piste . . .

Kimmage may have got carried away from time to time at the *Sunday Times*, but he could write brilliantly about cycling, as he proved with his first book, *Rough Ride*, the classic tale that lifted the lid on doping in his sport.

The fourth Irishman was Martin Earley, from Clonsilla, Dublin, who never seemed to stop smiling but who was to impress me more by finishing third on Stage 15 from Tarbes to Blagnac on a day of ludicrously heavy rain. Like Laurent Fignon, Earley was one of few pro cyclists who rode wearing spectacles (Malcolm Elliott, among others, wore contacts), and to this day I can't work out how he managed to see where he was going when the rest of us needed windscreen wipers full on.

Lucky Des. If he needed an extra interview or two, he couldn't go wrong with two possible overall winners, a potential winner of a stage or two and a writing rider far more mentally acute than others of his breed.

If Cahill had his own daily radio drama series, I had my own soap opera with its own unique cast of characters. I might not have known all their names, but I had worked out that, in the case of ANC at least, a cycling team consists of three different groups of individuals, all with clearly defined roles, and each believing they are more important than any of the others. We had a similar arrangement at the *Star* – subs, page planners, reporters, in that order – but the *Star* staff were never as catty as those of ANC.

Many years after the Tour, I spotted their alter egos in the 2011 fly-on-the-wall documentary *The Model Agency*, which focused on bookers, talent scouts and models, most of whom seemed to spend their lives in bitchy office arguments and bad-tempered tantrums. For the agency's bookers, talent scouts and models read the *soigneurs*, mechanics and riders of ANC. Angus Fraser, the Scot who was to see himself as the 'head *soigneur*', was into daily hissy fits *à la Model Agency*. Full of frightening exaggeration after he had completed a rider's massage ('I think Adrian has broken his thumb' – Adrian had not broken his thumb) and forever offering us the tale of his latest punch-up or the time he almost died of asthma, Fraser certainly kept us entertained – and we needed all the entertainment we could find.

Like the middle-aged lady who ran the model agency, Capper also called them his 'team' and in the strictest sense of the word they were a team. But according to the dictionary definition – 'a group on the same side, as in a game; a group organised to work together' – this certainly was no team. Understandably, they all had the individual foibles of men everywhere, and there was animosity and hostility between some of them throughout, although it did take me several years to discover the depth of their likes and dislikes.

Paul Watson got on fine with Ward Woutters, as did I, while the majority of the others couldn't stand him. Ward had decided early on that he didn't like riders with bleached blond hair and earrings, but he recognised Watson's talent and plainly had a soft spot for him. Ward, to Watson, was like the Sam Jaffe character in *Lost Horizon*, the wizened high lama with his fund of homespun homilies, the accumulated wisdom of age and experience.

'I got on with Ward great,' says Watson. 'He was perfect for me. I'd get a piece of card given to me with all the times on it. Wake up, breakfast, bags packed, out the door, at the car. That was brilliant. That was what I needed to know. I just needed someone to do that calmly, no hassle, no drama, no shouting and screaming. Whenever I was around him, I could just relax and get on. Ward was organised, but he was being shot down by the others. There were loads of people shouting the odds, but only Ward knew what he was doing. He was the only one who'd experienced it.'

Graham Jones had a different opinion of Ward Woutters: 'The old git. I never got on with him at all. I didn't like him right from the start and I still don't know why they brought him in. He wound me up. I had a couple of dos with him even before the start of the Tour. I just couldn't work out why he was there.'

Ward himself did not think much of his riders. He told me on the very first day in Berlin: 'The British team is not professional. They have to learn patience. Graham Jones felt he had to complain. When the Tour starts, we'll see where he is. There are better riders in Britain than him.

They call Paul Watson a climber because they saw him go up one steep hill, but the Tour is about *col* after *col*. Malcolm Elliott – a playboy. He's a tremendous talent, but he doesn't know how to suffer. I don't think he will make Paris. Sutton is not good enough for the Tour.'

It goes without saying that after Watson's attempt at mutiny he and Phil Griffiths were never going to get on. Watson says: 'I am sure some guys loved it, all that whipping up and getting frenzied, but I was already off the clock before we started. I needed bringing down, not whipping up.'

Most of the staff thought the world of The Boss – but he was paying them, after all. Their views on him changed on the last day in the Alps, when he drove off into the sunset never to be seen again and it was discovered that they hadn't been paid after all.

Watson says: 'Capper was fat, big. He was imposing. He had a big, booming voice. You knew he had some money, but sometimes his behaviour made you question his boundaries. He had money, but you'd be in a restaurant and if he liked the look of the salt and pepper pots, he'd put them in his pocket.

'He tried to convince me he was in the SAS. He gave me a pep talk during the Tour: "When I was in the SAS . . ." and all this. I just let it go. By then, I wanted to go home. My head had come off and he couldn't say anything to me by that stage. He sat down on the edge of the bed and said, "You've got to tough it out." He was trying to convince me because he knew what I was going through, telling me about being up on the moors, going days without food.

'He stank. He really did. And he ate masses. At training camp, he went off to get the food for the team and he came back with huge tins of baked beans with sausages in, Fray Bentos pies and biscuits. He couldn't see what was wrong with it. He was OK, really. I even wrote to him after the Tour was over.'

Shane Sutton's opinion of Capper has never changed after all these years: 'For me, there was no integrity in the guy. He took us in almost like his family. He took me out to dinner in Stoke, for an Indian, and promised me the world. You felt you were close to him, so then for him to treat us like that. To know he had all that money in the bank and he couldn't put his hand in his pocket to sort us out – to pay us what he had promised. We weren't asking for a double-your-money bonus or anything like that. We wanted our salary. It wasn't a lot of money, even in those days. He'd sold that company for millions.'

There were even occasions when disagreements among the riders moved into violence. Jones says: 'Shane beat the fuck out of Palov one night during the Midi Libre. We were staying in this place where the walls were really thin. Shane was lying on his bed and you could hear the conversation next door. It was Palov talking to Swart, I think, and they were slagging off the whole team. Shane had taken so much. He got up and barged in and beat the fuck out of him! He said, "You can't go round talking to people like that."'

'Yeah, it's safe to say I didn't like him that much,' says Sutton, a man who, like many Australians, tends to call a spade a shovel. 'We had a bit of a set-to. We were in this dorm with thin walls. We were in one room, they were there in the other. He was talking to Swarty and he was bagging the shit out of Malcolm. Malc had been out for a beer that night or something. Now, to me, you don't do that in a team. You have something to say, you say it to their face or you keep your mouth shut. Be honest about it or don't say anything. We could hear every word and I was getting angry, so I went in there and beat seven bells out of him. Griffo came in in these tiny underpants and tried to separate us. He got me back to my room and I heard them moving the wardrobes up against the wall! If you're an Aussie, you have a punch-up and then a beer the next day.'

Even Malcolm Elliott, one of the most unflappable of men, is happy to offer his own opinions on staff and riders: 'There were things that got on your nerves during the Tour, things you could have done without. The Belgian *soigneur*, Roger [Van der Vloet], would come into your room in the morning and bang on the bed to wake you up. If Angus Fraser was rubbing my legs, I would have to listen to his problems. And Shane had never liked Palov. They had had their famous punch-up in the dark, but Shane always said, "Oh, that fellow Palov, how can you trust a guy who can run away and leave his family behind?"'

If the staff and riders were not arguing or fighting with each other, they weren't talking at all. Some of them were concerned about all this; I was delighted. After all, I was writing a book about the daily trials of ANC, and the more trials the better. Some of the riders, with little enough to laugh about during the stages, were also delighted to get some entertainment from the management. The morning they were preparing for Stage 12 from Brive to Bordeaux, the personnel had started a massive shouting match over who was at fault for not collecting *bidons* from race headquarters – as serious as that – and I happened to look up at the first-floor window of the ANC hotel to see Elliott framed there, his face a picture of blissful glee.

With inter-staff battles on a daily basis, I suddenly found that I was promoted from humble hack, and something of a nuisance, to the George J. Mitchell of British cycling, a peace envoy, a go-between and a message-passer for all the people who were at war with each other. During one famous occasion in Lourdes, on the night France celebrate Bastille Day, Capper, for some unannounced reason, was *persona non grata* with Angus Fraser. When the fish course arrived, I again found myself the unwilling, impartial middleman as the Antony Worrall Thompson and Gordon Ramsay of ANC laid into each other. Capper announced we were eating cod and Fraser insisted that it was turbot.

'Just what I fancied, a nice piece of cod,' Capper had said.

'This cod is turbot.'

'Cod.'

'Turbot.'

'I've been around harbours, I live in the Isle of Man, I know cod from turbot.'

'My brother's got a boat in Scotland and I've fished with him.'

And so it went on: potayto, potahto, tomayto, tomahto, let's call the whole thing off. Within a day, Capper and Fraser had called the whole thing on again, but soon our leader had moved on to someone else.

I arrived at La Plagne the day after the Iveco brakes had failed to find that Capper and Griffiths – the two surviving *directeurs sportifs*, who, strictly speaking, should have been on reasonable terms – had decided to take a mutual vow of silence over Capper's demand that he should drive the lead Peugeot during stages while Griffiths mopped up in the rear. Griffiths was also incensed by Capper's decision to fly over his wife and two sons. It was bad enough having been lumbered with a journalist on the tour, but this was too much for Griffiths.

'I'm definitely going to quit,' Griffiths told me dramatically. 'I'm on my way. I've had it up to here with Capper. He has been hogging the lead car and this business with his family has just finished me. The only thing that's stopping me setting off home now is that I haven't been paid.'

Hadn't been paid? That was a new one on me and the first hint that, financially in particular, all was not well in the ANC camp.

Capper and his cash flow apart, I had become used to waking up to what I called 'the Daily Disaster', and I had spotted problems even at the first dinner in Berlin. Six of the riders had English, but one of those was from New

Zealand and seemed to speak a different language from his fellow Antipodean from New South Wales. The two French riders had no English. Palov, the Czech, could speak some, but for obvious reasons hardly spoke at all, which was slightly more than Adrian Timmis, who seemingly *never* said much to anyone. The first words I got from Timmis were during a stage in which he flung a wet jersey through the Peugeot window, hit me in the face and shouted, 'Here, take that.'

But at least I understood Timmis. The rest of the ANC riders and staff were like the international police forces in post-war Berlin, with the French, Russians, British and Americans guarding the city but unable to understand a word the others were saying. Our first *directeur sportif* was a Belgian, as was one of the *soigneurs*. The other *soigneurs* were from Germany, France and Scotland, and anyone who has been to Linlithgow will tell you this is a place with a language of its own. Talking to the ANC staff was like walking through a minefield. Apart from speaking differing languages and having differing views on cycling, on life in general and even on humour, they all seemed to be from different planets.

The ANC rider Guy Gallopin had told me, in all seriousness, that Jerry Lewis was the most popular film comic in France, and at dinner Ward, obviously tired of the knackered old joke about the dearth of famous Belgians, insisted that they had 'Eddy Merckx, Tintin . . . and Audrey Hepburn'. Audrey Hepburn? Cue for another frustrating discussion, with one of the staff insisting, having seen *Breakfast at Tiffany's* twice, that anyone who spoke and looked like Audrey Hepburn, who had a cat called Cat, ate pastry and drank coffee at three in the morning and fell in love with George Peppard could not be a Belgian.

Ward (who was correct, and I knew he was correct but didn't feel like joining in with this one) gave up and tried again. In an effort to find another famous Belgian, he said,

'Many of my countrymen often spend large parts of their holidays taking family photos of our famous Manneken Pis in the famous Brussels fountain close to our famous town hall.'

'And what the fuck is a Manneken Pis?' was the response.

'What does it sound like?' said Ward.

'Are you taking the piss?'

All the Brits had a good laugh at that, but it didn't even raise a smile with the befuddled Belgians, who sat there like dogs who had just been shown a card trick. Ward's Belgian *soigneur* Roger Van der Vloet – who bore a resemblance to another famous countryman, the adventurer and film-maker Armand Denis – decided that *he* had a funny story, about his times working with the five-time Tour winner Jacques Anquetil and his love of fornicating before, during and after a race – apparently any race. One or two were surprised at this, but most of us guessed that cyclists were way behind, say, boxers in the league of sporting abstinence. A number of riders on this Tour obviously did not follow Muhammad Ali in his insistence that having sex the night before a big fight could diminish his athletic abilities.

Fisher, the ANC press officer, was on the side of Ali with that one, and was incensed when Paul Watson's friend, a vivacious brunette, walked unannounced into the ANC dining room.

'Disgraceful,' was Fisher's verdict. 'Girls do not belong on the Tour de France.'

Roger snorted in contempt: '*Non, non,* Anquetil, he won five Tours on champagne, and that –' the Belgian held his forefinger in the air and wiggled it graphically '– women never did him any harm.'

'But it's wrong. It'll affect his performance.'

'My friend,' said Roger, 'you have a lot to learn about *cyclisme.*'

If it was good enough for Anquetil, said Roger, it was OK for Watson, and, as I pointed out to Fisher, all the

ANC riders shared twin rooms. Wouldn't the thought of a room-mate, presumably with the same key to the same bedroom door, be an inhibiting presence for anyone? As far as sex went, this would be as good as two cups of bromide for supper.

Just to wind Fisher up a little more, I told him that most European hotels now had full-on, 100-per-cent-hardcore porn available in most rooms. 'And we all know what Mother used to say about the effects of that,' I said. Fisher didn't see the joke: 'I must warn Tony about that' was his response.

There *were* girls on tour, much to Fisher's dismay. Both 7-Eleven and Toshiba had female *soigneurs* and one of them was Shelley Verses, partner of the Panasonic star Phil Anderson, who less than a few months previously had come close to signing for ANC. Angus Fraser told me that Shelley, the Tour's first female *soigneur*, even did massage for Anderson. This seemed unlikely, as they worked for different teams, but I wasn't going to argue with Angus about that one.

Urs Zimmermann, of Roche's Carrera team, regularly saw his girlfriend, Caroline, who was on Tour working as a journalist, and, as Elliott later related, Dane Jesper Skibby of Roland-Skala fell lucky when a girl turned up from Germany to see his room-mate Didi Thurau. Thurau, who abandoned after the Blagnac–Millau stage and was also fined and banned for doping during the race, was not interested. Skibby, noted for his wit and, later, for his own admission that he had used steroids for ten years, did his best as an understudy. The obvious thing to tell Fisher in an effort to calm his fears about women wrecking the Tour was that, as far as sex went, steroids worked for some riders (a Skibby) . . . and not for others (a Thurau).

Malcolm Elliott, whose then girlfriend, Julie, appeared from time to time during the Tour, had his own problems with a band of cycling groupies, too: 'Three witches from

York – although one of them looked OK – arrived at the meal in Strasbourg, a mother and two daughters. They started off by stalking me for quite a while and there was trouble written all over them.'

And if Fisher threw a tantrum over Watson and the Berlin brunette, it was no fault of Watson's anyway – according to the man himself: 'Yeah! She followed me all round bloody Europe. She found out what hotel we were in and she came marching into the dining room. She was quite fit.' And in answer to the obvious question: 'Er . . . in a way . . . but she just turned up. Her timing was well wrong. It was quite odd, because we were all sat there in our dining room and she came right up to the table. Everyone was staring at me. I was so fed up with everything, I thought, well, it's not like they're paying me. I didn't know she was coming. I knew she was in Berlin, but we hadn't arranged it.'

By then on his third glass of wine in the Novotel, Ward's bedtime story about Anquetil was even more graphic than Roger's offering. Woutters loved his dramatic little speeches and he certainly knew how to tell a tale: 'Anquetil, he liked staying up all night, even during the Tour de France, and would also drink his wine in bed. He preferred a room alone, for obvious reasons, but during the Liège–Bastogne–Liège, maybe 20 years ago, he had to share with a young rider. So what do you think Anquetil do next at night?'

No one had a clue. The mind boggled, although Roger, having heard this one before, was already smirking. Ward, *à la* Davina McCall bombing out one of the *Big Brother* losers, kept us in intolerable suspense: 'Jacques . . . go for a shit . . . picked some of his shit up . . . then put it . . . inside rider's . . . BED!' Roger, despite having heard it dozens of times before, was in hysterics. The English among us were appalled and Fisher looked as though he was going to be sick.

Could things get worse in Berlin? They certainly could. My first attempt at actual work – as distinct from nightly attempts to find a pub that sold Guinness or listening to poor jokes in the Novotel bar – was not funny at the time, and it took several years for me to be able to have a laugh about it. Far from being amusing then, it became another good excuse to look up details of the next plane back to England.

The *Star*, who were desperately trying to sell a few copies in Scotland, had told me a couple of days before I flew out to Berlin that it might be a good idea to interview the Glaswegian cyclist Robert Millar, the 'Kingpin of the Mountains' (the *Star*'s words) and a man who was an outsider to take home the yellow jersey of the overall winner. I had looked him up in the library in the Manchester office and knew I would recognise him because, famously, he had one of the biggest conks in sport. I had seen the pictures of him and had also checked up on his details in the library. Most articles about Millar described him as obstinate, occasionally aggressive, a bit of an oddball, and stated that 'he doesn't suffer fools gladly'. In other words, in tabloidese, he doesn't talk to the press.

In Berlin, Ward felt he could do better. He had already managed to get me an interview with what he called 'my old friend' Bernard Hinault (known always as 'the five-times Tour de France winner'), who had retired the previous year and was now working for the Tour organisers as a posh greeter at stage finishes for winners and the various jersey holders. Hinault was one of the most frightening men I have ever come across and I think he knew it. I am not saying he looked angry, or evil, or even demented, but he had plainly worked on a scary thousand-yard stare and for scary thousand-yard stares I would put him up there with Hannibal Lecter, Jack Nicklaus, Charles Manson and the former East German 100 metres sprinter Marlies Göhr – and she *was* scary.

Hinault – like Sir Steven Redgrave and the American sprinter Michael Johnson shortly before they retired and were still full-time sportsmen – wasn't much of a talker. I had asked him the obvious question about Brits on the Tour and I can still recall his unsmiling reply: 'It is necessary for every country to take part in this event.' Not the quote I was looking for, but it went in the *Star*, and if I had got a quote from Hinault – and survived – no problems, surely, with a skinny little Jock.

'My paper has asked me to talk to Robert Millar,' I told Ward. 'But he's said to be a bit problematic.'

'Oooh, I know Millar and I know Peter Post, his manager. You *will* talk to Millar. A rider is duty-bound to talk to the press.'

Millar's team, Panasonic, were staying in the Novotel, too, and Ward marched off immediately. He was back within a minute.

'Millar,' he said, 'has told the journalist to fuck off.'

'Well, he can tell me that himself.'

'But they're eating,' said Ward.

'Well, I'll wait until they've finished eating.'

I stood outside the Panasonic dining room for an hour and a half (pro cyclists take some time over their food) until Millar, and his huge conk, walked out.

'Do you have problems talking to British journalists?' I demanded.

'Fire away. No probs at all, mate,' he replied.

Mate? It was Miller's Aussie teammate Allan Peiper.

The race itself hardly set the world on fire during the first two stages in Berlin. We all got excited when Shane Sutton was drawn first in the prologue time trial – 'I had arranged that,' said Ward – up one side and down the other of the Kurfürstendamm. But the excitement died when Shane was almost caught by his minute man, a Czech called Milan Jurco, at the finish. Jurco finished fifth, Shane 202nd, but at least he could tell his children he had once led the Tour de France – for a few seconds.

Ward had decided that I could climb in one of the Peugeots, the one with the name of Graham Jones along the front, to 'get a close view of a time trial'. Ward, however, was back in his disapproving mode and decided within a couple of minutes that 'Jones is finished', which seemed a bit harsh at the time.

On Stage 1 itself – a 105.5-km burn-up from the start at Hitler's former headquarters, the Reichstag, and around the suburbs of the divided city – I found I had already been demoted to Capper's vehicle at the rear. Ward was still *directeur sportif* top dog and in the lead car at the front of the race, and I missed most of the action, particularly a mini-crash that involved Steve Swart and Palov. The mechanic Steve Taylor dived in to change their tyres, and he was excellent at his job, but like me he would have preferred to have been up front with Ward.

Capper was in the Humphrey Bogart class as a smoker and refused to have the windows open. He was asked if we could get some fresh air – it was around 30 degrees inside the Peugeot – but he said no. 'I don't want my bald spot roasted by the sun,' he explained. 'Anyway, fags have never done me any harm.'

Capper was a 60-a-day man. If he got close to the end of one, he'd light up another and had worked out how to hold on to two cigarettes and drive a car at the same time. If he had a break from smoking, he would dive into a huge ice cream, a can of Coke, a pizza the size of the World Time Clock in Berlin's Alexanderplatz and a few frankfurters. According to Paul Watson, Capper preferred his usual tins of baked beans with sausages, Fray Bentos pies and biscuits – 'It's good stuff this, this'll get you going,' he would say – but he couldn't find those in Berlin.

The team time trial through the British sector on the same day was far from memorable either, until the Germans again demonstrated that their much-vaunted organisation had more than a few flaws. A police motorcyclist outrider, possibly the one who had come close to wiping out ANC the previous night, lost his way halfway down the Wall and took the Spanish team BH up the wrong street. They lost two minutes and asked for a rerun. The Tour officials refused, moving ANC up one place – from 20th to 19th.

Without the low-profile bikes and space-age helmets that characterised the top Continental teams, it might have helped if ANC's specialised time trial bikes, with lightweight frames and 'cow horn' handlebars, had arrived. Capper, however, had experienced some difficulty in getting supplies, and the team, with little expertise in this type of event anyway, had to go on their road bikes dressed up with a rear disc wheel. It was another hint that there were a few gaps in the colonel's operations.

Malcolm Elliott says: 'The stages in Berlin were flat and fast, and we just found ourselves sucked along from start to finish without having to give it much thought. We'd been shown up in the team time trial, but then the low-profile bikes had never turned up.

'We'd been promised them, along with carbon-fibre bikes for the mountain stages. I'd had a low-profile bike early on in 1987, but it stayed as a frame hung up in Capper's garage. It never got used and as far as I know it was quietly disposed of for some poxy amount in the Isle of Man. In the team time trial, every other team was on low-profiles and disc wheels, whereas we had five disc wheels between nine riders and, rather than give the weaker riders an advantage, we all went without. That sort of thing just makes you feel inferior from the start. This was the Tour de France, the pinnacle of the season, and we couldn't even get a few extra disc wheels. There were always reasons whenever you mentioned it. Capper would say, "Lads, I tried, but Campag let me down." We were always asking for more kit and he'd say, "I'm waiting for another delivery from Assos."'

Adrian Timmis, too, recalls his anger at what he regarded as the team's lack of professionalism: 'We rode our normal road bikes but with a disc wheel in the back and a low-profile rim in the front wheel. It was a slightly lighter front wheel and I had two bottle cages on. I may have taken one off, but basically it was the same standard road bike. I put my skinsuit on and got on with it. The time gaps were huge in the time trial and it didn't do much for us in the race as a whole.'

In Berlin, I had been approached by dozens of German prostitutes calling themselves Dagmar, Marlise or Elfriede, most of them amazingly attractive and prepared to take credit cards (or so I was told). I had also seen an army of gun-toting East German soldiers, the oddest professional sportsmen I had ever come across and two boring time trials in which the British had done rather poorly. It was disappointing. Knowing so little about cycling, I had assumed that the ANC riders were in the same class as all the other Tour teams. I thought winning the Milk Race or the Kellogg's Tour was as good as you could get.

Micky Morrison had tried to put me straight when I met him in Stoke before setting off, but neither of us had had much success there.

'Did you know Adrian Timmis won a stage in the Midi Libre before the Tour?'

'What's a Midi Libre?'

'He got away from the bunch near the finish.'

'What's a bunch?'

'Adrian's a very good climber, too.'

'Oh, right. I used to do a lot of rock and ice climbing in the Alps when I was younger. I can swap some memories with Adrian!'

'I don't think you will,' said Morrison.

I knew nothing about their sport, but in Berlin I had worked out that there were some very good riders in the Tour de France and others who were not very good. Some of the ANC riders had spotted that, too. Elliott says: 'I'd fancied my chances in the prologue and thought I could get in the top 15 or thereabouts. I knew how hard I had tried, but some guys had gone 20 seconds faster. I knew then I was in for a hard time.'

Apparently, many Tour followers are addicted to their time trials, but to me it was equivalent to watching an Olympics 1,500 metres final with all the runners heading off at one-minute intervals. Where on earth were those famous mass sprints, the frightening hills, the Tour's famous views and the riders' bloody falls I had watched on TV? The most remarkable sights of the Tour so far had been those skinny ANC riders scoffing three meals apiece at dinner – and then walking over to nick mine – and the incredible muscular development of their quads, so pronounced that a rider's patella was concealed. They had the huge legs of a Ben Johnson and the thin arms and chest of a Mick Jagger. Even without looking at the abdominal fat that appeared like balloons on them after every meal, I knew riders liked to eat a lot. Like actors and dancers, pro cyclists seemed to have uncontrollable hungers yet their weight seemed to stay the same. But my reaction to losing my lunch because 'they need food more than you', according to Capper, had moved from surprise to irritation.

So much for the divided city. Back in my room at the Novotel, it was time to sober up and get down to breakfast. At least this was to be the last meal in Berlin, the last day of broiling heat in Berlin, the last attempted chat-ups from the armies of tarts and the hundreds of drug addicts and dropouts of Berlin.

Above all, this would be the last time I would allow the ANC riders to steal my food in what they saw as their *droit de seigneur*. I would treat the ANC riders like I treated my dog and tell them to 'stay', or I'd do what I did at home and eat on my own in my bedroom.

The riders had a short plane journey through the air corridor out of Berlin past Frankfurt to Stuttgart, while the rest of the ANC personnel faced a nightmarish 500-mile drive in team vehicles through the road corridor and past the speed traps, the aggressive and ticket-hungry Polizei with their smelly nylon shirts, body odour and ancient put-putting two-stroke cars with weird names like Wartburg and Trabant. At the East German border, an armed guard stuck his head into the Citroën and ordered us to wait in line next to the sign that read 'Money in Excess Will Be Confiscated'. The same guard, possibly a closet Tour fan, asked the mechanic Geoff Shergold for a cycling cap before demanding the five Deutschmark for a visa and our escape to the West. A butch female guard, a lookalike of Tamara Press, the Russian discus thrower, wanted another fiver from us 'for use of the road'.

By the time we reached Stuttgart, any pleasure I'd taken in the *Daily Star*'s decision to send me on the Tour de France had vanished. Willard's words came back to me again: 'Everyone gets everything he wants. I wanted a mission. And for my sins, they gave me one. Brought it up to me like room service . . . It was a real choice mission. And when it was over, I'd never want another.'

The horror . . . the horror.

4

OUT WITH THE BOYS

Disneyland. Fuck, man, this is better than Disneyland!
Lance, *Apocalypse Now*

'WELL, THAT IS the end of his cycling career,' said Tony
Capper in the outspoken manner we had come to love.
Bernard Chesneau, who was seated a couple of feet away in
the Sofitel in Stuttgart, close to the French border with
south-west Germany, was waiting for a train to Paris. I
knew he had little English, but I thought he'd got the
message. The Frenchman's little Tour de France cameo was
over. He was inconsolable – and he still is. '*Le Tour de
France – mais pas en France*,' he sighs now.

Stage 3 had run a hilly 145 miles from Karlsruhe, and it
was the day I began to recognise the delights, and the
potential disasters, of this race, and that there were sports
players in the world who should be admired as much for
their inability as for their ability.

Twenty years after the '87 Tour, I wrote another fly-on-
the-wall book, called *Pointless*, described by the publishers
as 'the inside, in-depth story of a season with Britain's worst
football club'. I had also started my ten months with East
Stirlingshire as a scoffing cynic, longing for them to lose
every week for the sake of the book – so that they would
finish bottom of Scotland's Division Three for the third

consecutive season and we could all have a good laugh. In the end, I was lost in admiration for one of the dottiest sporting institutions in Britain (the footballers were paid £10 a week) and their first win of that season was as pleasurable for me as England winning the World Cup in 1966.

In other words, I had made the same mistake as I had made with ANC two decades earlier. At least by the time I reached Karlsruhe most of my Berlin scorn had vanished. I'm not saying that I was banking on a stage win *à la* Capper, but by then I was desperate for all of them to survive to Paris.

And in that respect, the ANC riders did somewhat better than their staff.

During his brief spell on the Tour, Ward Woutters stuck gamely to most of the race rules – although he wasn't averse to the occasional moment of disobedience – and he had applied to the Tour officials for permission for 'a representative of ANC-Halfords' to travel with him in the lead car, leaving Capper a mile behind in the second Peugeot. 'This,' said Ward, who for some reason seemed to have developed a soft spot for me, 'is a genuine honour for a journalist. Even President Mitterrand would have to ask permission from the Tour! Now you will see real *cyclisme*.'

I was flattered. I was delighted, too, about the chance of avoiding six hours of passive smoking, although I quickly found that I could see little of the race itself, even from the sharp end. The ANC riders discovered, too, that there would be no easy days on this Tour, none of what Adrian Timmis describes as a 'piano day'. Once they were past the neutralised zone outside whichever town or city they were leaving, all the teams got stuck in, and even Ward was shocked to find he had to motor at 40 mph to catch up.

'It was so fast,' recalls Timmis. 'I spoke to Robert Millar and Stephen Roche, and even they couldn't believe how fast it was in the first week and a half. It was partly because there was no "*patron*" of the *peloton*. Bernard Hinault had retired, so I think a lot of riders thought there was an opportunity to do something in the race. It was a lot more open and less controlled, apparently, than in previous years.

'The stages were hard from the gun because there was always a silly hot-spot sprint after 20 km. The last hour was ridiculous. Superconfex, the Dutch team, would get on the front to wind it up for Jean-Paul van Poppel, their sprinter, and it would get unbelievably fast. I had read about how they had these "piano days", where they'd ride for hours at a nice easy tempo, but I can only remember one day when it was like that. The racing was very intense all the time.'

The whole frantic experience of a stage of the Tour de France had won me over within an hour of leaving Karlsruhe. I recall likening it to a ride at Disneyland: a slow crank to the top, a downhill plunge, then high-speed cruising when the land levelled out.

After 14 miles, and the first Catch sprint, Ward strained his ears for Radio Tour: '*Premier, Bontempi, suivit par Kelly et Duclos-Lasalle,*' it announced.

'They are all afraid,' said Ward.

'Afraid of what?'

'All afraid to try. Our riders think they'll use all their energy and fail to reach Paris. At this level, we're not going to win any money. And look at Chesneau now. His mind is not right at all. What on earth is wrong with him?'

We were on the Côte de Volkersbach, a third-category climb so forgettable that it has barely even made it to Google. But I have kept to this day the Tour's official pasteboards, which showed villages, climbs, sprints, feed area and any difficulties en route. And in there is the Côte de Volkersbach, with my note reading, 'Chesneau in the shit,' and, later, 'Chesneau even deeper in the shit and dropped.'

'Finished,' said Woutters. 'Chesneau is finished. Give him a *bidon*,' he demanded of Steve Taylor, the mechanic.

Taylor whipped the plastic water bottle out of the window, but Ward exploded in rage – in what I assumed was some odd Belgian dialect – when Chesneau handed back a full one. 'You see,' grumbled Woutters. 'His mind . . . not right.'

When Paul Watson dropped back with some more bottles for his teammate, Ward went ballistic. 'That's not your job!' he roared. 'You are not a *domestique*. Your job is to ride. The *domestiques* must come back with the water.'

'But how is a *domestique* going to come back with water for himself?' asked Watson, with unanswerable logic.

By then, ANC's stage was turning into a disaster. Taylor did well to rescue Timmis when he had punctured, and with Chesneau left to the mercy of Capper at the rear of the field, with 30 miles to go and the attacks starting ahead of us, it was the turn of Graham Jones.

'Give us a *bidon*,' asked Jones, even though he had two full ones. Taylor handed the water bottle out of the window but obviously hadn't taken in Ward's tricks of the trade, and as we motored on past him Jones was left screaming: 'Pull! Pull!'

'What does he mean, pull?' asked Taylor.

'He needs a pull, a pull!' screamed Woutters, slowing down until Jones came back alongside.

'*Bidon*,' said Ward, handing one out of the window, then immediately accelerating as Jones hung on to the bottle.

'You see,' said Ward, 'only two metres, but it gives his legs a rest. Now he has impetus. Now he has the speed to catch the other riders.'

'So that's how it's done,' said Taylor.

'You remember all this now,' said Ward, and certainly we all remembered that from then on.

Ward wasn't averse to a little cheating and didn't even mind a few fines for Capper from the race *commissaires* if it meant he could save a rider's Tour, but he drew the line elsewhere. In the last 20 miles of a stage, when the racing was getting faster and faster, the danger of cars weaving in and out of the bunch was obvious and no feeding was allowed. Swart dropped back to ask for some water, but he got little change from Ward.

'No, no, it is not permitted now,' he told Swart.

'Oh, come on, everybody else is!'

Woutters eventually handed out a *bidon*: 'But you see, we will be fined for this and you will be penalised some time.' And, much to Capper's disgust, he was right.

The last 14 miles into Stuttgart proved too much for Watson and Gallopin, who both dropped off the back. On the Tour's first road stage proper, five ANC riders were left behind, one of them for good.

Chesneau finished almost half an hour behind the stage winner, and Ward had worked out long before the finish that the Frenchman would soon be on his way home. Woutters, who was in his 60s at the time, looked as weary and as baked as his riders after 140 miles in the desperate heat. 'Now for Chesneau,' he croaked as he began to look at his map of eastern France. 'Paris is still 2,000 miles away for you,' he said to me with a tiny smile. 'For Chesneau, it is over and he is only 150 miles to his home. Now, will it be a train or a flight for him?'

For reasons of his own, Capper preferred that he went by train.

Chesneau, who was 27 at the time, was what the cycling press would call a 'journeyman pro' – a *domestique* who spent his days bringing water and food from team cars, shielding teammates from rivals and even sacrificing his bicycle or a wheel to a teammate who had punctured. *Domestiques* could get the occasional chance to win a stage; Chesneau, who had spent a year racing in the US before arriving at ANC, was never going to win a stage of the Tour de France. He was a likeable man, intelligent and a hard worker. With ANC, he had helped all he could, but he was ill when he arrived in Berlin and ill when he left four days later. He would not have been a first-choice fetcher and carrier for most of the staff.

'We took the wrong French rider,' says Phil Griffiths. 'We shouldn't have taken Chesneau. We went for him because he was younger, but we should have gone with Patrice Thévenard. My choice wasn't Chesneau.'

Thévenard, however, had stuck with ANC for only a year before moving on to cyclo-cross, and in many ways Chesneau was to have the last laugh. After his disaster on Stage 3, where ANC came close to losing Sutton and Jones, too, Chesneau retired within 12 months and 24 years later I found him working for Coca-Cola, one of the major sponsors of the Tour de France.

Born in Blois, he began cycling with his local club and was a pro from 1984 to 1988, first in the United States with an American team, Mengoni, which managed to last 12 months, then with Spanish team Kas, then at ANC and finally with the Belgian team SEFB, who by then had taken on Ward Woutters as *directeur sportif*. So Capper had that one wrong in Stuttgart: Chesneau did have another year in pro cycling, and things went fine for him from then on.

'I think my victory in a race in Central Park in New York was the most rewarding of my life,' he says. 'There were 50,000 spectators there and as an environment of madness it was at least equal to arriving for the start of the Tour de France.'

His greatest regret? 'The first three stages were in Germany, around Berlin, then to Stuttgart. Unfortunately, with several fellow members of ANC, I was a victim of food poisoning, and I had to abandon before the race had even arrived in France. What a disappointment!'

Chesneau, like fellow Frenchman Gallopin, and both Swart and Sutton, was married when he raced for ANC, and had been for more than two years when he joined the team in 1987. He and his wife, Marie, now have two grown-up children.

'I practised cycling at the highest level as a professional, which not many men can say, but there are more important things in life. I joined Coca-Cola in 1989, and in those 21 years there has been a constant motivation and passion for the job. Coca-Cola sent me to the Winter Olympics in Albertville in 1992, and I have also worked at football World Cups, the Tour de France and rugby World Cups. I have had a good life. I love people and I still go cycling, jogging, swimming and skiing in winter. I like reading books – but not books on sport, sorry to say!'

Chesneau understandably doesn't recall much about the 1987 Tour de France, but he does recall getting his name in *L'Équipe* after he'd abandoned, which just about sums up the French passion for the Tour de France.

'Usual spelling of Chesneau?' asked Tommy, the infuriating male copy-taker, when I phoned in my story for the *Star* that night. Tommy, a tiny Mancunian in his 60s, was too clever by half. 'Usual spelling of Saint-Julien-en-Genevois?' he would ask. Finding the words for a story had never been difficult; getting the words into the paper's pages was the hard part for any reporter on the *Star* or virtually any other tabloid. We were still at the stage of delivering reports over a telephone line to a copy-taker, and the one-keystroke techniques of today were still a few years away. In 1987, I only had my bits of A4 paper, my biro, the use of the nearest telephone . . . and Tommy. Halfway through the Tour, I found a shop that sold me a voice recorder, which baffled me totally. The first person I tried it on was Tony Capper, but after ten minutes I realised I hadn't had it turned on. Amazingly, Capper agreed to start again and, even more amazingly, produced the precise same replies he had given the first time. After that, it was back to the biro.

Like me, the *Star* had been left miles behind by '87. Journalism had moved on dramatically in Europe – and even more so in the United States.

Three months after the '87 Tour de France, I realised that I had done my ten years with Express Newspapers and was owed a sabbatical. I had three weeks to go anywhere, and do anything, in the knowledge that my job would still be there when I got back. I did *not* count the three weeks on the Tour de France as a sabbatical. I decided to spend the time as a subeditor (or what I think they call a copy coordinator in the United States) on the sports desk of the *Orlando Sentinel* in Florida. It was an eye-opener. Most of the staff were in their 20s, did not smoke or drink (at least not in the office) and worked with Atex, a paper-free software system that allowed them to work on-screen instead of on typewriters. In other words, no more Tommys, no more compositors, no more typesetters and no more fathers of the numerous Express Newspapers chapels to suggest to their colleagues, every month, that a strike was a good idea. *Defence of the Realm*, the 1986 political thriller set largely in a Fleet Street newspaper and the local pubs, got virtually everything right – an ambitious young reporter, a drunken old colleague and a corrupt newspaper owner – but I still have to laugh at the sight of Gabriel Byrne holding a piece of hot metal to bang out one of the staff compositors. If a journalist had dared to do that in the 1980s, the comps would have walked out within 30 seconds.

There was no father of the chapel in Orlando and, apart from the fact that the *Sentinel* staff couldn't write a headline to save their lives, this was a different league altogether. It took the *Star* two years to follow suit – although Rupert Murdoch had brought Atex to Wapping in 1986 – and until then we were still using a small army of Tommys, biros on bits of paper when working out of the office and battered typewriters on desks covered by fag burns when working in the office.

However, while I might only have worked for the *Daily Star*, with all its foibles, I was one jump ahead of the field during the Tour de France. I had a cycling team to report on all to myself. Most of the journalists from every country travelled in shared cars and could see little of the daily drama from a distance. Invariably, they would watch the start, follow the race for 30 miles or so, find somewhere nice for lunch and then drive off at high speed to the stage finish, in time to follow *Le Tour*'s own blanket TV coverage before the gladiators arrived. They could then, quite often before the riders even stepped off their bikes, dive in for quotes. Thanks to Capper, and the ANC Peugeot, I had a view of what amounted to a daily dramatic play of my own. I am not being blasé about this, but to arrive in an official team car at a stage finish did tend to bring out the braggart in me.

'What did you get up to today, Jeff?'

'Oh, I handed Chesneau a *bidon*, saw Timmis puncture, one of the ANC riders was fined for having a pee near some spectators and Tony Capper gave me some of his lunch.'

It was hard to beat that when the best anyone else could come up with was who won the stage, who abandoned and who was still in the yellow jersey.

After we arrived in France, I quickly got into what became my daily routine of driving down with the riders to the stage start, watching them sign in at the pre-race staging area, in the unlikely hope that some of the Tour fans might give an ANC rider a round of applause, and then grabbing my free coffee at the Café de Colombia caravan. Every day, the same Tour official would sound the warning whistle and then it was back into one of the ANC cars, follow the stage, find the *salle de presse*, write five to six hundred words on my A4 and then phone my piece over, all the time praying that I would get one of the girl copy-takers and that Tommy would be out on his boozer break.

It was not a difficult job, if the truth is told, and the officials who ran the Tour de France and looked after the press made life even easier for all of us. They had got this down to perfection over the years. At every stage *salle de presse*, from Berlin onwards, there was the same formidable army of middle-aged lady telephonists, part of a 20-strong secretariat responsible for catering to the demands of the 800 or so press and TV journalists. Telephones, telex machines, a seat, food (and even a selection of biros) were supplied.

Already while we were still in Germany, though, I did have one concern about what I was coming to regard as a glorified busman's holiday. In the press room at Stuttgart, as an American journalist staggered past with his Nokia Cityman – inside a backpack – Tommy told me the sports desk had asked for a word with me – always a bad sign.

'When are you going to ride a stage of this Tour?' I was asked. 'We need to work out when a photographer has to be there.'

The possibility of my joining a stage was getting more remote by the day. What, I thought, would Millar, or Fignon, say – or even do – if I lined up alongside them at a start? And, judging by their reaction to rogue riders, the Tour officials would not be too happy, either. When we'd arrived for the stage finish that day, the Tour organisers had been baffled to discover an extra rider, a young West German who had cleverly nicked an official number plate and infiltrated the bunch as they crossed the line. He was carted off immediately by a brigade of the Stuttgart police, who obviously hadn't found this funny at all. I certainly didn't fancy a night in a German police cell or, even worse, a French one.

'I'm still working out the details of the Tour and its riders, so I'll probably ride a stage once we reach France,' I lied.

In any case, for now there were plenty of other daily stories for the *Star* – and they were easy to find. Robert Millar apart, it was simple to talk to a rider – virtually any rider – and since I was, quite literally, living next door to nine of them, I had as many quotes as I wanted.

As far as I could see, the European cycling press could grab whoever they wanted without having to ask their permission. With so many pressmen on the Tour, it was a fair bet that the majority of them were not going to get exclusives, or 'scoops', as the tabloids used to call them then. The next best thing was a quote or two, and this applied to the coverage of virtually every sport, for, make no mistake, sports editors love their quotes – even the most puerile of quotes – as much as reporters love their bylines. This was before the days of the curse of modern journalism, the press conference, and its horrible human addendum, the media officer. In the good old days, sports reporters all hung about in the corridors outside dressing-rooms and collared managers or players on their way out to the communal car park and their Ford Granadas. They all got different angles and different stories. Now, press conferences, with their useless ritualism, are carefully stage-managed by PR men and women whose main job is to ensure that everyone gets the same anodyne briefing.

There is so much competition among the tabloids for 'angles' on sports stories, and this has led to the distortions we see today. You had to be different, and given the lack of access to the sources of stories – to players, management or coaches – hacks just started to make things up.

No need for that on the Tour de France. The French press hunted down the French riders, the Spanish the Spaniards, the Colombian the Colombians, I had ANC – all to myself, seemingly – and the lot of us could also grab the stage winners and the top three race leaders.

I don't imagine this ever happened to Lance Armstrong after he arrived in 1999 to take the Tour apart, but in '87 everyone from Stephen Roche downwards – Roche attempting to hang on to the yellow jersey for most of the three weeks – was at the mercy of the press. Before long, I began to feel desperately sorry for the riders.

It got worse and worse for them the longer the race went

on. On Stage 20, with its 135 brutal miles from Villard over the Col du Coq to the uphill finish of Capper's favourite climb, Alpe d'Huez, I was asked to drive the ANC Citroën, complete with its '*Officiel*' insignia, up the hill's 21 switchbacks to the summit (ANC were running out of staff by then).

It was astonishing to be applauded by every Tour follower standing, or sitting, by the roadside. Carrying an '*Officiel*' sign was as good as driving de Gaulle to the Elysées Palace. But I wasn't there to take a nice car around nice countryside and carry medicines and clothing into hotels for a bunch of 20-something kids. I still had to find the 'words' for the paper.

But, as ANC's juvenile *soigneur* Sabino Pignatelli might admit, if you were driving the Citroën to a stage-finish hotel, you did tend to have some time on your hands. I arrived with an hour or so spare to unload the vehicle, and from the hotel – and my own choice of double bedroom – it was a short walk uphill to the finish line.

Roche had lost the yellow jersey to the new race leader, Pedro Delgado, and, as the *Daily Star* sports desk were by then more interested in Roche than the troubles of ANC, I followed the army of journalists as the Irishman disappeared into the inevitable crush on the line. Nor was there any problem in following a bunch of French journalists behind Roche into the tiny dope-control caravan, where the rider waited to give his sample to two dour French *commissaires*.

Roche was brutalised by the stage – and the press. In terms of talking to journalists, he pressed all the right buttons at all the right times, but he had had enough. Unshaven, with the pallor of a corpse and with his eyes unfocused, Roche stoically answered the same silly questions as he had done on every other day of the Tour, until finally we left him alone. No other game in the world would show such a lack of respect to a sportsman, and

Roche soon discovered that most of the UK reporters were still looking for their 'exclusives' by the middle of the evening. A bunch of British and Irish journalists (the French were either still eating or didn't go in for this sort of thing), including Des Cahill, marched into Roche's hotel after dinner and, according to Cahill: 'Roche really lost his temper, the first time I had ever seen that happen. He shouted, "All the French and Belgian journalists see me right after the race and then leave me alone. Why do you think you can call on me any time of the night?" One guy had flown out from England for one of the Sunday supplements and wanted a picture of Roche on his hotel bed wearing the yellow jersey, but Roche refused and your man went away empty-handed.'

It was true, as Roche said, that most of the French would not chase a sportsman around for hours after the end of any major event, but they certainly had odd principles of their own. In the UK, we were forced to stick to rules invented by someone else, usually press officers and their management; the French press did their own thing.

By the start of the new millennium, it was still possible in the UK to obtain a one-on-one interview with a sportsman – if sufficient notice was given. Invariably, that player would then be carefully briefed on what – or, more likely, what not – to say. Players considered high risk and/ or high profile (in other words, those who, by dint of age or experience or stature, were likely to speak their own minds) were usually accompanied by a minder from the appropriate press office. One Scottish rugby international told me when I first began covering the sport in 2001 that he knew he had 'arrived' when the Scottish Rugby Union media manager, Graham Law, began to sit in on his interviews. It was, he said, almost as rewarding as winning a first cap.

There was scarcely a peep of protest from us put-upon writers; we had become used to this state of affairs and most of us were not going to rock a boat that had supplied us with several years of pleasurable cruising. We might have been able to quote CVs that listed, like campaign medals, 'five World Cups, six Lions tours, fourteen Five/Six Nations campaigns', etc., etc., but we had become happy to operate in a limited theatre, with neither the ability or the ambition to move on.

In New Zealand, for the British and Irish Lions tour of 2005, we were putty in the hands of Alastair Campbell, the former spin doctor of the then prime minister Tony Blair. He was, if you like, the film director, with Lions head coach Clive Woodward as the star, and an awful lot of work must have gone into it. Woodward never lost his lines once.

The tone was set early on when the reporters and photographers arrived at the squad's first training session to find ten-foot-high black canvas screens shielding the players. Access was limited to the last five minutes, by which time all we could witness was the post-session stretching and (an injured) Jonny Wilkinson punting a ball about.

In case we hadn't got the message, three wiry men in their early 30s, who couldn't have advertised their day jobs more vividly if they had carried around large signs saying 'Regular Army, Probably SAS', patrolled the woods surrounding the training area, breaking off occasionally to look us over and work out whether a knee in the coccyx would bring down a fat, unfit journo quicker than an elbow to the philtrum.

To our undisguised fury, Bravo One, Two and Three, as they became known, sat on the bench during matches – and attended every press conference. Their commander-in-chief was also big into the art of organised manipulation. Aware that most bylined writers need little provocation to preen, Woodward addressed most of them by their first names. He plainly regarded press briefings and the subsequent question-and-answer sessions as his stage, and before each one he would give a little speech, his thoughts for the day. In other words, he was rugby's Tony Blair, a man carefully coached in the art of public presentation, and he knew exactly when to look up from his notes. He kept his hands flat on the table in front of him but occasionally, when emphasis was needed, lifted them in front of his chest into a cradle, fingers and thumbs together. He was bright, well briefed and informative. In a word, insufferable, as far as the probing journos were concerned.

Nos amis, however, didn't have to put up with any of this sort of thing, and not just on the Tour de France. In 2000, I had left the nationals to write about rugby union for *Scotland on Sunday*, based in Edinburgh, and the French press's modus operandi certainly hadn't changed by then. I was seated in the Murrayfield press-box next to the former French star Franck Mesnel, who was wearing what appeared to be ballet shoes. Mesnel, a player who won 56 caps as a midfield back in the 1980s, had made a fortune from his clothing company Eden Park, but he hadn't lost his charm, or his taste in clothing. As I had in 1987 with Ward Woutters, I decided to ask a man in the know what to do about getting an interview with some of the French players. I had ten minutes to get a quote and I had guessed, quite rightly, that it could take me a week to talk to one of the Scots.

No problems, said Mesnel: 'Simple. Give them five minutes, wait outside the French dressing-room and walk in with the French journalists.'

'But this surely isn't like the Tour de France,' I pointed out.

'No, it's not the Tour de France, but it is French sport.'

And, as in the 1987 press charge with Roche into the dope-control caravan, the quotes were easy to come by. The French man of the match, Olivier Magne, had already been collared in the corridor and, as suggested by Mesnel, I marched straight into the away dressing-room with 20 others to find a naked half-back, Thomas Castaignède, surrounded by French journalists while two other pressmen sat on the side of the bath as a rather large but extremely docile prop called Christian Califano gave them his version of the game. In two decades, French sporting journalism hadn't changed at all.

5

FIELD OF FIRE

In a war, there are many moments for compassion and tender action.

Willard, *Apocalypse Now*

THE MAJORITY OF writers won't admit to this, but they do spend far too long – and I am as bad as anyone – clicking through Amazon in an effort to find out if their masterpiece is still selling. If you get to '345,987 in Books' (and it happens to everyone eventually), forget it, but Google can also be the perfect place for writers to hunt for reviews and as many blogs that mention them as they can find. There's a large amount of egotism involved here, but it sure can make your day. Someone might have decided that yours is 'the worst book ever written', but at least someone has read it. Here's my favourite, exactly as it was written in April 2011, from a blog which calls itself (no relation to Watergate and Woodward and Bernstein) The Washingmachinepost:

Parachuted in as journalist in residence from the star newspaper was jeff connor, subsequent author of this testament to self-destruction, wide eyed and legless. having a journalist in tow was likely as popular then as it would be now; even more so perhaps, given that connor was a tabloid journalist, rather than one with any sort of pedigree in writing about the beautiful sport. there is doubtless [not] much worse than getting in above your neck while someone not only watches while you do so, but writes about it afterwards.

Boy, did the Washingmachinepost get that one right. I certainly had no pedigree in the 'beautiful sport' and I don't think there is 'much worse' for a rider than finding a journalist seated alongside him as his Tour de France falls apart. I had a front-row seat as all of them at ANC – and that includes the staff – self-destructed on a daily basis. And while most cycling fans are aware that a lot of suffering goes into their sport, they certainly never witness some of it, the individual problems and the occasional inabilities of ANC to perform their professional jobs. None of these details appeared in the *Daily Star*, although some readers may have got a few hints. Since it was also what the editor called 'a family newspaper', there was a lot missed out – until the appearance of *Wide-Eyed and Legless*.

I was delighted to have written a first book. It gave me as much of a thrill as finding my first byline in my first newspaper, but I have felt not guilty but certainly culpable of a wrongdoing ever since. The book amounted to a betrayal, my own decision to 'spit in the soup', particularly when I wrote the words that described the last days of Graham Jones and Paul Watson on the Tour.

It says a lot about them that 25 years later all, seemingly, had been forgiven. We may have been staying, on the night after the gruelling Stage 6 from Strasbourg, in Épinal's Hôtel Émile Zola, but they have never told me, '*J'accuse.*'

In Berlin, after the prologue time trial, I had written down – and thanks to Ward Woutters for the quotes – that Jones, who had struggled almost as soon as he left the ramp, 'used to be a good *rouleur*, now nothing'. Ward added, 'Look instead at Thurau,' pointing at the German in the colours of the Belgian Roland-Skala team. 'Look at him, there's an example of a good *rouleur*. He pedals easily, no wobbling, his torso is straight and his head doesn't move at all.' It was fine to be handed the definition of what amounts to a good *rouleur*, but how could that make me a critical expert? Jones, I reported, had rolling shoulders, his head was moving from side to side and he definitely had wobbling wheels.

On the day of the Massacre of the Field of Fire, I stuck the boot in on Jones again after he had packed. It was only much later that I realised he had been ill. I had watched a poorly man suffer for six hours without much in the way of support from the general public, had watched him cheating (mildly) in an attempt to save his career and had spent much of the day in the knowledge that he was certain to abandon. Having written it all down on my A4 in the back of the car that had followed Jones for 169 km from Strasbourg to Épinal, I suddenly found myself a foot away from him in the same hotel. Jones was not a pretty sight and I was desperately sorry for him, but it didn't stop me from telling everyone who would read it all about his disastrous day. I wanted to say something to him, but what on earth can you say to a sportsman who has failed?

When the inquests, with Phil Griffiths and Capper as the head coroners, began in Épinal, Watson looked like a man delighted to be on his way home. In fact, he later admitted that he had intended to abandon that day and that he had a new job with a new team lined up for the following year anyway. He says: 'After three days, I knew I was not going to finish the Tour. Then you're looking at the map thinking which is the best stage to pull out, where's the nearest airport. Even after Capper's encouragement, I just didn't want to be there.'

As the other riders, satisfied (at least I presumed they were satisfied) that they had survived another day, were getting ready to change out of their ANC outfits for dinner, Jones was seated alone with a beer, his cheeks and eyes sunken. He did not have a job for the following year. He must have lost seven or eight pounds in weight and, to put it mildly, he didn't look well at all. It turned out later that Jones, like Chesneau, had been ill from the start of what was his fifth Tour de France.

'It depends what you define as ill,' he says. 'I was completely run-down basically. It was partly due to the preparation we had. It had been a bit last-minute and panicky. We did the Midi Libre and others, but we weren't really ready for them. You can't do a couple of Belgian semi-classics and race at home and then hope to come into those races, which were in 90-degree heat, and use them as preparation for the Tour. I never felt right. I was knackered. I was totally struggling. When I came back after the Tour, I had some blood tests. My potassium levels were ridiculous and I had low iron. So I wasn't ill in the sense of having a bad cold or a stomach virus. I just wasn't well enough to do it.'

Griffiths went straight for the throat and wanted Watson banned from cycling for 'walking out of the Tour'. Jones, he said, had 'done one tour too many'. I was on the riders' side on this one, but what could I say to them, particularly my fellow Mancunian Jones? A similar conundrum has faced every newspaper, radio and TV sports journalist in the world, and most of them make a cock-up of it. When I saw him at the hotel, I'd had six hours to think about it, but the best I could come up with was 'sorry'. Or 'better luck next time'. Or the daftest one of all, 'Are you all right?', the one usually asked of a pedestrian who has just been knocked down by a car. They might put up with it, but a sportsman or woman doesn't want to hear that sort of banality from anyone – and that includes the winners who are awarded a 'well done' from a reporter. 'Sorry' is a word for people who have lost a relative or a close friend; 'better luck next time' would mean nothing in this case, because for Watson and Jones there wouldn't be a next time, at least not in the Tour de France.

Finally I took a deep breath and walked over to Jones.

'I'm sorry,' I said.

Jones didn't even look at me, took another huge swig from his beer and staggered off to his bedroom. But at least if I was sorry for Jones I wasn't alone.

'I felt for Graham, knowing what he'd done in his previous Tours,' says Phil Griffiths now. 'To step down so much . . . it was all right for Malcolm and Adrian to step into the Tour and struggle, because the romantic challenge was beyond their dreams and they were realising it. Graham had ridden in the best teams in the world. He could have been top five in the Tour had he not been ill in 1980. In 1987, he was ill, too, and he was really struggling. For Graham, that was a lot to handle. He was a big asset to us – always – but he must have had a lot of turmoil coping with that. It must have been really hard to deal with that step down at that Tour.'

For some of the other ANC riders, however, there was little sympathy for either Jones or Watson. Quite the reverse. 'They had been destroyed on the road from Strasbourg to Épinal on the big climb of the Champ du Feu and everyone went past them near the bottom,' says Malcolm Elliott. 'At the time they looked OK and I thought they'd get back on the last group, but at the finish they were waiting for us. We got back to the cars and we could tell by their faces they had packed. I thought to myself, "You lucky bastards," because at that moment I think I'd rather have been doing anything else anywhere in the world than riding the Tour de France.'

When I first made my little 'sorry' speech to Jones, we were in the capital of the Vosges *département*, and I had just seen the Tour's first hills. And then there were six, with Jones, ANC's most experienced rider, and Watson, their King of the Mountains, following Chesneau into the broom wagon. The Frenchman was already back in his home town of Blois with his wife and two young children, but the losses

111

of Jones and Watson were devastating. For ANC, it was the equivalent of a rowing eight losing Matthew Pinsent and Steve Redgrave, and some of the ANC staff were taking bets that Shane Sutton wouldn't be far behind. By this stage, *directeur sportif* Woutters and *soigneur* Van der Vloet had already departed to wherever they came from in Belgium. This Tour had become an Ypres for ANC-Halfords.

Jones was three months away from his 30th birthday – a senior in pro cycling terms – when he travelled to Europe with ANC. It had been a long, successful career that really deserved a happier ending, and he had the men to write it for him 25 years later.

'Fortunately, I know that the 1987 Tour is not the way people will remember Graham,' says Shane Sutton. 'When you look at it, we had guys with Graham Jones's ability, with Paul Watson's talent, and they were going home. Something wasn't right. People knew what Graham had achieved. Getting round the Tour for him should have been a formality, the talent he had. He'd been to the Tour and raced it. He was used to being up the front on the climbs, comfortable. That was his element. But he was ill, too. He was respected by everyone, and the Tour de France knew Graham Jones and respected him, too. To see him leave it was heart-wrenching. But with the best will in the world, we had all been put into the Tour virtually naked.'

'Graham had problems with his stomach,' says Adrian Timmis. 'I think he had an ulcer that kept popping its head up. I probably didn't ask him as much as I should have. But that was just me. I think Graham thought we shouldn't have been there. I think he thought we should have done something a little bit less dramatic than the Tour, maybe the Giro or something, although that is still a tough race. I think he was sceptical about us riding it.'

On his first Tour in 1980, a race won by Joop Zoetemelk of the Netherlands, Jones was the youngest rider in the race and was 12th overall after Stage 16 to Pra Loup, a climb to the French ski resort in the Alpes-de-Haute-Provence. Then the whole of his Peugeot team fell ill with a virus at Morzine, a familiar tale for Jones in the years to come.

'Gilbert Duclos-Lassalle abandoned and he was not the sort of rider to abandon easily, being the big ox that he was,' he recalls. 'I think if I hadn't been ill, I'd have finished quite comfortably in the top ten, because there was a time trial to come and I was better at that than some of the people ahead of me, so there would have been a chance to make up some ground. And I might well have won the white jersey as best young rider, too. In 1981, I finished 20th. That's 20th as a *domestique*, basically. I lost time in the Pyrenees and the Alps because I was helping other people in the team.

'I'd had a bad year in '84, fitness-wise, illness-wise and injury-wise. I was thinking at the time, "God, can I carry on doing this?" You think however bad things are they might get better. I was riding in France, but the scene was picking up in England and the opportunity was there to come home and make a reasonable living – well, make a living – and have a normal life, which I had probably not had since I was 16, 17. I'd been living like a pro since I was 18. I'd been full-on for eight or nine years.

'I had had an accident in 1984. I was training and a car door was opened in front of me [a regular occurrence for a cyclist] and it hit my knee. I still have problems with it now. I was out with Paul Sherwen and Alain Bondue up in Lille. We were riding down a line of traffic, approaching the traffic lights, and you don't expect a door to open. But I hit the very edge of the car door with my right knee. I had real problems with burst blood vessels. I never really did recover from it and I can't straighten my right leg fully even now.

'I had stopped enjoying it a bit in France by then. When you're in a good team you do enjoy it, even if you're not the one who's winning, and in 1983, with the Wolber team, we'd had a good year. We weren't one of the biggest teams, but we'd done really well. Jean-René Bernaudeau, the Wolber team leader, who these days is manager of the Europcar team, had had a great Tour and finished sixth. We'd ridden the Giro. I'd been given a free role early on, so I placed well in Paris–Nice. But the sponsor pulled the plug in July.

'Being the best team rider, though, I was probably never going to be a team leader. There's a knack to winning, it's a real confidence thing. As hard as bike riding is, there's a way to win. I was capable of winning races given the right opportunities, but I'd settled into being the sort of rider who could help on flat stages, be strong in team time trials and help in the mountains. And Bernaudeau was never going to struggle to get a team. He had a lot of really good offers, but the offers varied. With some he could bring three teammates, with others a couple of teammates and sometimes he was told he could bring only one.

'It still goes on now. A team will sign a star rider and say, "Well, you can bring a couple of teammates with you." I was basically the one Bernaudeau would have taken anywhere. He had an offer from Del Tongo, which was Giuseppe Saronni's team, and that would have been just me and him. We also had offers from some Spanish teams, Teka and a few of those. Teka would have taken him, me and maybe two others, but Bernaudeau wanted to look after everyone. And that's a trait that's still in him now. You look at the way he runs Europcar. He has built them up from being an amateur team and he's taken the riders with him. He's been loyal to them and they've been loyal in return, a lot of them. He was the one who got the Système U team going because he wanted to look after his mates, the people he trusted. He got Système U, which was a supermarket chain, involved. But what he got together was never really going to be quite good enough. Apart from him and one or two others, we were never going to do anything in the big races. We had an in-between year. I was ill or injured half of it. I was goosed because I'd never got 100 per cent fit.'

When Système U pulled out – another regular occurrence for Jones – he had to make a decision. Would he hang on to his mate Bernaudeau or come home? 'Italy should have been the place for me. I think the racing would have suited me better. I'd have raced a bit less, too, so I'd have been fresher. I hadn't fallen out with cycling, but I had started to find the lifestyle a bit difficult. We didn't make a lot of money back then and it was hard being away from home all year. You just made a living and that was it. I'd had a good year with Peugeot, though, with a lot of bonuses, and if the British thing hadn't been picking up I'd have stuck it out.

'When I joined Ever Ready in the UK, it was quite a good bunch of lads, including John Herety, Steve Sefton and Steve Fleetwood, who later became a dean at Lancaster University. He was always very intellectual and into politics and stuff. It was a good little team and we did well and had a few excursions into Belgium. The criterium races never suited me, but at that time there was enough pro road racing. There were 40 or 50 pros in Britain and there was a fair old circuit of road races. We had the Nissan Classic Tour of Ireland that year as well. You could race every weekend. But the crit thing depressed me. I wasn't made for those at all.'

To this day, Jones cannot work out why he joined ANC-Halfords, and it remains a time he prefers to forget. The ANC Tour de France virtually finished him as a professional rider, as it did Adrian Timmis. 'I just don't know why I joined them. I think there's a period of my life in cycling where I've blanked out so much. I think, like everyone, you relive certain times in your career, and I relive the Peugeot days and racing in Europe. There's so little about the British period that I can recall, not even why I left Ever Ready to join ANC. Maybe Ever Ready said they needed more crit riders for the Kellogg's criteriums, and I was pretty crap at that or, rather, couldn't be arsed racing round in circles. I think they thought the Kellogg's criteriums, which were going to be on TV, were more important than anything else – and why wouldn't they?

'I think I only just scraped into ANC for 1986. I don't think I got a lot of money for it. I think it was typical feeble negotiating by me and they said, "This is all we've got left, take it or leave it." I was tenth overall in the 1986 Milk Race, but I was working for Joey McLoughlin, who won overall. I used to drag the bunch along for half the fucking days. People actually did say to me, "Why were you only tenth in that? You were going better than they were." Which was probably half true.

'When I met Tony Capper, he seemed quite a likeable chap. I went round to his house and he was quite friendly and homely. He was into his shooting and once he took me clay-pigeon shooting at his house.'

In 1987, says Jones, the ANC team suddenly got larger. Steve Swart, Shane Sutton and Kvetoslav Palov were riding with them, along with two, sometimes three, of the Frenchmen. 'As for the Tour de France, I think it had been talked about during the winter, but we were like, "Yeah, yeah, we'll believe it when we see it." These were the days when you paid an entry fee to get into the Tour and there was no real selection process. I think it was Tony Capper's obsession. It was not realistic, but I was taken along with it. I guess everyone was. We were on *Blue Peter* when we heard the news that we were in and my reaction was that it was too soon – for the riders and for the team. I was right to think we weren't ready. Four finished. Well, we were just there making up the numbers, really.

'Despite my misgivings, having already been a part of the Tour, the idea of not going was not something I could live with. When we went into it, I knew none of us were going to do anything, myself included. I went into it with a lot of self-doubt and that was proved right, too. But you couldn't not be there, as a cyclist who'd done it before, and with a British team.

'I know there are nice quotes from the Tour organisation at the time. There was a guy called Albert Bouvet, who was part of the race direction, and he said one of the saddest things he'd had to say over the race radio was "*Jones en difficulté*". I've always got on with the Tour organisation. It was mutual respect. Even today, Jean Marie Leblanc calls me "*mon favorit*". At least on the Tour I won a bunch of flowers and the Prix de l'Amabilité, and I think that was back to the respect the Tour de France had for me as a person and a rider. When the Tour came to London, they asked me to work with ASO [the Amaury Sport Organisation, which runs the Tour] on the routes for the prologue and the first stage. But, yeah, that Prix de l'Amabilité would have been a token thing. I think I also got the elegance prize, too – and I think I got that on one of the days when I wasn't very elegant!'

Jones had returned for his last Tour de France to find he was to take part in what was one of the toughest Tours ever. He had been used to fields of 140 riders, but the 9 ANC riders were faced with 198 others. Bernard Hinault – the man who, on each stage, basically decided whether they would have a fast or a slow day – had retired. In '87, it was every man for himself.

Adrian Timmis recalls: 'Graham knew what it was about. He'd done it before. We all went there to do the best we could. But it was a lot tougher than some of us had imagined.'

Jones says: 'It was really, really nervous, full-on racing for the first few days. You couldn't settle into it, and it was really hot and humid as well. I was cramping up halfway through a stage most days. Berlin wasn't any worse than any of the rest of it and I think we did a reasonably respectable team time trial there. We didn't finish last or anything like that and we didn't make fools of ourselves. We had never done a serious team time trial together and we hadn't even trained for it.

'On my last stage from Strasbourg to Épinal and over the Champ du Feu, I felt completely empty every time it went uphill. I remember knowing that I wasn't going to make the time limit. Griffo knew the tricks of the trade, with sticky bottles and all that, but you can only do a certain amount of that on the Tour. There's commissaries everywhere. And sticky bottles on their own are not going to get you through a stage. It might help you out a bit if you're in touching distance, just off the back of the bunch, or you're trying to get back on on a climb. But you can't sit and hold on to the team car for any length of time. It's not going to get you through.

'When you climb off, you don't really take it in. You climb off and you finish and you don't think about it. But then you get to the hotel later and see the guys who have got through the stage. And it really hits home when you get to the airport to fly home and the Tour is going on without you. More than anything, it's the next day when the race is on TV and you are a million miles away that hurts. You feel like you might as well not have been there, and yet only a day ago you were there.

'There was a lot of other things going on, too. I don't think we'd been paid for ages, and I didn't get the money or bonuses I was owed from the Milk Race. That was about two grand, which is a decent sum now, let alone then. I hadn't been paid since May, and I had got my first mortgage off the back of my first year's wages with ANC. Some of the other guys did get paid. I didn't. I think we did get a token payment from Halfords to keep us going to the end of the season.

'I have to say, it's not as intimidating to go to Europe to race and try to make it as a pro now as it was then. Going to Europe now is no different from going from Birmingham to London. In all the time I've been involved in the sport, I've seen a lot of British bike riders, and it's a great period now, with some great riders and great prospects. But in my time, apart from Malc Elliott, there were two other people who would have made it if they'd been another nationality: Chris Lillywhite and Chris Walker. Walker could have been Mark Cavendish. If Lillywhite had been Belgian, he'd have won classics.

'Looking back on the '87 Tour now, I think it was part of life's rich tapestry. It was a bad experience, but you can't change the past. The team was doing a pioneering thing. But it was a year or two too soon.'

The riders arrived at the Col du Champ du Feu after 40 miles from Strasbourg. Earlier, Phil Griffiths, who must have thought I knew something about the Tour de France by then, had told me that Stephen Roche's Carrera team had decided to defend the yellow jersey of the Swiss rider Erich Mächler. Roche's man was to be the Tour leader for six days, but the French *directeur sportif* of the latest version of the Système U team was equally determined that one of their riders would take the yellow jersey. Apart from Jones and Watson, there were a number of other casualties on a day of desperate chasing.

Officially, the Col du Champ du Feu was rated a Category 1 – one below the *hors catégorie* status given to the likes of La Plagne, Alpe d'Huez and some of the Pyrenees stages – but I am adamant that the Champ du Feu, with its hill rising in a long straight line seemingly for ever, was as damaging as anything else on the Tour de France, particularly for ANC.

It was Phil Griffiths' first day on the Tour, having arrived from Stoke the night before, and in some ways he had picked the wrong day at the wrong time. He was to face losing another two riders with the race not yet a week old. He has always believed he could have done better as *directeur sportif* than Ward Woutters once the Belgian had left. Ward, however, had a few *directeur sportif* tricks new even to Griffiths.

'Woutters went to the Tour at the start because he had to work at the water board and he couldn't get the whole time off,' says Griffiths. 'We were stretched before we went in, but it suited me fine to take a little break and go in a bit later, after a few days. Ward had a little industry of his own. He came to us in the winter of '86–7, and I could write a book on him. We felt that if we were going to ride the Belgian classics, we needed someone who knew his way around, could do the contracts, speak the languages. But he had a full-time job. He was an organiser, but I didn't see him as a threat. It was good for me, because I was doing too much anyway.

'I think Capper thought Woutters could have done more. He was not a dynamic man. If I had been in the team car at Amstel Gold the day Malcolm got third, he'd have won it, I'm sure of it. Malcolm got worked over well and truly by the three Dutch at the finish, and I think I'd have had more of an effect. I tried to give a bit more. I had been a British rider, Woutters hadn't, so I think I knew a bit more than him.

'I turned up at a couple of races that Woutters couldn't make. I arrived with a faxed copy of the offer of the start money that said "10,000 Swiss Francs", but they handed me an envelope with "5,000 Swiss Francs" written on the front. The 5,000 must have gone to the team as start money, with 5,000 to the team manager! I said, "What's this?" I thought, "Bloody hell. Woutters, you fucking bandit." But this was how it went. I did quite nicely out of a few contracts; the team managers got a cut from what the offer was and the agents were then pocketing a few quid. It was all controlled, just like the Mafia.

'When I got to France, the lads were just, pfffff, in almost a state of shock. This was early on, but the whole speed of the Tour was another level up. They'd been riding with these guys before, but suddenly at the Tour it went up a notch. It was so full-on, at a level they'd never even seen. Even after the first few days, they were already on the rack. We were like, "Well, how do we get through this?" The thought was that things would level out a bit after a week, but the mental aspect of coping with the first week was everything. If you could get over the big shock and deal with it, you could get into it. Timmis, Malcolm and Swart adjusted, but others did not.'

Griffiths' own performance on the Champ du Feu was as unforgettable as any of the riders' efforts, and it taught me that there was more to the Tour de France than a number of men riding a bike. They also serve who sit and wait in a team car.

'*Les Anglais sont terminés!*' bawled that irritating teenage cycling fan in the Z-Peugeot top, and we all knew straight away, and without hearing the news on Radio Tour, that it was going to be a long day for Griffiths.

After Ward and Roger had left, Capper had seen the opportunity to take over in the lead Peugeot. Griffiths, much to his disgust, was left with the mopping-up operation in the rear. On the first rise to the *col*, Radio Tour crackled into life and, with immaculate timing, announced that two ANC riders had been dropped from the main bunch ahead, just as we spotted two more orange saddles moving up through the forest ahead of us.

'Christ, look at Graham, he's legless,' said Griffiths as we pulled alongside Jones and Watson. 'There's obviously not much wrong with Watto, though.'

Jones, with sweat pouring down his face, had his eyes glued firmly to the two feet of melting tarmac in front of his wheel, and it was plain that his Tour would soon be over. Watson had long ago made the same decision.

Malcolm Elliott says: 'I remember very well the Champ du Feu. Out of Strasbourg there had been some small climbs, but the racing was so fast that I was already struggling when we reached the steeper terrain. There were trees either side and the climb went straight up. When Graham Jones abandoned, it made it easier for the other one to join him. Paul's head fell off and he was like a man liberated after a week of hard labour. Losing people didn't make life any harder; if you stick at something long enough things might get better and something will happen.'

Watson had asked Griffiths, 'What's happening up front?', almost as if he was passing the time of day with an old friend he had just met again.

'Never mind that,' snapped Griffiths. 'You've got two choices now, Paul. You can either make an effort and ride strongly to the finish and maybe get blown out, or you can stay back here and get eliminated. Graham's gone, you've still got it, so either way tomorrow doesn't exist. Now drop down a gear and ride away from Graham. Don't wait for him at all. I want you apart on this climb. The *commissaires* can't watch both of you.' Watson nodded in agreement and put space between himself and Jones within a few seconds.

'Right, Graham, bottle,' said Griffiths. Time for the sticky-bottle trick, but this time Griffiths and Jones were out of luck. A *commissaire* on a motorcycle appeared from nowhere, wagging his finger in smiling rebuke. 'That's another fine mess for Capper,' said Griffiths, 'but I don't care. We have to keep the boys going.'

Jones was past all help and after 60 miles came to seek the aid of Griffiths, who knew by then his priorities were elsewhere.

'It's no good,' said Jones.

'Are you going to get off?'

Jones nodded and was left to the mercies of the broom wagon, closely followed by Watson.

'I thought if I carried on I might jeopardise my move to Hitachi,' says Watson. 'I'd already been approached by

122

them, so I knew I had something for 1988, but I really wanted to do well with ANC. The TV was there and my parents and my friends were watching, and I wanted to do a good ride. I knew I could have done if things had been a bit different, but I couldn't wait to get away. There was all the backbiting. People were lashing out at each other and it wasn't organised. I had one jersey – one short-sleeve jersey for the Tour and that was it. It wasn't any different from how it had been all year, but you suddenly realised that to do the Tour you had to be much more organised.'

Griffiths had lost half his English contingent on the race's first major climb, and there was a good chance Gallopin would soon be heading back to his home in Corbeil, 60 miles south-west of Paris. With no *commissaires* in sight, Griffiths could use the sticky-bottle trick for 20 seconds at a time, and on lonely stretches Gallopin simply hung on to the car door while Griffiths motored along at 20 mph. Finally, with the stage finish at Épinal in sight, Griffiths produced his last stroke of genius, pulling out an ANC cap as a bribe for a motorcyclist from the Garde républicaine to pace Gallopin the last few miles. '*Vous allez juste avant?*' Griffiths asked, and the policeman, who plainly had done this before, agreed without saying a word. Gallopin made the time limit with less than a minute to spare.

'That was brilliant,' I told Griffiths later, and I believed it. 'But what will happen with Jones and Watson now?'

'Well, there was nothing wrong with Paul. Graham Jones has had one Tour too many – he was in his lowest gear possible and still legless, while Watson was cruising, doing nothing. It's more a question of what Paul wants to do. It wasn't his legs. He's got the strength as you yourself could see.'

More than two decades later, the Champ du Feu disaster was still preying on Griffiths' mind: 'We had three different riders with three different problems. Watto, it was frustrating, because you knew he was capable of so much more. Gallopin was a fighter to the end. That guy, really, you'd have had to lock him up to stop him reaching Paris. If you'd told him he was out of the time limit, he'd have topped himself. It was his job to ride the Tour and he was going to finish it. He was going to fight tooth and nail to the finish. Watto didn't even have to be on top form to ride and finish the stage that day. His was a mental state. Graham was sick, ill, so you had three different situations.

'You're sitting in the car thinking, "Whoa, what do we do?" You don't have to make that decision in a split second, but after the climb we had to do something. You can slow the car down and wait for riders, but at some point we had to concentrate on Guy, who had a chance of making the time limit. We had to make that decision and stick by it.'

As Malcolm Elliott told me, there had been a personality clash between Griffiths and Watson long before Griffiths arrived in Strasbourg. Earlier in '87, Watson and a couple of other riders had done a *Mutiny on the Bounty* and tried, unsuccessfully, to end Griffiths' career as ANC team manager. Griffiths had never forgotten that. In the hotel in Épinal, they ignored each other after Watson abandoned, but 25 years later they were talking again.

'Paul Watson frustrated me no end,' says Griffiths. 'He had the talent and on the days he wanted to he could do anything on a bike. I put it down to a weakness in himself, that he didn't realise how good he was. It was a mental thing. Watto, for me, could have developed, especially with the carrot of money. I didn't see his short attention span – something he'd admit to – as a shortcoming, but he should have stuck at it. When he went to Hitachi after ANC, getting there is almost the easy bit. You then have to get in the team for the races and fight for your place.

'Eventually, he found out how difficult being in a team car could be. Many years after '87, he had a few days' work driving the VIPs for Skoda at the Tour de France when his stickers came off his car and the *commissaires* wanted to get him off the route. Or the day he locked the car keys in the boot and he had some VIPs waiting and there's three minutes to the start. He said to me, "Now I've seen the other side of it. I've seen what you had to do."'

Watson says: 'I've spoken to Griffo and we had a good old chat. We get on fine. With Griffo, I think we were a bit too similar. I shot from the hip. I wasn't measured. That's probably why he and Malc get on so well, because they're opposites. Me and Phil was a clash of personalities, nothing major. He was hyper, I was hyper. I preferred Ward Woutters, cos he was calming. That was great for me. I was like a racehorse, all twitchy.'

'Watto was a nutcase,' says Shane Sutton. 'In the nicest possible sense of the word. He had so much energy and was always up for a laugh. He was funny, upbeat, he would always see the joke in something. But he wasn't like that at the Tour. You could see something was wrong with him. That wasn't the Watto we knew. It got the better of him. Earlier in the season, Watto and I had driven 25 hours to the south of France to do a race. I would never say to [the British cycling director] Dave Brailsford now, "Let's get Ben Swift" – one of our Sky riders – "to drive from Sheffield to Paris to do Paris–Nice." You wouldn't contemplate it. I don't think the top teams at the time would have done that, either.'

At the time, Capper had had his own unforgettable views on the Massacre of the Field of Fire: 'Chesneau and Graham Jones were legless, Watson was headless. You could see the difference between Guy Gallopin and Paul. Guy was carrying on even though he was suffering just as much as Paul. The trouble now is Paul has got to start from scratch again. Any reputation he had is gone and he'll have to prove himself all over again.'

Capper had missed the mark with that one. Watson was happy to tell anyone, Capper apart, that he had signed a contract for the following year with Hitachi months before the Tour de France. No wonder he wasn't too worried about his reputation.

On his last day on the Tour, Watson managed to upset Sabino, the youngest (and tiniest) *soigneur*, as the other riders set off to drive back into Épinal for Stage 7 to Troyes. Watson wanted a lift to Paris, but Sabino, whose brother was a *soigneur* for Sean Kelly at Kas, didn't fancy the 100-km trip and plainly didn't see himself as an ANC dogsbody – which, strictly speaking, he was. But if Watson was getting a lift with Sabino, I wished him all the luck in the world; as far as driving skills went, I put the young Frenchman in the class of the 26-year-old lady from south London who had famously failed her driving test 90 times.

His principal job with ANC was to take the Citroën estate and its baggage full of medicine the 100 miles or so from the stage start to the stage finish, with the Iveco – full of the riders' spare clothing and any spare bikes – following him at its maximum speed of 40–50 mph. When I first hitched a ride in the Citroën with Sabino, in an effort to get away from another white-knuckle day with Capper, I had been looking forward to a leisurely drive through the French countryside. It turned out that Sabino was the original boy racer.

By then, Stage 16, Nick Rawling had arrived from England to take over from mechanic Geoff Shergold, who had had to return to his work with British Gas in Southampton, and Sabino wasn't prepared to wait for Rawling, either. Within minutes of setting out from Blagnac, he was doing 140 kph in a race with the Kas Mercedes van driven by his grinning brother. When he realised the Iveco hadn't managed to keep up, he was astonished. '*Merde! Où est l'autre homme?*' he asked.

Because of his age – 22 – and diminutive stature, Sabino took a lot of 'you stupid boy' reprimands from the likes of Capper and Griffiths. But no fool he. When he reached any stage hotel, Sabino would find a good room for himself before dining and drinking on the ANC bill and then relaxing in his bedroom, usually by watching the porn channel Satellite X on TV. Like most Frenchmen, he had no problems about admitting this, and by the time the bosses arrived to wonder what he had done all day, Sabino could tell them, in all honesty, *'J'ai été à pied d'oeuvre.'* ('I've been hard at work.') He did think of himself as a ladies' man, whistling at any girl he passed in the Citroën, and outside Millau he drove down the middle of one of the town's pavements in his search for a Mademoiselle Right.

Malcolm Elliott says: 'Sabino, the other *soigneur*? He would drive with one eye on the road and one eye on the pavement, and he was always pestering me to fix him up with an English girl when he came over.'

Elliott apart, Sabino thought little of the ANC riders and staff.

'Capper told me to drive Watson to Paris. One hundred kilometres, that *con* Watson! He rang his *copine* in Paris first to tell her he was coming.' In case I hadn't got the message first time, Sabino repeated, 'Watson . . . *petit con*. And Sutton! He asked me to wash his jersey, but I said, "*Non, non.*" Even Sean Kelly does not ask that of his *soigneur*, I said to Sutton. Sutton said to me, "Fucking, fucking this and that," but I still said, "*Non.*" Sutton, *petit con* . . . Capper, *grand con* . . . Watson, *très grand con.*'

Watson got his lift to Paris.

Dear Mr Connor:
I notice when reading your book about the Tour de France that you had done a lot of the French translations for Mr Capper and the other members of the ANC-Halfords team. I don't think much of your French translations. You mentioned that Paul Watson had left the Tour to meet his '*copain*' in Paris. A *copain*

is a boyfriend and I suggest that Mr Watson travelled to Paris to meet his *copine* (girlfriend). I suggest that you are nothing but a *chatte*, Mr Connor. In other words, a cunt.

Best wishes – and better luck with your translations. January 2, 1989. Name withheld.

Paul Watson was not the author, he insists, although he does add, 'I hope your French has improved a bit by now.' When *Wide-Eyed and Legless* came out in 1988, Watson wrote a scathing review of the book in a cycling magazine – possibly *Cycling Weekly* – above a headline reading something on the lines: 'Top Pro Slams ANC Book'. Watson was to admit later, 'I don't think I've read it. I read the bits I'm in.' But at the time, in the belief that there is no such thing as bad publicity for a writer as long as you get your name in the paper, I had a good laugh at Watson's review and left it at that.

But towards the end of 1988, he rang me at home in Eskdale, presumably to have it out with me in person. I was at work in Manchester and my mother took the call. His main complaint seemed to be, 'I don't think I come out of the book very well.'

'But I thought you all came out of it very well,' said my mother.

That was the end of that, but Watson had a point.

'I don't remember that call,' he says now. 'But it's the sort of thing I'd have done. I got wound up by that sort of thing.'

As Shane Sutton says, Watson has a great sense of humour, with the cynicism of many professional cyclists, and he has a lyrical gift for describing his own life and ANC and cycling in general. Like Malcolm Elliott, he must have a picture in his attic; although the earring and bleached blond hair have gone, he looks more or less the same today as he did 25 years ago. He could probably write a bestselling

The *Daily Star* sports desk and its 'organised' chaos during the '80s. The author, in his chaotic clothing, on the right. (© Express Newspapers)

The author meets Malcolm Elliott at Heathrow, 29 June 1987, with both trying their best to keep apart. (© Express Newspapers)

Tony Capper. The Boss gets
ready for work during the '87
Tour. (© Phil O'Connor)

Micky Morrison poses by the ANC
'motor' in 1985. (courtesy of Micky
Morrison)

Morrison, Paul Watson and Milk Race winner the
Belgian Eric Van Lancker fight it out in 1985.
(© John Pierce, PhotoSport International)

Morrison sprinting for a King of the Mountains prime during the Nissan Classic in 1985. (© John Pierce, PhotoSport International)

Greg LeMond and Bernard Hinault on Alpe d'Huez in 1986, during the race that 'blew the mind' of Tony Capper. (© Getty Images)

ABOVE LEFT: The individual time trial on Kurfürstendamm, West Berlin – prostitutes by night and the world's greatest bike race the next day (© Phil O'Connor) **ABOVE RIGHT**: The late Laurent Fignon. (© Getty Images)

ABOVE: ANC go to war. Right to left, Timmis, Palov and Elliott. (© Phil O'Connor) **BELOW**: Sutton, Palov, Swart and Elliott during the team time trial in Berlin. (© Phil O'Connor)

A smile from Steve Swart and a few thoughts from the enigmatic Kvetoslav Palov. (© Phil O'Connor)

Guy Gallopin in action. (© Phil O'Connor)

Belgian Stefan Morjean of Hitachi gets a lift from Timmis and Elliott on Alpe d'Huez. (© Phil O'Connor)

The pride of Ireland, Stephen Roche, and his yellow jersey. (© Getty Images)

TOP: We'll always have Paris . . . Timmis, Elliott, Gallopin and Palov when it was all over. Sabino Pignatelli is riding shotgun in the second team car. (© Phil O'Connor) **MIDDLE**: Malcolm Elliott wins the first stage of the 1995 Tour DuPont in Wilmington, Virginia, with Adriano Baffi second and fellow Italian Massimo Strazzer third. (© Getty Images) **BOTTOM**: Former ANC *directeur sportif* Phil Griffiths and Rotherham's Russ Downing celebrating the rider's Lincoln GP win in 2009. (© Andy Jones)

TOP: Graham Jones, right, with his BBC Radio 5 Live team, Peter Slater and Phil Sheenan, on Alpe d'Huez during the 2008 Tour de France (© Andy Jones) **MIDDLE**: British superstar Bradley Wiggins CBE gets some words of advice from Shane Sutton OBE during the 2011 Tour. (© Andy Jones) **BOTTOM**: ANC's head mechanic, Steve Snowling, in his workshop at Wevelgem, Belgium. (Courtesy of Geoff Shergold)

ABOVE LEFT: Malcolm Elliott with wife Clare and daughters Ruby, left, and Evie at their home in Sheffield. (© Jeff Connor) **ABOVE RIGHT**: Paul Watson in his new role as a cycling super-snapper. (© Andy Jones)

ABOVE LEFT: Adrian Timmis, still addicted to cycling. (© Andy Jones)
ABOVE RIGHT: Steve Swart, the curse of Lance Armstrong, in his Auckland work gear. (© Alex Wallace)

autobiography – if he could get some of it past the lawyers. He is a comedian, but definitely a Bill Hicks rather than a Bill Cosby.

On his life as a pro cyclist: 'I was once riding up this mountain in a race, it was probably the Midi Libre. It was a long climb and it was boiling hot. I was struggling on and I spotted this girl, a pretty girl, in the crowd. Next to her was her boyfriend. I looked at him and there was just this exchange of glances between us: I would've given anything to be standing on the side of the road with his bird and he would've given anything to be in my position, riding the bike race.'

And on life after cycling: 'I can see how sportsmen struggle. You come out of that environment, having been pretty good at it, and because you've been good at bike riding, you think you must be pretty good at everything. I can see why it comes as a shock when they don't do so well in business. You've been isolated, cocooned in a particular world, worrying about training, and then you realise your spelling isn't as good as it should be. You're coming out way behind people who've been working in business for years.'

Watson was spot-on. Playing professional sport doesn't necessarily equip you for very much else when the time comes to retire, as any televised interview with the likes of Steven Gerrard or Alex Higgins will demonstrate. The brains of most performers are embedded firmly in their sports gear. (Although I did once catch the England goalkeeper David James using the word 'ambivalence' on BBC Radio 5 Live. Eamonn Holmes had to ask him what that meant.)

But what does a pro cyclist do on retirement? Well, if your name is Paul Watson, you can do all right for yourself.

As is often the case with cyclists, it was Watson's father, Brian, who got his teenage son interested in the sport. 'He encouraged me to ride a bike when I was 13. My dad was a bit pushy and I almost certainly wouldn't have done it otherwise. I didn't really like it. Well, I liked it because I was good at it and I could win races, but I didn't really like the training. I was brought up in Hemel Hempstead and I went to JFK School there. We lived in Warners End, Hemel, and I used to go training round Ivinghoe Beacon. I'd do my cyclo-cross training: ride there, run up the hill and then ride home. Dad encouraged me, definitely, but it wasn't like he forced me to go out or anything. There was definitely a need to please, which was why I did it. Today, I'd rather go for a run than ride a bike.

'I wasn't particularly good at school. I wasn't stupid, but – and a lot of cyclists will probably relate to this – I was the guy staring out of the window. I'd see the fella on the tractor cutting the grass on the playing fields on a nice sunny day, with his top off, getting a suntan, and think, "Yeah, that's the job for me." I wasn't daft, I could get through, but I got bored.

'I was schoolboy cyclo-cross champion at 14, then I went to the road. I was 18 when I went to France, with a club in Alençon, and I was there for a summer. Then I raced cyclo-cross for the La Redoute amateur team. Paul Sherwen was in the La Redoute pro team, so I was training with him and the other pros who were in the same area, Graham Jones, Robert Millar, Sean Yates among them. I came back and did well in the Milk Race, with a third place in 1985, riding for Great Britain. I was national amateur road race champion that year, and then I turned pro after riding as part of a combine team in the 1985 Nissan Tour of Ireland along with Stephen Roche. And that's where it got a bit messy!

'I rode for Raleigh in 1986, then joined Lycra in 1987, and at the time Capper ran two teams – ANC and Lycra-Halfords – to avoid the rules preventing British pro teams being too big. To compete abroad, they needed a bigger pool of riders, so Capper's riders were split between the two teams in the UK but came together to form ANC-Halfords in Europe. I did like the friendships. The guys were great and with the British amateur team it was just such a giggle. In the amateur Tour of Italy, I had the climber's jersey, and we had a great spirit. But when you turn professional, you have to have that love for it to get through it. That's why I was constantly thinking, "I don't like this." The laughter stops when you turn pro. There just wasn't any laughter.'

Watson's first race with ANC was the Étoile de Bessèges, an early-season five-day stage race in the south of France, and the 24-year-old Englishman caught the eye from the start at Spa. It also saw his first clash with Phil Griffiths.

'I'd met Capper when I agreed to join the team, but I guess the first proper time I met him was in Bessèges – when I finally got there. The plan was to get picked up by Phil Griffiths on the way. We'd arranged to meet at a service station, but they never turned up. Eventually, Shane and I drove down there overnight, getting there at 3 a.m., just a few hours before the race. I was livid, but Phil said, "We pulled in and you weren't there." I swear now, I was there. I only had my training bike, a Motobecane from my old team in France. I thought my race bike would be there for me, but it wasn't. I had to take the mudguards and everything else off. It was a right state. The mechanic, Phil Corley, daren't touch it in case something fell off it. I lined up on the start line next to Gilbert Duclos-Lassalle, an established French pro, and he looked at me as if I was something on the bottom of his shoe. I was so wound up, so angry, I got in the break and ended up with third place.

'I could always climb on the short climbs as well as anyone. I used to get the climber's jersey in the stage races we did. I'm not talking about the big *cols*, but on the shorter climbs I was good. I got in the break at the Flèche Wallonne in 1987. It was all new to us and we didn't know what to expect. The first time we hit the narrow, 25 per cent Mur de Huy, it was chaos. There was a crash and the race split, but on the second climb of Huy I led all the way up. Then there were the top five riders and just me.'

Watson's rivals were former world champion Claude Criquielion, Rolf Gölz, Stephen Roche, Jean-Claude Leclerq and Yvon Madiot. 'It was like a dream being in that break with those guys,' says Watson. 'I was feeling really good, but then I broke a spoke. In the end, Leclerq won and I was sixth.'

Watson's ride earned him a contract with Hitachi for 1988, although obviously he didn't tell Capper at ANC.

'After the Milk Race in 1987, I had one day to wash my clothes and the next day we were doing this race in France. Griffo put some pressure on me to go. They were getting paid start money on the condition me and Malc rode. We'd had some results in the spring and now the team was getting these invites, but they wanted me and Malc to turn up. My head was already coming off and we had the Tour coming up. We were doing these long, 200-km stages and it was hot, in the middle of nowhere and there were no crowds. I was thinking, "What am I doing here?"

'I was riding alongside Malcolm trying to get him to climb off with me. "Come on, Malc, let's get off."

'Finally I convinced him and he said, "Where?"

'I said, "I don't know, anywhere. Let's just get off." Then I said, "OK, the next left, we go left."

'We were coming into this town and the race went straight on and we went left, but it was a dead end. I thought the race would go on and forget about us, but as the officials came past in the cars, they saw us, so we're crouching down behind a car, trying not to be spotted. God knows what they thought, but I was already on the verge of cracking. I just wanted to stop.

'Malc reckoned he could windsurf and I didn't believe him. So after one of the stages in the Midi Libre, we got in one of the team cars and nipped down to the beach. He hired a windsurfing board and a wetsuit, and he wasn't bad. He was pretty good in fact. I think I went out but wasn't so good at it, so I sat on the beach. It's obvious I was looking for anything to get out, to find a release from the boredom. I couldn't hack it.

'At least now they have laptops and the Internet and DVDs, but we didn't have any of that. I didn't really want to go on the Tour, but, on the other hand, I didn't want to miss it. It was a big deal. I knew it was the chance of a lifetime and I hoped I might get better as it went on. There was a medical, before the start in Berlin, and they did their tests and said to me, "You're not very well. You need to see your doctor." Well, we didn't have one. They did blood-pressure tests and heart monitors and whatever, and something was flagging up. But I didn't need them to tell me. I knew myself I wasn't well. I needed a rest. I'd done too much racing. Because me and Malc had got the results in the spring, we were thrown into every race. Even the bikes were shit, just basic Peugeots, 531 tubes, and they were really heavy. You wouldn't even go training on one of them now.

'By Berlin, I don't think we were getting paid. I think the last pay cheque was in June, and we had this action plan to slash the tyres of every ANC van we could find if we didn't get paid. But it was a catch-22. Should we ride, even though we weren't being paid? There was already an atmosphere of fear going into the race but also anger at not getting paid. There wasn't a good team feeling as we set off.

'Berlin was bad, too hot and the speed was unbelievable. It just didn't let up. Palov didn't want to be in West Berlin. He was terrified of being caught by the authorities. Sutton didn't want to be there either. In the first few days, I was feeling the way I'd have expected to feel in the third week. Looking back, you wonder what the others might have been on. I can only speak for myself, but we didn't have anything, nothing whatsoever, because we were so naive. Even when I went to Hitachi a year later, I stuck to multivitamins when they wanted me on a programme. You have a choice and I didn't want to. In Paris–Nice in '87, I was riding next to Bert Oosterbosch, the Dutch rider, on the Ventoux. He died two years later and he was only in his early 30s.'

6

THE BFG

Hey, man, you don't talk to the colonel. Well, you listen to him.

Photojournalist, *Apocalypse Now*

I HAD A Capper of my very own at the *Daily Star* offices in Manchester. If Capper could be considered overweight, quite bald, aggressive and at times very rude, so could his spitting image in Ancoats Street. Ray Mills, the *Star* deputy editor, was a rough, tough Northerner who revelled in being obnoxious and uncultured. We knew him as 'Docker' (often striking about something or striking someone), 'Dark Satanic' (Mills) or 'Biffo'. Of the three noms de plume, Mills preferred Biffo, as he saw that as a term of endearment for a character who was pugnacious, a bit of a hard man but sort of nice with it. Mills later realised that 'Biffo' stood for 'Big Ignorant Fucker from Oldham'. When he fell from a ladder at home, his nickname was changed to 'Biffol' ('Big Ignorant Fucker Fell Off Ladder') and suddenly he preferred to be known as Docker, or 'BFG', after Roald Dahl's Big Friendly Giant.

One night when I was in the paper's composing room, the back page was late and by way of a reprimand he came out with his favourite line when giving a bollocking: 'I'm gonna cut your balls off with a rusty saw.' I liked him.

135

Like Capper, he was a big man with a big heart, but Mills had his weaknesses. He had a habit of sleeping in his office after a night's boozing. (By way of a change, the *Star* assistant editor, another legend in his own lunchtime, would regularly fall asleep during the morning conference and we would simply tiptoe past him and leave him to it.) And Mills, rather than going to the WC, preferred to pee into his office waste bin, which precipitated a strike by the cleaning staff.

Cleaners, mainly ladies, had a hard time in national newspapers in those days and dreaded some of their early-morning jobs. When I was on the Northern *Daily Mirror* in the mid-'60s, Mike Terry, the editor at the time, was another who liked to pee in his office bin. One day when a cleaner arrived to do his office she found no Terry but his glass eye. His monument to some German shrapnel in France during D-Day was leering at her from his desk. I'm not suggesting that Capper was in that class of hedonism – unlike Mills and Terry, he drank very little – but their general demeanour, their views on life and how to deal with staff were amazingly similar.

When I went out to get a mid-race report from Capper at Tulle, after Stage 11 of the Tour, I found myself squashed under a café umbrella with him on the town's boulevard as he drank wine I had paid for and smoked cigarettes I had bought for him. It was an excellent interview, but most of the time I had to stop myself from saying, 'Have you got a twin brother who works at the *Daily Star*?'

Capper, like Mills, was a BFG – and a great talker, although he didn't attempt – as he had with Paul Watson and some of the other riders – to tell me about his past in the SAS, not once I had told him that anyone who knows anything about the army is aware that most members of the SAS are under 5 ft 10 in., light in weight and never talk about their peculiar job of work, all of which left Tony Capper out of the equation. I thought later he had perhaps been watching TV back in 1980 and had caught the Iranian Embassy syndrome that had swept the country; overnight, local pubs across the UK had been full of hundreds of fantasists claiming membership of the SAS. Capper certainly hadn't been in the special forces, but I guessed that, like Ray Mills, when push came to shove he could look after himself. 'You couldn't take Tony at arm's length,' warned Griffiths when one of his unpaid mechanics decided that someone should give him a doing.

How much could anyone believe about Capper and his life and his plans for ANC-Halfords? Over his wine in Tulle – he took the half-full bottle away with him – I thought this had to be a man who looked at the world through rose-coloured glasses, a man who saw his wide imagination as reality. He admitted that losing three of his riders was 'just a bit of a setback', but he certainly wasn't going to lower his sights. 'I think we are still entitled to a stage win from one or two riders,' he said. 'My team have shown all the character we thought possible from them.'

Malcolm Elliott, said Capper, was the next Sean Kelly; Adrian Timmis was the next British Tour de France winner; and Gallopin was going to be his next *directeur sportif* (albeit second in command to Capper himself). Angus Fraser, the man with whom he was to have the sort of shouting match I remembered from primary school during dinner in Lourdes a couple of days later, would be his full-time *soigneur*. At times, I thought Capper was looking at a different Tour de France than the one I had been following – and a different Tour de France team. 'The instances where the riders have suffered because of any difficulties, or maybe "differences" is a better word, have been very few and far between,' he said. 'Only once have we had problems with a race start in terms of equipment being there, only once in the whole race to date. Not once have we had problems in terms of timing or anything else – and the whole thing is totally uncontrollable by us.'

Many of his troubles, said Capper, had been the fault of

the team personnel. There had been problems after a race in picking riders up and a problem when they had forgotten to fill up one of the Peugeots with petrol before a stage. 'Oh,' said Capper, 'an instruction will now be given to all people concerned that the radios should stay on during and after the race.'

He was honest, but at times he still appeared to be away somewhere in his own cloud cuckoo land. In terms of organisation, he said, ANC were not in the top ten on the Tour, but that would change within a year: 'We will be in the top ten because we can organise well. The number of hiccups that we haven't solved I could count on the fingers of one hand – in a whole year. We're talking about two or three occasions and they've been solved instantly. Success to me is not not making mistakes but is recognising them when you make them and correcting them. Because anyone who thinks they can do summat and not make mistakes is a fool.'

Capper was certainly no fool, and I didn't consider him a fibber; he was more a Walter Mitty than a Billy Liar. I think he genuinely believed that one day all his fantasies would come true and that, like Walter Mitty, he would go to sleep a stoker heating a boiler and wake up an RAF fighter pilot. But then, as his Action Sports colleagues Micky Morrison and Phil Griffiths point out, a former Stoke taxi driver had, as he had promised, produced a team that won the Milk Race and the Kellogg's city-centre series; he had had a rider on the podium of a classic; and he had taken an English team on to the Tour de France. Many of his fantasies did come true.

He told me that in his time he had been a policeman, a taxi driver, a managing director and a millionaire, all of which I believed. He had no qualms about describing the reasons why he had been forced to leave the police; in his own words, 'I went off my beat and what I did was wrong.' He even told me that when he split from the co-owner of his first taxi business in Stoke, his former partner committed suicide, a story I would probably have preferred to keep to myself if I were him. He also revealed that during the early stages of ANC he'd had debts of £250,000 – again a detail that most people would keep private. It was much more difficult to get any details about how, in 1981, he had founded his overnight express delivery service, and it was only many years later that I found out a part of the whole.

After his taxi company gave him the idea of a franchise business, he managed to find a venture capitalist, *à la Dragons' Den*, to get ANC started. Public company boss Sir Aubrey Brocklebank, formerly of the Guinness Mahon merchant bank and once the owner of Irton Hall in Eskdale, Cumbria – which in the wildest sense of the word makes him a former neighbour of mine – recalls that 'ANC, a delivery business, had been started by two entrepreneurs, Vic Barnes and Tony Capper, an ex-policeman'. In other words, Capper had had a partner from the start.

Brocklebank, whose venture-capital group was called ReInVenture (now dissolved), helped Capper and Barnes with the early development of the business. They had tried and failed to get financing until they spoke to Brocklebank. He had long espoused what he called 'the need for flexibility about the roles of a number one and a number two in a business'. He says: 'Some years later, they realised they would need to change their ways to take the business securely to a higher plane and exchanged jobs, Barnes becoming chief executive and Capper non-executive chairman – a move later rewarded with a multimillion-pound trade sale. The clever entrepreneur knows what his level is. He or she will either stay there or seek an appropriate number two to help cope with life at a higher level.'

Capper certainly never struck me as a natural 'number two'. A former colleague of his in Bristol recalls: 'When I worked for ANC Parcels, I met Tony Capper and he was larger than life, a bit of a rogue, approachable, but strong in character and he didn't take any crap. He was a man able to discover openings in the parcel business and bring the ideas to fruition. Tony rejoined ANC's Bristol franchise with his stepbrother, Rod, who at the time owned that franchise. Tony improved certain aspects of the business and secured a new fleet of VW LT35s vans, complete with ANC logos, and he brought in new business opportunities. I think if he had gone back to ANC in Bristol with more financial backing, the business would have blossomed at an even faster rate than it did. He was a man of vision, good judgement and business acumen.'

Despite the glasses of wine I fed him in Tulle, Capper would never say exactly how much he was worth. If his declaration 'I'm a millionaire' – the nearest anyone could get to a figure from him – was true, it became clear several years later that if he had stayed with ANC he could have owned a good section of the Isle of Man by now. According to the business section of the *Daily Telegraph* in 2006:

> Lloyds Development Capital has made more than a three-fold return on its investment in just 10 months after selling parcel delivery business ANC Group to FedEx for £120m.
>
> LDC, the venture capital arm of Lloyds TSB, took a 27.25pc stake in ANC in February, backing a management-led buyout that valued the group at £37.3m including debt. Management, led by ANC chief executive Mark Gittins, owned the remaining 72.75pc of shares in the logistics firm.
>
> The surprising speed of the "flip" by LDC is thought to have been prompted by an approach to buy the business from FedEx. FedEx will place ANC in its FedEx Express arm, the focus of which is on serving the entire UK domestic market with a parcel service.

Capper could have been a multimillionaire by now – instead

of a mere millionaire. But of course, by the mid-'80s, like
Toad of Toad Hall, he had found a new toy: professional
cycling and in particular the Tour de France. He had given
away the chance of what could have been millions for what
many others would call a daft game.

Was he a cycling fan? He certainly liked the concept of
being a team manager in one of the greatest sporting events
in the world, and he loved the limelight (he had basically
ordered me to take him for an interview in Tulle). There is
little doubt that he thought the world of his riders, too. He
was addicted to almost everything involved in the Tour,
and in particular his days in one of the team cars. He saw
himself as cycling's Stig Blomqvist; he was a man who loved
driving in situations where the normal rules of the road did
not apply. And the best place in the world for driving like a
maniac without breaking the law is in France on the Tour.

For anyone who has missed the delights of travelling in a
team car, it goes something like this: most of the drivers are
crazy; they are supposed to drive in single file, but quite
often they don't; the lead team vehicle must be driven by
the *directeur sportif* on the right-hand side of the road;
their order is based on which teams are doing well (e.g.
Carrera) down to teams doing not so well (ANC); the first
team car follows riders who are performing well on any
given day, and the second team vehicle follows riders who
are not doing well, in an effort to persuade them to start
doing well again.

Driving a team vehicle, then, whether first or second,
could turn a stage into a long, often tedious day, followed
by what I considered a scary session of reckless driving.
Capper, however, had his own way of mollifying the
boredom – and feeding himself at the same time. I wondered
what he was up to when he told a delighted Griffiths to
take over as Car 1 while he fell behind the convoy to stop
for an ice cream. It gave him a chance of doing his Stig
Blomqvist and speeding flat out in pursuit. Unfortunately

for him, if ANC had a Stig Blomqvist, other team cars had a Carlos Sainz or a Sébastien Loeb.

After the start of one of the longer stages of the Tour, the 11th between Poitiers and Chaumeil, most of the riders had decided that, with the Pyrenees only a day hence, they should have an easy few hours. And if it was an easy day for the riders, by necessity it was an easy day for the drivers, too. 'Time for some snap,' said Capper signalling Griffiths that, for a time at least, he could take over in the front. Capper got his 'snap' and was driving back to the convoy when a Z-Peugeot lead car, heading in the same direction, cut him up. 'I'm not standing for that,' said Capper, and immediately gave chase. With each determined that the next place in the long line of team drivers was theirs, they roared down the middle of the E11 like the drivers in *Bullitt*. The Z-Peugeot man chickened out first and Capper, with a V-sign out of the window, shouted at the loser, 'That showed you!'

'How are you spelling dehydrated?' asked Tommy the copy-taker by way of a change.

'D-E-H-Y-D-R-A-T-E-D. It means someone has lost a lot of water. It means someone has been deprived of something.'

'Couldn't you find a pub, then?' asked Tommy.

'Just put me through to the sports desk. By the way, Tommy, when do you retire?' I was not in the best of moods.

'Sports desk.'

'It's Jeff. I've done the stage, but it didn't quite work out as we'd planned.'

'Oh, yeah?' said a Scottish voice I didn't recognise.

'I rode 100 miles and I saw most of the riders, but I had to follow them, rather than ride alongside them. That wouldn't have been allowed.'

'Oh, yeah?'

'I did my best.'

'Oh, yeah? So we're not getting a piece about you doing a stage of the Tour de France, then?'

'You are getting a piece about me doing a stage on the Tour de France, but it's . . . different.'

'Oh, yeah?'

'Look, mate, I have just ridden 100 miles through 30-degree heat on a bike that was a foot too small for me. I've fallen off it at least three times, I've lost six pounds in weight and I've got third-degree heat burns, and if you say "Oh, yeah?" once more, I'll do a Ray Mills on you.'

'And what's doing a Ray Mills?'

'I'll cut your balls off with a rusty saw.'

'Oh, yeah?'

If there was little sympathy from the *Star* sports desk, there was even less sympathy from the ANC riders, who didn't even bat an eyelid – the odd snigger apart – as I staggered past them and hobbled slowly and painfully into the dining room of the Hotel Ibis in Poitiers. A smiling Steve Snowling was heading in the opposite direction and, like Tommy, he was in comic mode: 'You look a bit wasted, Jeff, a touch dehydrated,' he said.

Poitiers is undoubtedly a beautiful city, but I could have done without it on the night of Friday, 10 July. The *Daily Star* had made what amounted to their final demand (something on the lines of 'Get on the bike or get on the plane') the night before Stage 10 from Saumur to a theme park called Futuroscope. I plainly couldn't join a stage from the start, but Stage 10 was yet another time trial, this one a ludicrous 87 km, and if I followed at a discreet distance not many of the Tour commissioners would see me. Since I was facing an extra 40 miles, with ANC heading from our overnight stop in Angers to Saumur, then on to Futuroscope and from there to our hotel in Poitiers, the *Star* were going to get their money's worth with this one.

Phil Griffiths and the rest of the ANC staff were delighted. 'A great suggestion,' said Griffiths. 'You can use Watto's spare and we'll give you a *bidon*, a *musette* and a map of the stage. But don't forget some food and lotsa water. Oh, and there's some Lycra shorts and an ANC-Halfords jersey that should fit you.' They had handed me the ANC equivalent of Blind Pew's black spot and now I understood. Griffiths had come up with a way of getting rid of the Pig for good.

'And don't forget this,' said Snowling, strapping a spare tube under the seat.

'What's this for?'

'It's for if you puncture.'

'But what do you do with it? Don't I need something to blow it up with?'

Snowling looked at Griffiths; Griffiths looked at Snowling.

'You'll manage, Jeff,' said Griffiths. 'And don't forget, you're not a real rider until you've fallen off a few times.'

I was to join the ranks of the 'real riders' within a mile of leaving Angers.

'*Pardon, monsieur, la route à Poitiers, s'il vous plaît?*'

I was lost already and I hadn't even got out of Angers. It gave the middle-aged Frenchman a good laugh. I asked for the way at the first set of red lights, toppling slowly over sideways onto the pavement, unable to free my trainers from the clips (Griffiths had failed to find me a road-cycling shoe big enough). I hit the ground, landing painfully on my elbow, but between giggles the Frenchman did point me in the right direction.

The Loire Valley, the Garden of France: its vineyards, its orchards, its artichoke and asparagus and cherry fields, its river and medieval chateaux – and its 30-degree heat. I saw nothing of the beauty of the Loire Valley, but I will certainly never forget the heat. It was pleasant at first. The Loire plain had hundreds of fields of yellow sunflowers, and the shimmering heat of the distant horizon was almost ethereal. I cruised along in a big gear enjoying the day until the gradient, a headwind and the juggernauts suddenly streaming past me down the D748 made me wonder if this had been a good idea after all.

Before long, I was in the lowest gear possible, had to stand up to ride and was finding that the worst foes of a rider – even a pro rider who has to spend six or seven hours on a bike during a race – are saddle sores. By the time I'd reached Loudun, as I sank down on a straw bale alongside *soigneur* Friedhelm, I had developed the syndrome of journalists everywhere and in every job: I wanted to blame someone – in this case, the *Daily Star*.

'Ha, ha, ha,' laughed Friedhelm when he saw me. 'Ha, ha, ha, you are the big racer now.'

'How far to go?' I asked.

'Only *fünfundzwanzig Meilen* now,' said Friedhelm, who was there looking after the halfway feed. 'You will be able to catch some of the Tour riders before long. Maybe tomorrow!'

The laugh was on Friedhelm. I finished with third-degree burns, but he was in a far worse state by the end of the day.

'In case you're interested, Friedhelm is back,' Steve Snowling said sarcastically to Capper in Poitiers. Capper had told Friedhelm that he would pick up the German – and his huge ice box – at the feed point and would take him to the finish. But Capper's sports plan had failed somewhere along the line, and while he opened the door of the Peugeot to let Friedhelm in, he waited until he'd got his foot in the door before driving off without him. Friedhelm was stranded in mid-stage with the finish line, and his hotel, a long way away. At least I had a bicycle.

'Only 25 miles to go now,' I shouted to Friedhelm as I set off again towards Poitiers.

Little should be said about my last 20 miles aboard a bike that had become what amounted to a lethal weapon on an 80-km-plus time trial that had been tough even for the ANC's professional riders.

'Even the time trials were very hard work in the Tour,'

145

says Adrian Timmis. 'That 87-km time trial at Futuroscope was horrendous. Although I'd done the odd hilly 25-mile time trial at home, that was ridiculous. More than 50 miles and the roads were heavy. I rode the 10 km back to the hotel after the stage and I couldn't sit down after pushing the big gear all the way.'

Out of curiosity, I later asked a psychiatrist friend of mine – as distinct from a friendly psychiatrist – what was going on when I found that the sound of the traffic was becoming more and more distant and I caught myself singing 'Raindrops Keep Fallin' on My Head' repeatedly; despite constant efforts, I had been unable to stop myself from singing the same daft song to myself.

'It sounds like you were in an epiphenomenon dream phase,' said my friend. 'It's a form of delirium, an acutely disturbed state of mind that occurs in fever, intoxication and other disorders. If I were you, I would give up cycling, particularly in very hot weather.'

I found I could drink water, lotsa water and lotsa Coke, but I couldn't eat a thing, even when I stepped off the bike. At a roadside café, I was tempted to ask for a room for the night. I walked up the final hill into Poitiers, found the hotel and shambled into my room, leaving Watson's bike with Snowling. Like a man who has spent a night on too much alcohol, unwilling to check out the damage, I finally found the courage to look at myself in the mirror. I saw there the wrecked face of Graham Jones at Épinal, with the same sunken cheeks and glassy eyes. Virtually every part of my body was aching and I had the raw sunburn of a holidaymaker who has only two days in Majorca to get a tan.

'Friedhelm's got third-degree burns, just like you,' chortled Griffiths at dinner. 'You should form a little club.'

The 17-stone German had walked, still carting the ANC ice box, almost to the outskirts of Poitiers, where he had been picked up by Jan Raas, the manager of the Dutch

Superconfex team. He had refused to come down to dinner.

'He's not angry,' said Snowling. 'He just feels humiliated. Raas couldn't believe that a team would leave one of its *soigneurs* like that.'

Capper, who had thought that the second Peugeot was following him, put it all down to a 'hiccup' and admitted it was his mistake. 'He'll come round in the end,' said Capper.

I came round eventually, too, and was well on the road to recovery until I saw my *Star* report and the results for Stage 9: '1: S. Roche (Ire) 1hr 58min 11sec . . . Nowhere: J. Connor (GB) 4hr 32min 17sec.' Very funny.

7

DOCTOR WHO?

*Sometimes, the dark side overcomes what Lincoln
called the better angels of our nature.*
General Corman, *Apocalypse Now*

WITH HIS BULK, his aggression and the scarred face of
one of the Glasgow razor gangsters from *No Mean City*,
Angus Fraser was a hard man to like.

'It is never difficult,' wrote P.G. Wodehouse, 'to
distinguish between a Scotsman with a grievance and a ray
of sunshine.' That was Angus: up one day, down the next
and nothing in between. But he was a *soigneur*, a necessity
for stage racing, and had a job recently rated one of the
toughest in sport (racing grooms were voted No. 1) by the
writers of *USA Today*. When I read that, I began to
understand some of the reasons for Fraser's regular daily
strops during the 1987 Tour.

Shelley Verses, who was the first female *soigneur* –
working with Toshiba – at the time, told the magazine:

> The worst job in sports? That sounds about right.
> There's so much more than giving a massage after the
> race. We're valets, cooks, washers, drivers, wound
> cleaners, psychiatrists and confessors. It is long hours,
> hard days, tough conditions and a wonderful way of life.

Another American *soigneur* likens it to being a roadie with a heavy-metal band. Sex, drugs and rock and roll? Maybe.

By the time we arrived in Pau after Stage 13, ANC having lost their fourth rider in Shane Sutton, I had begun to quite like Angus Fraser, to think that he wasn't such a bad guy after all. David Boon, one of the ANC sponsors, had asked if I would drive his BMW to Lourdes while he spent a day at the sharp end with Capper in his Peugeot. Lourdes being Lourdes, and awash with the ill, the injured and the dying, all looking for a miracle from Jennifer Jones, there was nowhere to park. In the end, I found a space, marked 'Cardinals Only', close to the Domain, the sanctuary surrounding the Grotto. It was an area I recognised from *The Song of Bernadette* (a film that had frightened me to death when I watched it as a seven year old). After fighting off the vendors trying to sell me a candle, I walked back into town and was in a shop buying Capper a Miraculous Medal (which was nicked later) when I heard loud American voices outside. I guessed that either Ronald Reagan had bombed East Germany or someone from the States had won something somewhere.

Sure enough, Dag Otto Lauritzen of 7-Eleven had taken the stage, and that night a bunch of Americans appeared from nowhere in the Hôtel Adriatic. They were insufferable, telling everyone how it was done while not listening to a word anyone else was saying. I recognised one of them, a radio man working for something like the Cluttsville *Daybreak Show*, and I remembered his hilarious commentary from the team time trial in Berlin. 'A nice play by the 7-Eleven guys there. A little give and go in the switch,' he had told his listeners. It was John Motson commentating on baseball.

We had been devastated to lose Sutton, who in every sense of the word had fought the good fight, and we certainly could have done without this. Half a dozen of them were bawling, 'USA, USA,' and another one was bellowing at the manageress because the hotel wouldn't accept his American Express card – and because the bar didn't sell Buds. 'What kinda joint is this, anyway?' he demanded.

Americans abroad know that the louder they speak and the bigger words they can find the more likely they are to be noticed. This bunch were either doing a dress rehearsal for the Ryder Cup's 'War on the Shore' or had been reading *The Best Speeches of American Football Coaches*.

'That 7-Eleven guy kicked their asses big time, but our man really won because he managed to keep eternal vigilance,' said one.

'The outcome could have far-reaching effects on the process of this race,' said American Express man, who was on Kronenbourg by then.

'I'm a Yankee Doodle Dandy,' shouted a third.

That was enough for Angus: 'Hey, son, that Dag Otto Lauritzen is a fuckin' Norwegian!'

Once he had seen off the Yankee dandies, Angus went into overdrive, bawling at Laurent Fignon and the rest of the French Système U riders (fame meant nothing to Angus) for allegedly taking the mickey out of the same manageress, then regaling us with a story about how he'd hit someone – the wrong man, as it turned out – for tying a can to the Peugeot estate during one of the feeds. Not a damaging practical joke, really, but Angus carried on as if someone had stolen his wheels.

But I liked Fraser. Unlike Capper, with his aggressive high-speed tourism and his delight in frightening me to death, the Scot was one of the safest drivers on any road. Off the road, he could be a different proposition altogether. At times, he looked as though he was heading for a total breakdown.

In Poitiers, where both Friedhelm and myself had finished the day with third-degree burns, Angus threw a serious wobbler at the dinner table, announcing that he was 'pissed off with him [Sabino]. He's done nothing except watch the porn channels and he thinks he knows everything. I am the *chef* round here and people do what I say.' Riders and personnel had stopped eating in amazement as he thumped the table before announcing as he stormed off, 'If I tell them, even the waiters will change their trousers.'

I'm still trying to work that one out, but for all his tall stories and afflictions, imagined or otherwise, Angus was popular with most of the riders. Timmis got on fine with him and he was one of the few men the young Englishman was prepared to talk to at length. Fraser saw himself as a surrogate parent to the likes of Timmis, and he told me, 'I'm their father confessor. The only trouble is, I've no one to confess to. Who does the father confessor confess to?' To some extent he had a few confessions for me.

Before Stage 8 from Troyes to Épinay-sous-Sénart, the day that Palov actually won some cash for Capper by taking a Catch sprint, I climbed into the Peugeot brake behind Angus and the man he liked to call 'my German subordinate, Friedhelm'. To widen my knowledge of the Tour de France, I was to witness the *ravitaillement*, the halfway feed. Driving in a 23-strong convoy of identical vehicles, we travelled 80 miles to the village of Bologne in the Haute-Marne. It was there that I remembered that, like many Scots, Angus liked to call a spade a spade. Team car officials are almost as celebrated as many of the riders, but the novelty of being applauded on the roadside can become a bit wearing. French children and their fathers would even stick their heads through the window to demand a cycling cap, and every British cyclist following the Tour believed they were owed a spare tube or a spare strap just for turning up to say hello to anyone from ANC. I knew that they were the cycling equivalents of the Scottish fans who took home the Wembley grass after the 1977 defeat of England, just looking for something to remember the event by; Angus did not see it that way at all. 'Fuck off, son' was his standard response.

He also made it clear who was the boss *soigneur* in this outfit. 'Roger,' he sneered, 'always wanted tea in a *bidon*. That's what the *soigneurs* do in Belgium, but it's a load of bollocks. Malcolm Elliott asked for tea in his *bidon* one day and Roger said, "Ah, I told you so." I think water or Isostar is a lot better . . . and that's all they get from me.'

I had no answer to that, no interest in that at all, and didn't even know what Isostar was, so to pass the time of day I tried a different tack. 'Angus, isn't it odd that the policemen on the roadside near the finish of stages all look exactly the same as the day before?'

Fraser looked at me as if I was mad: 'Of course. They're the same fuckin' cops, man. Look, man, this Tour is really four Tours in one. You've got the riders, the publicity caravan, the personnel and the police who travel ahead of the convoy all the time. They're the same fuckin' bunch.' Fraser sighed at Friedhelm with the look of a man carrying the weight of the world on his shoulders. 'What do you do for a living again?' he asked of me.

But what was he doing for a living? At Bologne, the stage's halfway point, Angus and Friedhelm had to squeeze their 17 stones into identical jerseys two sizes too small and, with the other team *soigneurs*, settle down to wait, dangling the cloth *musettes* full of the riders' high-energy foods. Once the riders had sped through, with Angus handing them their grub like the last but one man in a 400-metre race, we all headed off to the finish and his evening as ANC's heavy-metal roadie.

There was no doubt that Fraser was good at his odd job, and presumably got paid for it, but it baffled me how, and why, he had chosen this job in the first place. I thought he knew as little about the intricacies of cycling as me and, although he plainly liked the idea of being in charge of something, anything, I wondered what he was doing here. He had told me that his full-time job was at Meadowbank

Stadium in Edinburgh, where he worked as a sports therapist, with the Olympic gold-medal-winning sprinter Allan Wells among his clients.

On the basis of that and the rest of Fraser's CV, Capper had a lot of time for him, but I don't think even he worked out what the Scot was up to half the time. In Tulle, after I – or rather the *Star* – had paid up for all the wine and cigarettes, Capper announced that he was hoping to take Fraser on full-time to help with 'those electrodes things'. As always, I couldn't work out whether Capper was serious, Capper was joking, Fraser had been telling Capper a fib or Capper was in his nightly fantasy world. In the end, I decided it was a bit of each.

'We need a full-time contracted masseur who is responsible for bringing in more when required,' said Capper. 'Then it's his responsibility and there's no question of people coming in and saying, "Hey, I'm number one." That's up to the bloke who's employed them, because it's part of his budget. They know they're quite clear they go to Angus first to be paid and it's no good them arguing they're a better masseur than Angus, because he's paying them out.

'Yeah, we've got Angus for this period of time because he was our first choice and he's the best *soigneur* in Britain and probably the only one who can be compared to a Continental one. He's a fully qualified masseur, he's a qualified physiotherapist and he knows sports medicine, so that he's able to recognise troubles with a rider, give advice and be able to put them right in terms of diet, exercise and things like that.

'His problem is that he's got two *soigneurs* he personally wouldn't have picked and of course that gives him every opportunity to say, "I don't agree with this or that." OK, he's a bit of a moaner, but he's the best in Britain. He can tell a rider what's wrong with him and that rider will bloody well believe him. Now if I stand there and say, "You've got a cold," he would almost certainly go and ask Angus and he'd tell him, "You've got a little minor touch of influenza."'

A subtle difference, but that was Capper's view of Dr Fraser.

For various reasons, the two men were never to get together again and I thought I had heard the last of both when the Tour ended in Paris on 26 July. In the case of Capper, I was correct, but I happened to be reading the *Mail on Sunday* of 28 July 1991 when this caught my eye on page 80: 'DRUGS SHAME OF CYCLING'S MR FITNESS' with a subhead of 'REVEALED: THE SCOT WHO SUPPLIED BANNED AUSSIE WITH STEROIDS'. I knew at once that the 'Banned Aussie' would not be Shane Sutton, but I certainly knew who the Scot was.

The piece had been written by the *Mail on Sunday*'s sportswriter Ian Stafford. The fact that the Aussie, Martin Vinnicombe, had been caught doping was not new, but Stafford had taken the trouble of heading up to Scotland to track down Fraser. Knowing a little about Angus Fraser, I would definitely not have fancied that job. Stafford would later 'do a Plimpton' with a book called *Playground of the Gods*, for which, among other things, he boxed a round with the middleweight world champion Roy Jones (who apparently did not hold back and treated Stafford as he would treat his regular training partner) and joined a scrum during a Leicester Tigers rugby union match. He was obviously made of stern stuff and Angus was plainly small beer alongside Jones or the Leicester captain at the time, Martin Johnson. But I had to laugh when Angus was quoted as saying: 'Now you can go and talk to my solicitor.'

Stafford wrote:

> A top international cyclist, banned after testing positive
> for steroids, was told how to use and sell drugs by a

British sports adviser. The *Mail on Sunday* can reveal a direct link 12,000 miles away with sports adviser Angus Fraser who works at Edinburgh's Meadowbank Stadium. Vinnicombe, whose outstanding international career is effectively finished, received information about steroid use in a series of damning letters from Fraser starting in 1986.

If it was the end of the Australian's career, it was the end for Fraser, too.

He had been seconded to the Australian cycling team as their masseur during the 1986 Commonwealth Games in Edinburgh and had been advising about sports injuries and psychology. A letter to Vinnicombe from Fraser was signed 'Angus' and it outlined which drugs to take, dosages and when to stop using them to avoid detection.

In a letter dated 2 October 1986, Fraser revealed he had just returned from Colombia and Mexico and advised Vinnicombe to 'sell drugs brought from South America'. The effect of Synacthen could, according to Fraser, 'make you walk through walls', and he concluded, 'I have (and you have) everything you need to win the Olympic Gold so stay out of trouble.' Fraser also explained the correct dosage for the anabolic steroids Dianabol and Pronabol, which were not only illegal but very hard to get hold of. Fraser must have found a chemist somewhere.

Fraser, employed by Edinburgh District Council, had been cornered by Stafford at the Meadowbank velodrome and he told the reporter:

> I'm out of a job if this comes out. I haven't got any way of disputing these letters. I have no defence, but now you can go and speak to my lawyer. Vinnicombe was killing himself. He had some guy in Australia giving him all kinds of drugs and he was using massive amounts. He never told me who he was. I'd like to

know why Vinnicombe's done this to me. I thought he was a genuine guy. If someone asks me specific questions, I'll help them. I was answering all the questions Vinnicombe asked me. He telephoned me and asked me to send him the details. He never even paid me. My job's in jeopardy now.

Fraser was right about that and Edinburgh District Council first suspended and then sacked their £15,000-a-year 'cycling coach and print operator'.

The thing that surprised me most about the Stafford story was that most of the damning letters sent by Fraser dated from 1986, one year before he was taken on as a *soigneur* by ANC-Halfords. The implication was obvious, but I knew for a fact that if Fraser was there to dope some of the ANC riders he could only have succeeded with one. Certainly none of the English and Antipodean riders or Palov were involved. Palov even refused to take part in the sticky-bottle trick throughout the Tour, although he was offered the opportunity several times.

Fraser did massage for Adrian Timmis and Guy Gallopin during the Tour once Graham Jones and Paul Watson had abandoned and the Belgian *soigneur* Roger had gone home. Fraser joined the ANC party the evening after the Field of Fire, but Watson had met him before: 'The guy scared me. I just didn't trust him. He didn't know what he was doing. He was a fucking witch doctor.' Timmis was also asked the obvious question, to which he gave the obvious reply: 'I never wanted to get involved in doping. I didn't want to face my mum or my family, because they backed me all the way as a rider. I saw Angus a few years later and I had heard stories, but I don't know what went on. I don't know the ins and outs of what happened.'

On the same day that Watson and Jones were slaughtered on the Field of Fire, Guy Gallopin came within a minute of joining them on the train home, and it was only the efforts of Phil Griffiths that saved him. The bet was he would last for a couple of hours of the next stage from Épinal to Troyes, but astonishingly the Frenchman had found a new lease of life. After 20 miles, he actually made a break for a short period – much to the delight of the *Le Tour* TV people, who told the world at once that the president of the French Cycling Federation was suddenly *tête de la course*. I thought at the time that Gallopin had either overdosed on protein drinks, had 12 hours sleep the night before or was the hardest man in the world. If there were any suggestion of doping (because of his proximity to Fraser), it was never raised, and for good reason. His impressive stamina was legendary and this was a more plausible reason for his renewed energy.

All the riders liked him. 'Guy was great,' says Shane Sutton. 'Calm, but a real hard case. A real gentle giant and a lovely guy, who was always in control. You're right, he didn't speak much English, but he was trying to learn bits and bobs. He would write stuff down on bits of paper. I'm not sure how much help I was teaching him English, mind! He'd have ended up speaking Aussie. He taught me bits of French. We roomed after Watto had gone and we were opposites, which is probably why we got on. I heard he's managing a little French team now and is doing well.'

During the Tour, at the Hôtel au Bon Accueil in Tulle, Gallopin – one of four brothers, all riders – walked into the bar where I'd set up my 'office' and accepted a glass of wine. He'd turned out to be one of the hardest men in the world after all. Since the Field of Fire, Gallopin had managed four 'same time' stage finishes, and most of us were now convinced that he would make it to Paris after all.

'Will no one object to you drinking a wine?' I asked him. 'Do you think Mr Capper will see you?'

'*Je ne donne pas une baise à ce sujet.* I do not give a fuck about that,' he replied in two different languages, in case I didn't understand the first one. 'Shane, my room-mate, told me how to say that in English.' I also got the message when he told me he was a former gymnast and had a black belt in karate.

'I was in a bad state on the Champ du Feu, but I came out of it . . . with some help, of course,' he smiled. 'But I had to get through that because we were close to my home in the next day's stage and my wife was to come and see me go past. Also, I recalled my misadventures in 1983 when I had no morale at all. My wife was in hospital and I did the whole Alpine stage to Morzine just in front of the broom wagon. From start to finish, I did not see another rider. Except of course the 35 who had already been picked up by the broom wagon! This Tour, I've had a chest infection since Berlin. Jones, Watson and Chesneau, I believe, had the same complaint, but I'm still here and they are gone. That's not bad.'

Capper liked to call him 'my dark horse' and said that he would 'make a good Welsh miner'. Like everyone else he was amazed at Gallopin's powers of recovery. 'I think he's been able to suffer the two days' illness, get through it and regain his strength,' said Capper. 'We were coming up the last climb today and, having seen him on the first three days, we were sort of looking up and saying, the next guy around the corner is going to be Guy, but there he was in the second group behind the main bunch. In the last four days, he's never been out of the action. That takes a special sort of genius who won't give in, so in fact Guy has been a revelation. Guy would make a good Welsh miner, he'd make a superb blacksmith, he'd make a good bosun's mate – he's that kind of man, hard as bloody nails.'

The 1987 Tour was the last for Gallopin. With no offers forthcoming from Capper, for obvious reasons, he became a *directeur sportif*, most notably with BigMat-Auber 93, a French professional team, and, later, AS Corbeil.

'I've got a story for you,' I proudly told the guy on the

Star's dog shift when I rang the office a couple of hours after the stage from Épinal to Troyes, the day after the Massacre of the Field of Fire. It was a Tuesday and, as is usual in summer, a quiet sports night. I thought I had a chance, perhaps even a page lead.

'Whatyagot?' It was the Scotsman again. With Tommy, he had become the bane of my life.

'One of the stage winners has been caught doping.'

'One of those ABC boys?'

'No, an Italian sprinter called Guido Bontempi who's in the same team as Roche. And it's ANC, not ABC.'

'Whatever. Has anyone else carried it?'

'Er, not really.'

'Forget it then. No, hang on a minute, send us 200 words.'

'Usual spelling of Bontempi?' asked Tommy the copy-taker when I got through to him, and even with a story of just 200 words, I did file a quote. It had been offered to the Tour press office by Davide Boifava, the Carrera *directeur sportif*. This was a classic: 'They found in the analysis a small amount of testosterone, the natural hormone secreted by the body. Guido swears by God that he has taken nothing. To show everyone the injustice of it all Guido has decided to stay on the Tour and to win another stage.' Guido certainly stayed on in the Tour of '87. He didn't win another stage that year, but he did win three more from 1988 to 1992.

A couple of other European papers did carry the Bontempi story, but the news that the winner of one of the major stages of the Tour had tested positive didn't cut much ice with them either, being relegated in the sports newspaper *L'Équipe* to seven or eight paragraphs down page. I understood at the time why the *Star* weren't interested, but surely in terms of *L'Équipe*'s blanket coverage of the Tour this was similar to Ben Johnson getting caught after winning the Olympic 100 metres. In my ignorance, I didn't realise that doping was endemic in pro cycling, that there were dozens of cyclists in the Tour de France taking illegal substances and that the French press in particular had done so many stories about steroid abuse that it had become old hat.

I knew that many specialist sportswriters (cricket being the prime example) tended to keep their whistles in their pockets when scandal threatened to invade their own little province, but I didn't believe that applied to the Tour de France journalists, not in the '80s at least. But, like the cricket writers, they were not going to dive into a cesspit and pull out the corpses when it could mean no cyclist would ever talk to them again and end their annual month-long jolly round one of the most civilised countries in Europe. Channel 4, who gave otherwise exemplary coverage, showed the start and finish of the Bontempi stage and then briefly mentioned the fact that the Italian hadn't made it past doping control. I thought this sportsman should have been hanged, drawn and quartered, until I decided that he was just a small part of a whole and had simply carried out team orders anyway.

In the end, Bontempi did lose his stage win, was fined £500 and given a ten-minute time penalty and a one-month suspended ban. I was appalled then, but my only instinct now is: 'Good on you, Guido.' For him, and many other riders, it was a case of no dope, no hope. The length and difficulty of the race, as demanded by the Société du Tour de France, meant that it was near impossible without some doping. On that basis, I could always put up with the race's dubious ethics.

Despite the loss of two men, the Champ du Feu disaster had demonstrated to me that the remaining ANC riders were able to show their mettle when necessary. But once we reached the Pyrenees and followed the climbs there, I began to think that the pro cyclists as a group were being asked to do too much, regardless of the fact that they are the hardest men in any sport. Sportswriters and pundits have an annoying habit of calling every British sportsperson, win or lose, 'brave', but brave to me is a man who will ride down a mountain at 60 mph dressed only in a Lycra skinsuit – no head guards in those days – in the knowledge that there is a good chance he could crash and be seriously injured. 'You're not a real rider until you've fallen off,' in the words of Phil Griffiths.

Adrian Timmis, the quiet, shy boy from Stoke, certainly was a real rider, a man prepared to endure danger and pain for the sport he loved – even for Capper's £0 a month.

The riders had made a two-hour train journey from Bordeaux to the Bayonne on the France–Spain border. The map of Stage 13 from Bayonne to Pau showed three major climbs, one of them over the Col de Marie-Blanque, a mountain so famous and notorious that being the leader over the top is almost as good as winning the stage itself.

'That was my first real experience of racing in the high mountains,' says Timmis. 'That was my first real taste of what it's like. The Marie-Blanque is a hard, hard climb. I was the "climber" and I had a free rein, but you soon realise you're not going to be at the front with those other guys. There were no hairpins. It just pointed straight up. People laugh when you say you get a rest on the climbs with hairpins, but generally they flatten out, so you do get a bit of a rest. But Marie-Blanque was just relentless. On and on. And then we did it again the next day – the other way.'

By the next day, Timmis looked like what Griffiths described as 'something out of a butcher's shop'. Angus Fraser thought he could do better than that, announcing to all of us that Timmis 'is like a bucket of blood, a right mess', that he had broken his thumb and could be out of the race. Bucket of blood, broken thumb or no, nothing was going to stop Timmis.

'On the descent, I looked down and there was a big

bulge in my tyre where I'd been braking too much and the rims had got that hot the tyre expanded,' he says. 'I thought, "That's going to go bang in a minute." I looked down thinking, "I'd better stop and change that." But before I could stop, my tyre blew out and I crashed before the next corner. I got going again and there were three or four riders picking themselves up, Anderson and Kimmage among them.

'I got to Pau in bits – ripped to bits with blood on my hands, cuts on my arms and legs. I didn't know about the Hitachi rider. I saw that on TV that night and saw him getting airlifted to hospital. He'd gone over the edge.'

The hospitalised rider was the Belgian Hendrik Devos, who was to have a year off work with concussion before riding the Tour again in 1989. We knew there had been an accident when we spotted a gaggle of photographers and white-clad medics on the side of the hill. Timmis, who had been one of the following pack, crashed and slid head-first down the road, ripping the exposed flesh on his arms and legs and tearing his shorts. His bike was wrecked and Steve Snowling had to give him a spare. Timmis climbed back on and, without saying a word, as was his wont, carried on.

The stage had become a battlefield, total bedlam. Riders who had lost touch with their service vehicles were screaming for wheel changes from any passing car as the heat of braking melted the glue on the rims and whole tyres slid off. Steve Taylor, who changed for one of the Del Tongo Italians, burned his hand on the damaged wheel, and, lower down, a furious Bontempi gave him an earful of Italian abuse for offering him a rear wheel instead of a front one. On another sharp corner, Capper took his eye off the mirror and cut straight across Jurco, racing down at high speed, and the giant Czech demonstrated his command of English with a string of profanities. Capper wound his window up at once. 'I don't want the bastard gobbing all over me,' he said.

163

When we arrived in Pau, we discovered that Timmis was on his way to see Dr Fraser and that Shane Sutton, along with 12 other riders from various teams, was dressed and ready for the trip home.

'The Saronni brothers climbed in the broom wagon steaming,' said Sutton in the Hôtel Campanile on the outskirts of Pau. 'All they could say was "Madmen, madmen", over and over, and you should have heard Frank Hoste and his language in the wagon.'

If the Saronni brothers and Shane thought this was a sport for madmen, they must have been right. I'd put the Tour de France on a par with cage fighting, where men are happy to be seriously injured in the cause of a ludicrously small amount of money and for fans who like to watch that sort of thing.

'Do those guys who run the Tour de France call this a sport?' I asked David Boon when he arrived at Pau with his PR man in his BMW. 'I'm beginning to think that the Tour de France is less a sport than an armed conflict.'

Like many sponsors, Boon seemingly had a gift for saying the wrong thing at the wrong time. Timmis was just walking past us after a session with Angus, his arms and legs scraped raw by the gravel and a haematoma the size of a cricket ball high on his thigh, when Boon offered me his reply: 'Of course it's a sport. Do you know anything about sport? Do you know anything about cycling? Didn't you notice that Timmis bottled it on that descent today?'

So Timmis bottled it on the descent? Boon was like a younger version of Capper, full of enthusiasm for the days ahead, and working out, *à la* Capper, where and when ANC would win a stage. At dinner, he became embroiled, again *à la* Capper, in an argument with a huge Dutch journalist with a handlebar moustache the size of Salvador Dalí's.

'You see, Elliott will win a stage yet,' said Boon.

'But, my friend, you need a team to win a stage,' said the Dutchman, quite correctly.

'Elliott will win in Paris,' insisted Boon.

'If he reaches Paris,' said the Dutchman, who was winning this one hands down. 'Tell me, are you with the team?'

'Well, I'm from ANC, yes,' said Boon.

'But what has the African National Congress got to do with bike racing?'

'What the hell is the African National Congress?' asked Capper.

By the time we reached the Alps, Boon had left us and in his place we had another ANC-Halfords sponsor; he had the gift of saying the wrong thing *all* the time. When Stephen Roche collapsed on Stage 21 to La Plagne, after a dramatic attempt to catch the Spaniard Pedro Delgado close to the finish, our new friend asked me, 'Was Roche that stiff I saw being carried down in an ambulance?'

It was 11 p.m. by this point, and there had been much wining and dining with Capper in La Plagne's Résidence Aime, with its spectacular view over the nearby mountain. It had turned into a memorable night, and the riders felt the same way. With only the stage from La Plagne to Morzine and two flat days left – one of them a time trial – Paris was not far away, and many of the riders had stayed up late. The yellow jersey, Delgado, was seated a few feet away, with a smug smile on his face, and the stage winner, Laurent Fignon, was close by, holding court, with a number of the Système U team.

That was when Palov, still with his ANC top on, walked past us on one of his futile missions to nowhere.

'That guy [meaning Palov] does have a Slav look about him, don't you think?' the ANC sponsor asked.

'He's from Czechoslovakia,' I said.

'Thought so.'

'He's with ANC.'

'Oooooh, is he?'

Personally, I had developed a strong objection to what

Griffiths called 'bloody civilians' joining the ANC squad. I didn't count myself as a bloody civilian by then. Griffiths had warned me on one of the last days in the Alps, 'They'll never accuse me of bringing outsiders into the camp. There's no room for civilians in a racing team.'

Did he mean me?

'Of course I mean you. I've never known a situation where a journalist was allowed to travel with a cycling team.'

'But, Phil, you could have been lumbered with a real tabloid pig, you know, like the characters who put mikes under beds.'

'Yeah, but if you had been a pig, you wouldn't have lasted the first two days. We'd have just bombed you out. We'd have left you on the roadside. It would have been you out of the bus, then your bag a mile later, and that would have been that.'

I'm glad to say that the Pig did behave himself once I had learned more about cyclists, their teams and above all the people who run the Tour de France. Boon had got it wrong. I had asked him, 'Do those guys who run the Tour de France call this a sport?' and his response was 'Of course it's a sport'.

But that was not what I had asked him; for me, the people who ran the Tour de France, at least the '87 version, cared little about sport; we were watching a monument to greed and ambition, a sport governed by commercialism.

After 1986, and despite the unforgettable battle between teammates LeMond and Hinault, the Société had decided that their race wasn't tough enough, that there would be an extra 137 km and 50 more riders and that the first four days would be spent in Germany, with Berlin paying £1 million for the privilege. They also thought the riders could occasionally manage two stages a day and that there would also be two long transfers by train between stage towns. The riders didn't like that at all, but there was no Hinault there to object.

Riders were the bit players in all this and I quickly understood that if any of them were going to survive in a Tour de France there had to be some short cuts along the way. Even a runner, of sorts, like myself knew that the human body was not built to stay physically and mentally attuned to a race that lasted almost four weeks. I was not the only one who believed that.

Graham Jones, like virtually every other rider, was never going to accuse his sport of doping, but he does say: 'One or two people might disagree with me, but I still think that the Tour can almost ruin you if you're not prepared and not careful. You have to dig very deep and it can scar you. Adrian Timmis was a talent, and he won stages in Midi Libre, but he might agree that he was never the same after the '87 Tour. I think fatigue-wise it puts a lot more strain on you than any other race.

'Whatever you think, the Tour de France is not natural. It is impossible to recover 100 per cent from doing a 100-mile bike race. You can't recover from one day to the next, so you're always going downhill. The stronger riders are the ones who can limit that, but you cannot recover from a 120-mile mountain stage because you don't get 24 hours to recover. You get a night's sleep, but your muscles cannot cope. Being a good Tour rider is about recovering as best you can. If you don't have the preparation and the build-up to an event like that, it can damage you.'

At least the organisers recognised this by turning half a blind eye to various wrongdoings. After his stage win at Troyes, Bontempi was given what amounted to a little slap on his backside because he was a first-time offender. This leniency on the Tour's part in itself suggests that many other riders had been doping, too, and that the organisers took it for granted. If Bontempi had been the only rider in the race using steroids, the organisers would surely have 'done a Ben Johnson' and banned him for a couple of years at least. But the Tour was not going to lose all its star names, and the cycling public were not going to watch a race between men who would suddenly look quite ordinary. The Tour and its public would not welcome a race in which 20 or 30 'clean' riders arrived on their own in Paris on the last day.

On the 1987 Tour, the yellow jersey and the first three finishers on the day were tested in dope control along with a couple at random . . . which still left plenty of odds for the gamblers. EPO was still a twinkle in some mad doctor's eye, but as one *directeur sportif* told me in Bordeaux, 'They are one step ahead of the testers all the time. And the drugs are so easy to get. They just go round Europe and ask in chemists. Most will refuse, but they can always find one who will sell them eventually.' Pressed on the number of riders in the Tour using drugs, the same manager said, '95 per cent.'

Doping was a banned topic in cycling before Paul Kimmage spat in the soup with the publication of *Rough Ride* in 1990 and the Festina scandal of 1998 erupted. Following his arrest by the French police that year, the Swiss rider Alex Zülle bravely decided to come clean, telling reporters:

> I've been in this business for a long time. I know what goes on. And not just me, everyone knows. The riders, the team leaders, the organisers, the officials, the journalists. As a rider you feel tied into this system. It's like being on the highway. The law says there's a speed limit of 65, but everyone is driving 70 or faster. Why should I be the one who obeys the speed limit? So I had two alternatives: either fit in and go along with the others or go back to being a house painter. And who in my situation would have done that?

Having heard the views of Zülle, the cycling press decided they had to come clean, too, and that they would depart from their unspoken agreement not to write too much about doping. The Tour had been a European ritual for 100 years, an integral part of the myth of France, and no one in a position to expose the culture of doping was going to spoil the spectacle – until the Festina affair.

Journalists I have spoken to since claim that the Festina team and the police who raided their hotel 'almost destroyed the Tour'. It went on, however, for, as the organisers knew so well, the cycling public have been able to put up with almost anything down the years and still have their favourite riders and favourite teams.

In 1966, the first five finishers in the World Championships refused a dope test, including the five-times Tour de France winner Jacques Anquetil, the 'good friend' of Ward Woutters and his *soigneur* mate Roger. Anquetil, a man noted for his indiscretions, admitted, 'Everyone in cycling dopes themselves and those who claim they don't are liars.' He was subsequently banned – and reinstated within a few months. Once he retired, he became a respected TV and newspaper commentator. Anquetil, who was suffering from stomach cancer as he worked on the 1987 Tour, died shortly after the four surviving ANC riders arrived in Paris. He was fifty-three – but lasted three years longer than Lauren Fignon, who had quite rightly asked me to 'fuck off' when I got in his way at the start of Stage 5 in Strasbourg. Fignon died 19 days after his 50th birthday, on 21 August 2010, having suffered with metastatic cancer for more than 12 months. Despite the severity of his illness, he managed to finish his biography, in which he admitted to the use of amphetamines and cortisone during his career. This is not intended as a mantra about the evils of doping in cycling, but the thought of the number of cycling dopers who die young is frightening.

Bontempi apart, the history of the Tour is littered with (inside, down page) headlines of positive tests and includes a lot of famous names. Dutchman Joop Zoetemelk, winner in 1980 and still competing at the age of 42 in 1987, tested positive for steroids during the Tours of '77, '79 and '83. Two months before the 1987 Tour de France, Zoetemelk won the Amstel Gold Race, the Dutch classic, with his countryman Steven Rooks second and Malcolm Elliott of ANC-Halfords third.

Elliott, who, like many cyclists, looks on it as part of the game, wasn't bothered in the slightest – even when Rooks later went on the Dutch TV show *Reporter* and admitted to amphetamine use during his 13-year career. Later still, in 2009, Rooks confessed he had been using the performance-enhancing drug EPO (erythropoietin) after 1989.

The Belgian Eddy Merckx was disqualified from the 1969 Giro d'Italia after testing positive, although he claimed successfully that a spectator had handed him a spiked drink on one of the stages. Merckx, however, was less fortunate in 1977, towards the end of his career, when his test results, along with those of former world champion and fellow Belgian Freddy Maertens, showed positive for use of stimulants.

Perhaps the most bizarre incident came in the 1978 Tour de France, when race leader Michel Pollentier of Belgium and Spaniard Antoine Guttierez were caught attempting an elaborate fraud to avoid detection during a urine test. Both riders had a bag of 'clean' urine strapped to their chests, kept warm by body heat to allay suspicion, and a tube ran down their arms so, they hoped, that they could squeeze out a safe sample for the tester. The tester wasn't fooled.

Even before the *Daily Star* sent me on the Tour de France in 1987, I knew the Tommy Simpson story and the fact that his death on Ventoux owed as much to the two tubes of amphetamines found in the rear pocket of his racing jersey as to the awful heat of that day.

But the game had become more sophisticated by the late '80s. Looking down the naughty list of those starting the

1987 Tour, Sean Kelly had tested positive in 1984 – making the prolonged persecution of Lance Armstrong by Kelly's biographer David Walsh in the pages of the *Sunday Times* somewhat ironic – and Fignon had been caught in 1987, just before the Tour began.

His countryman Bernard Thévenet, Tour victor in 1975 and 1977, once admitted that he had 'ruined his health' by using corticosteroids. When he was pointed out to me in '87, he was managing the RMO team, which included Paul Kimmage, who, in *Rough Ride*, admitted having a little dabble himself at a post-Tour criterium.

During the 1987 Tour, testers found positive readings on Bontempi of Roche's Carrera team, Silvano Contini of the Italian Del Tongo team and Didi Thurau of Roland-Skala, the same Thurau who had pursued Graham Jones down the Kurfürstendamm and so impressed Ward Woutters. All protested their innocence, as riders invariably do.

The 1998 Tour was dubbed 'the Tour of Shame', and is considered the most scandal-ridden modern Tour, which is saying something. On 8 July that year, French customs arrested Willy Voet, one of the *soigneurs* for Festina, for possession of drugs including narcotics, EPO, growth hormones, testosterone and amphetamines. Voet had been a busy man and later described many common doping practices in a book. Two weeks after his arrest, the French police raided several teams in their hotels and found doping products among the TVM team. But, with the race seemingly on its last legs and unlikely to be able to talk its way out of this one, the Tour organisers and the riders found an answer: first a sit-down strike during Stage 17 from Albertville to Aix-les-Bains, and then some canny mediation from Jean-Marie Leblanc, the director of the Tour. The French police were persuaded to hold back with potential arrests and their country's greatest sporting event went on. Many riders and teams had already abandoned and only 111 completed Stage 17, riding without race numbers and at a pace even I could have followed. But the Tour had gone on.

Festina were forced into a criminal trial in 2000 and it soon became clear that the team management had deliberately organised doping. Richard Virenque, a top Festina rider and a French cult hero, finally confessed at the trial, having been ridiculed for maintaining that 'if I was doping I was somehow not consciously aware of it'. Like many others, Virenque seemed more concerned about his image with the general public than the fact that he had been doping for much of his professional career. He need not have worried. The Morocco-born rider returned to the big time by winning Paris–Tours in 2001, crossing the line with thousands of his fans cheering, whereupon he told the press that he had done it 'for all those who tried to destroy me'. In 2003, Virenque held the yellow jersey for a short time, and a year later he was the King of the Mountains for a record seventh time. Perhaps the Tour de France had suddenly become a level playing field.

In the years following the Festina scandal, anti-doping tests were tightened, but that was not the end of that. Suddenly, dozens of riders were prepared to spit in the soup. In 2004, Philippe Gaumont of the Cofidis team told the press that doping with steroids, human growth hormone, EPO and amphetamines was endemic in his team. In June, British cyclist David Millar, also of Cofidis, and reigning time trial world champion, was arrested by French police after two used EPO syringes were found in his apartment. Then Jesús Manzano, a Spanish rider with Kelme, claimed he had been ordered by his team to take banned substances and also told the world how to evade detection.

French newspapers have been after Lance Armstrong for years, partly because of his unwillingness to learn and speak their language, and also because they are convinced that anyone who could win seven of their Tours had to be on something. A French rider, incidentally, hasn't won the Tour de France since Bernard Hinault in 1985. In August 2005, one month after Armstrong's seventh consecutive win, *L'Équipe*, which until then had shown little interest in Tour doping stories, claimed to have evidence that Armstrong had used EPO in the 1999 Tour, along with his main rival, Jan Ullrich of Germany. Ullrich and Italian Ivan Basso were later thrown out on the eve of the 2006 race amid allegations from the Spanish police. No team, however, had sacked a Tour winner until 27 July 2006, when the Phonak cycling team announced that Floyd Landis, the overall yellow jersey, had tested positive after Stage 17.

None of these incidents, however, seemed to affect the Tour's credibility in the eyes of the general cycling public. Nor did it affect my view that this was a race for lions, organised by donkeys.

'Do you remember that piss-up in that disco in Villard-de-Lans?'

'What piss-up in Villard-de-Lans?' asked Steve Swart. 'I don't remember anything about a piss-up in Villard-de-Lans.'

I had telephoned him at his home in Auckland, midday for him, the middle of the night for me. I had been tempted to get a flight to New Zealand to talk to him about ANC and the '87 Tour – until I remembered. Along with dozens of other British and Irish Lions fans on the 2005 tour there, I still owed $120 for alleged speeding just outside Dunedin. The cop, who had been driving in the opposite direction until he turned round and pulled me over, had chatted for half an hour about rugby and I'd assumed I was going to get off – until he gave me the ticket and told me it was payable 'at any Westpac branch'. Before he left, he handed me a laminated plastic card headed 'Welcome to New Zealand'. I definitely was never going back there. Seven years later, I am still getting demand letters.

Until then, I'd had a soft spot for New Zealanders: great travellers, inordinately fit sportsmen and women, laid-back and great boozers. I had put Swart in every category – until he told me he couldn't recall the night out in Villard-de-Lans.

Swart, who has lived in Auckland since retiring from professional cycling at the end of 1995, and who now runs his own construction company, was 22 when he joined ANC, but was already married to Jan. Of the nine riders, he was the man I would have backed to get to Paris. I can only recall him having two bad days: Stage 12 into Bordeaux and the day he climbed off between Valréas and Villard-de-Lans.

'Swart was the one rider I thought would never pack in,' says Malcolm Elliott. 'He had a problem with his foot, but he just seemed so laid-back. His attitude seemed to be, "It doesn't matter, it's only a race, it's only the Tour de France, we'll get through it." His morale seemed the best of anybody's.'

Swart did appear to enjoy himself, despite the foibles of ANC. The heavens opened during the stage from Tarbes to Blagnac. With 35 miles left to the finish, a thunderstorm heralded the waterworks. Within minutes, the roads were flooded and as we passed Swart the water was almost up to his knees. 'It was ridiculous,' says Elliott. 'I thought we were going to ride and ride until we disappeared.' Swart thought it was hilarious and he was still smiling when he told me later, 'See, it does rain in France during the summer!'

Swart had been suffering for a week with pulled knee tendons by the time we set off for Stage 19 and the 120 miles from Valréas, a tiny town in the Vaucluse, through the limestone rock-climbing playground of the Vercors to the ski resort of Villard-de-Lans. 'I just couldn't push any more,' says Swart. 'I tried, but when I stood on the pedals the pain was killing me.'

He was due to leave at five the following morning – hardly worth going to bed for – and the three mechanics and I decided to say farewell in style. After a few beers in the dining room, we set off for the disco in the depths of the hotel. Drinks were £5 a piece, the first one being free if you had a ticket. Swart had plainly got round this before and helped himself to a number of tickets when the doorman moved aside to answer the door. When these ran out, Swart found us a bottle of tequila, much to the delight of its owner, who apparently thought it was an honour to have his booze nicked by a Tour de France rider.

Swart appeared to have an astonishing capacity for drink, despite not having touched a drop for a month. But in 2011 he couldn't remember a thing about his night out in Villard-de-Lans. Maybe he wasn't much of a drinker after all.

Like many Kiwis, Swart was a bit of a nomad. He had landed in Britain from Hamilton in 1986, looking for a professional contract. He says: 'It was weird because there was another Kiwi called Brian Andrew Fowler, whose finest hour came when he claimed the gold medal at the men's team time trial at the 1990 Commonwealth Games. ANC-Halfords offered him a contract in 1986, but he declined it. And then, for some reason, my name was put forward. I was told I was going on the Tour de France after the Milk Race. Ward Woutters was looking after the European side of ANC, but when it came to the Tour he wasn't there, so to speak.

'When I went on the Tour, I was only 22. Jan was already living in the UK, and, looking back at '87 now, the Tour is the hardest thing I have ever done. Something like ANC wouldn't happen again under those circumstances, but not many guys get an opportunity like that, and you have to take every opportunity you can.

'I've got memorabilia and stuff like that, but my kids don't ask about it and don't really understand it. Sometimes the kids might tell their mates Dad had been on the Tour de France, but it wasn't the biggest deal in the world even to me.

'Looking back at it now, it was obvious even after the first day that we were well out of our depth. There were riders who did well for themselves – Malcolm almost won at Bordeaux – but my right foot got worse and worse and worse, and the team didn't help. I was looking at another stage of suffering. I was quite happy to be going. Once the decision is made, the pressure goes off you.

'I always got on well with Phil Griffiths and most of the other guys. Capper I spoke a minimal amount to, and I could never work that guy out. The Tour made me grow up. It made me stronger and able to ride with the best. I never got paid by ANC, but the money wasn't the objective; it was more important just to ride the Tour. Like I said, I got along well with most of the guys, but kept myself to myself. That's part of my nature, and I thought it was the best thing to do under the circumstances with ANC.'

After ANC collapsed in '87, Swart spent a year, along with Kvetoslav Palov, with CEFB, run by none other than Ward Woutters, before joining Lance Armstrong's Motorola, the American team that had once been called 7-Eleven.

'How did you get on with Lance Armstrong when you moved to Motorola?' I asked him.

'I can't really talk about that,' he said, which was what I had expected, since I had seen Swart's name on the Internet in relation to his admission of doping and what had become another round for Lance Armstrong in the numerous episodes of litigation that kept him busy after his first retirement in 2005.

In 2006, Swart was asked to appear at an arbitration hearing in Dallas on behalf of SCA Promotions, a company that provided risk cover for sports. Armstrong, the world's third most powerful sportsman in 2005, according to *Forbes* magazine, had gone to court to force the arbitration after SCA failed to pay him a $5 million bonus for winning a record sixth Tour. SCA had been happy to pay $4.5 million for Armstrong's previous tour wins, but withheld the 2004 payment because it wanted to investigate doping claims made in *L.A. Confidentiel: Les secrets de Lance Armstrong*. The book was published in France for legal reasons and the co-author was David Walsh, the *Sunday Times* sports reporter. This was another round in Walsh's long-term effort to nail Armstrong and prove that he had been doping since 1996, when he was still recovering from testicular cancer.

Swart was to earn more headlines with the Armstrong imbroglio than he had in the whole of his cycling career. The book claimed that Armstrong had taken performance-enhancing drugs, including EPO, human growth hormone and steroids, and had covered it up. Swart was quoted by the authors as saying that the decision to take EPO was made during the early part of 1995 by some senior team riders, including himself and Armstrong.

The book was at the centre of three cases brought by Armstrong. In June 2004, the American brought a defamation suit in London against the *Sunday Times* for an article it printed about Walsh's book. Then, in September 2004, he filed a defamation suit in France against the book's publisher and authors, and a magazine that had printed an extract. In the same month, he went to court in the United States to force SCA into arbitration. Walsh and co-author Pierre Ballester had provided no source for the charge that Armstrong had admitted to his cancer doctors in 1996 that he had used EPO and human growth hormone.

Armstrong was as unbeatable in the law courts as he was on a bike, and the newspaper settled out of court. Walsh left the *Sunday Times* and the paper's lawyers said in a statement: 'The *Sunday Times* has confirmed to Mr Armstrong that it never intended to accuse him of being guilty of taking any performance-enhancing drugs and sincerely apologised for any such impression.' Armstrong later dropped the similar lawsuits in France.

Armstrong has never filed litigation against Swart, although he's always denied his claims. Armstrong has challenged the credibility of his accusers, but there appeared no obvious reason for the New Zealander to stick in the boot. He didn't have a known grudge against Armstrong – he has never had a grudge against anyone to my knowledge, because that is not his style – and he certainly did not get paid by Walsh. And so, the debate continues: is Armstrong one of the greatest athletes who ever lived, or an out-and-out cheat?

Americans call them 'mega-risers', sportsmen and women who attain a different, unreachable league from the rest of the world. There is always suspicion about them somewhere, but the East German 400-metre sprinter Marita Koch (her world record of 47.60 seconds hasn't been touched in more than 25 years), the Jamaican sprinter Usain Bolt (his 100-metre world record of 9.58 seconds is the largest ever margin of improvement) and Armstrong himself have never tested positive for banned substances.

Because she represented East Germany, it was always assumed, by Americans in particular, that Koch (who never earned a penny from athletics) was part of a doping programme; the same Americans will insist that Armstrong has always been clean and that, anyway, you can't take cheap shots at a man who had almost died of cancer.

Believe him or believe him not, it is always going to be hard, if not impossible, to destroy the Armstrong brand. David Walsh must know that by now. At the last count,

Armstrong had more than 3 million followers on Twitter, close to 2 million 'likes' on Facebook, earned £7 million a year, including endorsements, and charged twice as much as former US president Bill Clinton for speaking engagements.

8

BAD DAY AT BLACK ROCK

They were gonna make me a major for this, and I
wasn't even in their fucking army anymore.
                                   Willard, *Apocalypse Now*

IN THE KNOWLEDGE that the holiday resort you have
enjoyed the first time is never the same the second time
around, I never returned to the Tour de France after 1987.
I watched it on TV in 1988 simply because Malcolm Elliott
was there riding for Stephen Roche's Fagor team. Nor had
I made an attempt to find out what had happened to the
ANC riders, Elliott apart.

But in June 1990, my wife pointed out that the Milk
Race would be passing close to where we lived in Cumbria
and we could catch Stage 10, from Penrith to Morecambe,
by driving the ten miles from Eskdale to the Burlington
slate quarries at Foxfield. There are easier ways of cycling
from northern Cumbria to northern Lancashire, but the
Milk Race organisers were obviously looking for their own
little Alpe d'Huez.

'That's one of their biggest hills,' said my wife. 'And one
of those guys in *Wide-Eyed* is in it.'

'Which guy is that?'

'That Aussie guy, Shane Sutton.'

It wasn't much of a hill and we got there in time to see

Sutton, who was leading overall, buried inside a huge pack as they went past at speed. Once again, I realised that cycling followers don't get much for their money (the racing may be free, but think of all the food, drink and petrol needed), but, like the thousands of Tour de France fans who yell for their favourites, I did my few seconds for Shane.

'Go, Shane!' I shouted as they reached the top.

Sutton either didn't hear me, had spotted me but felt it better not to recognise me, or had his mind on other things. But my wife got a smile from the Australian when she shouted, 'Shane, Shane! Come back, Shane!'

And that was the end of that. Shane never did come back, but ten years later, by then the ultimate couch potato when any sport was on TV, I caught an individual pursuit race on the BBC. As one of the competitors roared past, I spotted on the side of the track a slim guy in shorts, and in GB colours, giving what appeared to be a mega-bollocking to the rider.

Shane Sutton, later Shane Sutton OBE, hadn't changed much at all.

The revolving doors of pro cycling are well known to the sport's public – Elliott from ANC to Fagor to Teka; Roche from Carrera to Fagor to Histor Sigma and back to Carrera, etc. – but I, and several others, would have put money against Shane staying in the game after his retirement and becoming one of the most revered coaches in the business. When he was awarded the Order of the British Empire in 2010, some of his former ANC companions were even more surprised.

'You know what Shane's like,' says Graham Jones. 'I'm sort of amazed that Shane is where he is now, really! I don't think I've met a more volatile person in my life. The amount of little scraps he got into! We'd be out on a training ride and if someone cut him up he'd be up for a fight.'

When he was a pro rider, Sutton weighed little over ten

stone, but, as Micky Morrison puts it: 'Shane was quite an aggressive character. He wasn't frightened to have a fight. We went to the Isle of Man to see Tony Capper, and Shane was telling me what he was going to do when we got there. "I don't care how big he is," and all that. Tony owed Shane some money, but, Tony being Tony, if you came to repossess the furniture, you'd end up giving him some more. You'd have an issue with him and he'd be clearly in the wrong, but you'd go into the office and end up apologising to him!'

Sutton's '87 Tour ended on Stage 13 and in sight of the Pyrenees, but he put in a remarkable performance to get that far. He had had trouble from the opening time trial in Berlin and from then on he had spent every day on the rack. On the stage out of Poitiers, the heat was so ferocious the roads were melting, and Sutton finished the stage more than 30 minutes down, having had long periods hanging on to the car door and costing Capper a small fortune in fines. But still, he wouldn't give in.

'Shane was riding on guts alone,' says Malcolm Elliott. 'His reserves had gone, but he still managed to raise a smile with us from time to time.'

Shane was not smiling when he rang his wife at home and discovered his bank account hadn't been credited with that month's pay. 'By then, I was getting a bit of pressure from home because we weren't getting paid,' he says. 'Adrian and Malc could put it to the back of their minds because they were young and single, but I was 30, I had a family. My wife at the time, Joanne, had given birth to my first child, Emma, when I was away racing in February that year. She was born on the 4th and they got a message to me at some hotel in the French countryside on the 5th. Now I was at the Tour, my wife was at home with a baby and the money wasn't coming in. If you're younger, like Geraint Thomas now, if he was in the Tour not getting paid, he'd crack on and sort it out afterwards. I was told the money would be in, but it wasn't and after a while you're just being told something over and over and nothing is happening. So I climbed off.'

Like every other ANC rider who had climbed off, after Sutton retired on the way to Pau he was forced to sit with the staff at dinner. He could eat and drink what he liked from then on – as an Australian, he liked the odd beer – and suddenly he had his extrovert face back on. He even had time for a laugh and a joke with the staff – until Capper told him that he hadn't yet managed to find him a flight home. 'Have you got a crowbar, Shane?' asked Griffiths. 'Because you'll need it to get some cash for the trip home.'

Sutton says: 'On the day to Pau, I wanted to get home as quick as I could. But I had to stay on an extra day because I couldn't get a flight. I had to go in a team car and spend a day in the cavalcade. I went up to Luz Ardiden in the car and it was hard, it was horrible. Quitting the Tour is not something anyone wants to do and you do it because you want to get out of there. Physically and mentally, I had had it, and then I had to hang around and go up the mountains in a car at 20 km an hour. There's a lesson in that – quit near the airport. Or, failing that, near a train station!

'I'd been ill at Paris–Nice in the spring and I'd stopped racing for a bit and tried to rest. I had some tests and I had swollen liver enzymes off the back of a bout of food poisoning at Paris–Nice. I felt really rough. Capper, Griffo and Morrison told me about Joey not going on the Tour, and I knew I was making up the numbers.

'I didn't have the preparation for the Tour. I hadn't done the races you needed to do it. I'd been ill, but I rode OK. I did the best I could. The whole Tour was special. The fact it started in Berlin, the fact Rochey won it and I was going OK at times. I was doing pretty well in the team time trial, but then the next day you could be swinging like a dunny door.

'Of all of my stages, the day to Bordeaux stands out.

Malcolm won a few hot-spot sprints and then got third in the sprint that Davis Phinney won. I came into the city over the bridge thinking, "I feel great." But next day I pinned my number on and I felt terrible.

'It was a really fast Tour. The start was unbelievable at times and you just wondered when they'd ease up, but they never seemed to. On the same day to Bordeaux, Sean Kelly crashed right near me in the *peloton* and that didn't make me feel better at all.'

Kelly. I remember him well. Millar was scary, Fignon slightly more scary and Hinault in a class of his own for scariness. Put all three together and you get Sean Kelly. Des Cahill had warned me that should I try to interview him, 'Kelly can spot a civilian [i.e. me] at a mile and he doesn't talk much. One time, he did an interview on RTÉ and just sat there and nodded his head for yes and shook his head for no, which can make life difficult on the radio.'

All the ANC riders got on fine with him and one of them told me that Kelly had a real keen sense of humour: 'When I saw him in Berlin, he came right over to say hello and good luck and then asked me, "What are you on?" I told him we were on nothing, nothing at all except the usual stuff you get from a chemist, and Kelly said, "Jeezus, have you got a *soigneur* who works for Boots or something?"'

During the years after the '87 Tour, I quite regularly told people I had spoken to the great Sean Kelly before a race, which was true. I went into the 'I once met someone famous' syndrome on several occasions in an attempt to grab some reflected glory from a sportsman or woman, and that included Kelly.

It's a bit puerile, but I don't feel the slightest guilt about it, because 90 per cent of sportswriters will have done the same thing. I once got an autograph from Marita Koch during a race at Crystal Palace, which later became one of my favourite pub brags: 'Yes, I met Marita Koch, a really nice girl.' Koch didn't speak a word of English at the time and I certainly didn't speak German. But she had a nice smile and put a 'Marita x' on my autograph.

In Edinburgh in 2005, I had followed a band of journalists in pursuit of the extremely statuesque Swedish high jumper Kajsa Bergqvist and, having thought of nothing else to say, I asked her as she was walking out where she was going on holiday that year.

'The Maldives,' she said.

'I've been there.'

That was that, but from then on, if anyone was asking, I knew Kajsa Bergqvist 'quite well' and she was 'a really nice girl'.

And so to Kelly. I can still claim that I spoke to him during the 1987 Tour de France, but let's say I didn't get much by way of response. I got two words and a nice smile from Ms Bergqvist over a couple of minutes in Edinburgh, which is two more words than I got from Sean Kelly in Brive.

I'd spotted him seated on top of his Kas team's Peugeot, looking mean as hell, unsmiling, aggressive and plainly not in the mood to talk to anyone. Not that that worried the ANC mechanic Geoff Shergold, who had also spotted Kelly and immediately told me, 'I once beat Sean Kelly, you know. It was in the GS Europa two-day event in Southampton and I outsprinted him. It was his first race outside Ireland and he was 15 at the time. I'll go over and ask him if he remembers.'

'Geoff, are you sure? He looks in a pretty bad mood and he might not appreciate that just before the start of a race. See what I mean?'

A middle-aged Frenchman had just found a way through the riders' cordon and shoved a pencil and a grubby piece of paper into Kelly's face. Kelly said nothing, didn't pick up the pen and paper, and petrified his fan with a long stare. The man retreated in confusion.

'Oh, he just got his approach wrong,' said Shergold,

who charged over towards Kelly and his car, handing me his camera on the way and asking me to take a snap of the pair of them.

Standing at a safe distance, I watched as the mechanic approached the rider and started talking to him animatedly. Kelly sat there impassively until he suddenly produced a huge grin and a handshake, and then posed with a delighted Shergold as I took the snap.

'You see,' said Shergold, 'he does remember me.'

Maybe Kelly wasn't the man of dour legend. When a few minutes later he agreed to pose with some of the people from the publicity caravan, who seemed to be selling condoms, in I went.

'Excuse me, Mr Kelly, my name is Jeff Connor and I'm a sportswriter for the *Daily Star* in Manchester?'

That was as far as I got. Kelly said nothing, didn't even glance at me, climbed slowly off the car bonnet onto his bike, pulled his gloves on tight and rode slowly away.

If that was the end of my interview with Kelly, it was also the end of Kelly's '87 Tour de France. Sutton says: 'We were on this little country road, nothing going on, and we were just rolling along when it happened. He just hit a wheel and went down. When you have a crash at real speed, you skid and roll and you get road rash, but you can ride on with road rash. It's just nasty. But when you fall like Kelly did, you just hit the deck and you break bones. It was terrible, because Kelly was a real gent. Someone like him could have looked down his nose at us and thought, "Who the hell are these guys?" but he didn't at all. When word went round the bunch that Kelly was down and he was in trouble, there was a terrible atmosphere. We slowed right down. We were going slow anyway, but we almost came to a halt and no one wanted to race. It was really moving. He tried to carry on, but he'd broken his collarbone. Eventually, he had to quit and the race went on without him. Then Malc did well, so it was a day of mixed feelings.'

Returning to his own experience of the Tour, Sutton says: 'Yeah, on the first day in Berlin I led the Tour de France – briefly. I don't know why I went first. Maybe it's because the teams went off in alphabetical order, ANC were off first and someone had said, "Well, who's going to go first then?" and I'd said, "Well, I'm not bothered, I'll do it." Yeah, one thing to tell the kids about.

'Mind you, I failed the pre-race medical the first time I went in. I knew I wasn't right and obviously the doc could tell, too. I had to go back in and somehow I passed it second time. I didn't ask too many questions.

'I don't think I made much of it at the time, but starting the whole Tour off is a pretty nice thing. It's hard looking back to know what the thought processes were. It was quite weird there on the start ramp, about to start the Tour, in West Berlin. It was odd, the atmosphere was quite strange in that city, what with the Wall and everything you knew about what life must be like on the other side.'

Sutton had originally been part of ANC's sister squad, Lycra-Halfords, but when it became clear that the injured Joey McLoughlin was not going to be fit for the Tour he got the call. 'I didn't feel right at the time. I'd won Eastbourne–London, or one of those races, and I'd said to Phil Griffiths in the car, "There's something wrong." It sounds odd, winning a race and saying you're not right, but I could sense it. The way they sold it to me was they said, "Would you start the Tour for us?" I knew I wasn't right but it was the Tour, so . . .

'Even before the team had set off, the cheques had stopped arriving. We weren't getting paid and I had a family and a mortgage. Riding the Tour in those circumstances, it's hard to appreciate what that does to a person. I was given repeated assurances that the money would go in, but for me it was dead simple. The cut-off point would be that if my money wasn't in by the Pyrenees, I'd come home.

'You're going to ask me if I regret it. Well, what would I

have proved? You can get round the Tour, OK. You can put up with the crap hotels and the bad food. But I didn't think there was anything more to get out of it. I had no real form. My only regret is starting it in the state I was in. The terms and conditions we were working under never left our minds, on the bike, off the bike, every day. You need to be compensated for riding an event like the Tour de France.

'We had minimal back-up and it was a pretty big task just to ride. I carried on mainly out of the respect I had for Phil Griffiths, and I still respect him. I did it for him, more than myself and certainly more than for ANC or Capper.

'I didn't ride the rest of the season after the Tour. Some of the guys carried on, but I didn't. I was getting over my illness anyway, but when it came to the Nissan Classic in Ireland, Halfords came up with this offer of 600 or 700 quid for us to ride for ANC-Halfords. I'm not going to go into the figures of what I was owed, but 700 quid was not compensation for me. I refused and rode for Watertech-Dawes instead, got in the big split that decided the race and picked my career up.'

Sutton continued on the British circuit during the 1990s, before taking over as Welsh national coach, where he oversaw the youthful career of the future Olympic road race champion Nicole Cooke. He is now a British Cycling head coach looking after Britain's Olympic track cycling team.

'I rode the Tour. I can say I rode it. And I've had 25 years in a sport I love, working with people I love. To make a damn good living doing what you love, you can't complain about that. When I look back at my Tour experience, none of the boxes were ticked. Now I make sure I tick all the boxes in everything I do. I did learn a lot from that Tour.'

With Shane on his way home and the ANC team down to five, I had begun to wonder if it was a pre-defined plan that the fewer riders you had left the worse the accommodation was to be. Lourdes was passable, despite the hotel being full of unbearable Americans, and it would have taken a hard heart not to have enjoyed any hotel in Toulouse. But the Tour really stuck the boot in when we arrived in Millau after Stage 16. I had even lost my personal bed space. It was an awful night, but it still makes all of us laugh now.

When he arrived at our 'hotel' to find me waiting for him, I asked Capper, 'Have you ever watched that film *If. . .*?'

'I don't watch many movies,' said Capper, who was looking somewhat stressed out anyway – too stressed out to talk about his favourite films.

'Well, it's about all these kids in a public school who eat crappy food, hate the masters and they all sleep in the same dormitory.'

'So what?' asked Capper.

'Well, it's a lot like where we'll be staying tonight.'

I had travelled with Sabino in the Citroën to the overnight stop in Millau, a medieval town in the south, and he was looking forward to his two or three hours of rest and recreation before the riders and staff arrived. His face was a picture when we were shown the accommodation.

ANC's billet was an ancient college dormitory. Well, not just any ancient college dormitory: the Collège Marcel Aymard was, and still is, an approved school for the sinning juveniles of the Tarn region. It specialised in dealing with, as the prospectus wrote, '*démotivation, violences verbales ou physiques et absenteeism*'. Or, as Google Translate would put it, 'motivation and the stopping of verbal and physical abuse and absenteeism'. Fortunately, the boys and school staff were away for the summer (or had all decided on the absenteeism) but a lady in her 70s was happy to show us round.

'These are pictures of the boys who went on to better things,' she told Sabino and me, pointing out some ancient photographs on the wall of young men who looked like characters from French Foreign Legion movies.

'Here is where the boys work,' she said, opening a door to a room full of desks with names written on them by large knives, 'And here are the toilets.'

We left that one alone for the time being and Sabino asked her, '*Et où les cavaliers du sommeil ce soir?*' ('Where do the riders sleep tonight?')

'*Ici.*'

Sabino, who at least hadn't asked where the televisions were, was appalled to find that all the riders, plus most of the management, *soigneurs*, mechanics and journalist, were to do a night's bird in one long bedroom with the beds divided by hardboard partitions. Only '*le patron*' (as the school receptionist had described Capper) would have a room to himself and even that was close to the huge communal wash area and its faulty, dripping plumbing.

'I'm dreading Malcolm seeing this,' Capper said when he arrived. 'I've found the place where we're eating and it's 300 bloody yards from the main road. And it's uphill. But at least I've got a kip of my own.'

The only man able to consider Collège Marcel Aymard one of the Tour's home-from-home nights and who thought that staff and riders of the race should be happy to take the rough with the smooth was Phil Griffiths.

'This was the dormitory,' he laughs now, reminded about it. 'You're a nice chap, but you obviously hadn't slept in tents in Morocco on the Tour of Morocco, hadn't been through Milk Races or Peace Races. I don't know whether you thought the Tour was all five-star luxury. I mean, the riders were used to the accommodation being less than the best. When we went to the Étoile de Bessèges with ANC, the rooms were so bad. The last guest to have used them must've been Napoleon. Phil Thomas looked at the room and said, "I'll be ill tonight." He was asthmatic and he could smell the dust and, yes, he was ill. We'd seen the good and the bad. Of course, Malcolm would be having a wobbler about the dormitories. Millau was not great, but if you're a journalist writing a book, you're going to write in a bit of drama. Someone like Fignon would have had a bit of a problem with it, but Millau wasn't the shock it was to some people, obviously.'

I took the point, but I also had to point out to Griffiths that spending nights in the open during a storm on Mont Blanc was far worse than lying in a tent in Morocco, or even a dormitory in a south of France approved school.

I had some support on the subject, especially from Malcolm Elliott. He says: 'Millau was just a little village. The place was so desolate it was as if we had gone into a squat like one of the *EastEnders* sets. It was pretty much a low. I had been talking to one of the PDM guys and he told me they had won a *prime* and the prize was a week's stay in this region; the second prize was two weeks away from the region. My pet hate is small beds and we were in camp beds about an inch wider than your shoulder. Why did we get shafted like this? We had been hung out to dry in the worst place they could find for us. We were the poor relations of this Tour.'

Like everyone else, I was also 'dreading Malcolm seeing this' when he arrived in Millau, and I surreptitiously headed off to the press centre and left the staff to it. I watched a memorable stage finish, won by the French champion Régis Clère, who had beaten off most of the Tour big boys on the final climb, but I got my timing wrong again when I headed back to the barracks. The silence there spoke volumes as the ANC riders arrived and, Capper included, the staff were standing there like squaddies waiting for the RSM to march into their dormitory for inspection. As Capper had feared, Elliott walked in carrying one of his memorable strops and it was obvious he didn't like this place at all. He took one glance at the school dining room, spotted its wooden seats and plastic tabletops and demanded querulously, 'Where am I supposed to sit?'

'Over here, Malc,' said Capper, as always desperate to

keep his team leader happy. 'There's a nice seat for you and the food doesn't look so bad and we've got a nice bedroom for you, too.'

Elliott clattered his table irons in response, but as always his mood couldn't last. Friedhelm was mixing a huge bowl of muesli and yoghurt for the riders' breakfasts, pretending it was his dinner, which amazed a serving staff member in his 80s. Capper, sensing Elliott's mood was shifting, said, 'That old bugger's won third prize in a competition and his reward is dinner with the ANC-Halfords Tour de France team.'

While the old man's relatives lined the bottom of the table like spectators at a chimps' tea party, he happily tucked in with the riders. 'At least he has something now to tell his grandchildren,' said Capper.

We all had something to tell our grandchildren. I had been worried that I might snore in the dormitory that night and keep everyone awake, but Capper managed that for me with an 80 decibels world record – and he was sleeping next door. The last thing I heard was the slap of flip-flops on the floor echoing down the corridor and a distant voice: 'I'm not coming on this fucking little Tour again.'

It sounded a bit like Malcolm Elliott, but he was wrong about that one.

9

THIS IS THE END, MY FRIEND

This colonel guy, he's wacko, man. He's worse
than crazy, he's evil!

Chef, *Apocalypse Now*

BY THE TIME we were buried into the Alpine stages, ANC's
options, for the riders at least, had become somewhat
limited. We did have a staff with as many members as a
rugby team, but having three times more personnel than
cyclists wasn't going to get Capper his stage win. It was
depressing, too, to see the glum-looking riders sitting alone
on one side of a restaurant while the staff sat together on
another; the naughty schoolboys still on detention while
their teachers laughed and joked ahead of their Christmas
holidays. And we had plenty of teachers all of a sudden: the
wives of Capper and Donald Fisher, the two teenage sons
of Capper, a couple of representatives of ANC and Halfords,
three *soigneurs* (if you include Sabino), three mechanics,
two *directeurs sportifs*, a tabloid journalist and the poodle
of Mrs Fisher. ANC's Tour de France was beginning to
resemble a huge family outing.

Fisher, after spending a couple of days catching up with
some work there, had reappeared from Paris with his wife
– a tiny, aggressive blonde – and their minuscule poodle.
Mrs Capper and two teenage Cappers had also appeared en

masse and there was much muttering in the ranks.

'As we were losing riders – and this is one of Capper's big mistakes – he invited people out and all of a sudden we had this entourage,' says Phil Griffiths. 'But the thing was, Capper had paid £37,000 to get into the Tour and he was in charge. This is how it worked for Tony: you went to the start village and you had the bank of the Tour. It wasn't a shed, it was a mobile office with desks and staff. As your riders abandoned, the organisation cancelled those hotel rooms and then you went to the Tour bank and you got refunded some money for each rider. You weren't paying for those riders any more, so you got a cash refund every day. But then he decided family members could come instead.

'I remember one mechanic was talking to another and said, "Do you stand up to put the tyres on the wheels or do you sit down?" And one of Tony's kids said, "My dad doesn't pay anyone to sit down." This was in front of the riders.

'The last week of the Tour was very sombre. There was no laughter and banter like there is when you're on top of things. And for me and the staff, it wasn't a case of we had to understand what the riders were going through. We were affected just the same as them. But to have people along who were not going through it was too much for the riders to take.'

Capper's family even managed to upset Adrian Timmis, which took some doing: 'It seemed every time a rider packed, another member of Tony's family turned up. I know we upset Tony's wife. Malc and I were taking the piss out of the kids, but they were at the dinner table with us and that was the last thing we riders wanted. We were riding the Tour, after all. That was Capper's first excuse for leaving. We'd upset his wife. We were told that he'd gone because of that. But I knew that wasn't the real reason.'

Elliott says: 'Capper's missus arrived with two of their

kids and Capper decided they could sit with the riders for meals. That was the last thing we wanted, a couple of kids sitting around asking questions, making comments. They were tactless at the best of times, but at the end of a hard stage and after two weeks of continuous racing – the hardest thing you'd done in your life – you just wanted to be on your own, with your own kind. We had to tell Capper, "Tony, we don't want your kids around." That upset him, but later they left with Mrs Capper.'

By Avignon, only Elliott, Timmis, Gallopin and Palov were left from a starting team of nine and, apart from F1, cycling must be the only team sport that does not allow replacements. The general feeling among the staff was that all four would now survive to Paris. But were the staff going to survive to Paris?

Capper had something weighty on his mind and all of a sudden he seemed to have lost his enthusiasm and his will to carry on with the Tour. He basically relegated himself to number-two *directeur sportif*, with Griffiths the man in charge from then on. Griffiths was good at that; he was in his element. His organisation was exemplary, even if he was a bit bossy with his staff and even the journalist at times. If Capper was the colonel, Griffiths was definitely the regimental sergeant major. Steve Snowling, the head mechanic, found that hard to take at times. At Avignon, Griffiths and Snowling became involved in a long and protracted argument over seat adjustments for Timmis, while Capper and Fisher, the laymen, hovered impotently on the fringes.

'Adrian has got a very long back,' said Griffiths. 'You'll have to move his saddle back a centimetre.' The mechanic was equally adamant that he had got it right, but the contretemps blew over, with Snowling sarcastically pointing out to Griffiths, 'I didn't get this job just for blowing up tyres, you know.'

Griffiths had a tough job, but life had probably been

made easier for the rest of the staff, with two *soigneurs* – Angus and Friedhelm – to look after four riders for halfway feeding and massage after stages, three mechanics to take care of four lead bikes, and, if the worst came to the worst, Griffiths could take his pick from a number of drivers.

This being ANC, the worst did come to the worst when Capper decided it was time he went home and took the Citroën estate with him. It was difficult to dislike him, despite all his foibles, and I have said to as many people as will listen that he was never a man to lose his cool. But his enthusiasm for the Tour de France had vanished somewhere between Avignon and La Plagne. The same must have applied to his press officer, Donald Fisher, after the Day of the Dead Dog.

We had survived the night in the dormitory at Millau, but after Stage 17 to Avignon it was obvious some of the ANC members hadn't slept too well. Elliott, who finished sixth in the stage, gave me a sarcastic response when I asked him how close he had been to the win and, with time to kill before dinner, and the Tour on an official rest day, he found himself a deckchair in the hotel garden, where he fell asleep while working on his tan. He had been joined for a kip by Griffiths (so much for his insistence that he had the ability to get a night's sleep anywhere), but both were woken within minutes by screams from Mrs Fisher.

During the boiling hot afternoon, she had left the poodle inside the family Rover . . . with the windows closed.

'It was awful,' says Griffiths. 'It was bad enough having all the families there because they were smokers and that wasn't good. But when the Fishers left their dog in the car in Avignon and it died, that was terrible. For them, it was like losing a member of the family, and it was traumatic for all of us. And we're trying to ride the bloody Tour with all that going on. But before long we lost Capper, too, and we *really* lost something with that.'

The youngest Capper managed to upset Griffiths even

more by announcing that he would be following the next stage, the time trial up Mont Ventoux, in the team director's car. In the manner of many teenagers with rich fathers, he announced this as a fait accompli, rather than making a polite request, and that didn't go down well with Griffiths at all. 'Oh no, you're not,' he said. 'You go with your dad if you go with anyone. I'm the team director and in charge of the cars and I say there's no more than three in a car. Boys shouldn't be allowed on this Tour.'

The departure of the poodle – Nick Rawling buried the dog in the Avignon hotel garden – did leave some free space in the back seat of Fisher's Rover. It gave the team an extra option for Mont Ventoux.

The mountain, which earned most of its notoriety from the death of Tommy Simpson there while tackling its airless 1,900-metre climb, was to host yet another time trial, which, while not exactly putting smiles on the faces of the ANC riders, did mean they could climb at their own pace.

'It still seemed a hell of a way to Paris,' says Elliott, 'but I was viewing Ventoux as a bit of a rest day, just riding within ourselves and not trying too hard.'

The stage start was in Carpentras, which once called itself a capital (of the old Comtat Venaissin papal territory) but is in effect a large village, and there had been problems sorting the various team cars into the correct order. Vehicles were lined up like a traffic jam in Turin. Griffiths had asked me to travel in Fisher's Rover and, as I was the only person prepared to sit in what amounted to the dead man's seat, I found myself in the spot that had once belonged to the poor dog.

Somewhere between Avignon and Arcadia, the poodle, which strictly speaking had been a victim of manslaughter, must have decided to get its revenge. Fisher couldn't attach the billboard, with the name of Palov on it, to the front of the Rover and eventually it was left on the radiator grille. 'Dig in, Omar,' shouted Fisher from time to time, fag in hand, as Palov fought his way up the hill. But he changed his tune when the Rover started to overheat. 'Dig in, Rover,' pleaded Fisher as the possibility loomed of ANC providing another belly laugh for the Tour officials and fans. Palov nearly had to finish the stage on his own, without a team car in attendance, but the cooler air near the summit rescued us.

In the end, one or two of the staff apart, ANC did rather well. A large number of riders had followed Elliott's lead and decided that this was as good as a rest day (pro riders are pretty good at ham acting when it comes to showing Tour followers that they are really suffering), but some of them did take it seriously. The eventual stage winner, Jean-François Bernard, screamed and cried his way to the top, and such was his effort that at one stage he looked ready to do a Tommy Simpson. It gave him the yellow jersey for a day, but he was almost matched by Adrian Timmis.

'I had a good day, although I probably overdid it,' says Timmis. 'I was 30th on the time trial, or thereabouts, and I'm sure someone told me I was fifth-fastest to the bottom of the climb. Having a proper go on a normal stage did me good. On Ventoux, I admit I didn't think about Tommy Simpson too much. I knew what it was and why it was important, because of Tom, but it was just a blur, and the climb was relentless. The first part is in the trees and then you come out into the open. People said normally it was like a furnace, but it was pretty cold. I'd had my skinsuit zipped down in the trees, but it felt cold above the tree line so I zipped it up. I'd been halfway up there, to Chalet-Reynard, in Paris–Nice, but after that I knew nothing about the climb. I was off fairly early and I was getting time checks from people on the side of the road saying I was top five at the time, which was nice. But I did feel like packing the day after Alpe d'Huez.'

Timmis and ANC ran into more problems the day before the climb to Alpe d'Huez, the mountain that, a year previously, had given Griffiths and Capper the notion of taking a British team to the Tour de France. We arrived in Villard-de-Lans ahead of Stage 20 to find that ANC had drawn the short straw with the billeting again. The Guichard Immobilier reminded me of one of the two-star places I had stayed in as a youth in Majorca. It was as bad as that.

Griffiths' girlfriend, Judy, had arrived from England, but Griffiths was keeping her well out of the way following his insistence that 'they'll never accuse me of bringing outsiders into the camp'. Mrs Capper and Mrs Fisher had no such concerns, and we arrived to find them busy sorting out their rooms with a stroppy receptionist.

Alpe d'Huez was certain to be the stage of the race for ANC, myself included, but I sniffed something nasty in the air as soon as I arrived for breakfast next morning. Capper and his wife were doing an inordinate amount of whispering, and the riders and staff looked even more unhappy than usual.

There had been a few mutterings that things were not well in the ANC camp back home, and Griffiths finally admitted that the bailiffs had been into the offices in Stoke in an effort to remove furniture and office equipment. No wonder Capper looked so worried.

Micky Morrison was the man who opened the door to the bailiffs, and he says now: 'Basically, Action Sports went into receivership and it just closed down, but we didn't have anything for the bailiffs to take. We were out of a job. It had credit cards that had been used to pay for fuel and expenses. I was owed money. And so was Griffo.'

Back in France, the riders were facing three Alpine stages knowing they would not get paid for their month of hard labour. Mrs Capper did solve one of the problems by returning home, Mrs Fisher, minus poodle, close behind.

Not that that helped the riders. Swart had abandoned on Stage 19 and Adrian Timmis came close to joining him two days later. 'It was only three years ago that I realised how far it is from Bourg d'Oisans to the top of the Galibier,' he says. 'It's climbing for 50 km. There's a few little dips, but that's all they are. It's false flat for miles before you get to what people think of as the climb proper. We rolled down Alpe d'Huez that morning because we stayed at the top and the start was at the bottom. I think Roche put all his men on the front and drilled it from the start. I kept thinking, "The *autobus* has got to start soon, it's got to start soon." Eventually, I cracked and I thought, "I can't take this any more."

'So I swung out and Paul Kimmage shouted at me to get back in the line: "It's too early." Meaning that if I sat up there, I'd never make the time cut. I had to hang in until the *autobus* group formed. It was horrible. I got back into the line and it did split into groups, but, because it was so early, we still went hard to the top of the Galibier, and then we did through-and-off down the valley road because it was too early to lose too much time.

'When we got to La Plagne, the elder statesmen knew we could go up at a fairly steady pace. That was the only day I thought I wouldn't finish. There's a myth in cycling that says that being in that back group is somehow easy, but it's not. It's survival. You've got guys who've done it for a few years and they know how much time they can lose in a kilometre on a climb and they're calculating to make sure they can make the time limit. It's not a club run down the valley road. You're racing to make sure you stay in.'

Timmis and the other three were to survive the Alps, but Capper had had enough. At La Plagne, he climbed into his vehicle and, without a word to the riders, drove out of their lives.

'I'll see you in Paris, Jeff,' he said, still able to look me in the eye. 'I've got to go back on business, but I'll be there for the last-night dinner.'

Morrison says: 'Griffo rang us in the office from France – no mobiles then, of course – to say Tony had gone. Steve

Snowling hadn't been paid and I think they sold some wheels or bikes to get them through to the end. I did hear Malcolm had lost his temper with Capper's kids, who were running around the hotel, but this was the man who'd created the team, ducked and dived, put his own money in, now he's hearing people say they don't want his family there. His way was to think, "Well, the hotel rooms are empty, I'll keep them on and get some people out here to see the Tour." It wasn't the right thing, but he didn't do it with any malice.'

'In the last days in France, we didn't know where he'd gone,' says Griffiths. 'I rang the office, but my feeling is it came down to his wife saying, "Right, them or me," and Tony was in a corner. But then, if the family hadn't been there, there would have been no problem.

'It was a very successful team and he was the visionary, the energy. It was his team. It wasn't Phil Griffiths' or Malcolm Elliott's, it was Tony Capper's. When Capper went, we did have small money issues. He took the credit cards and stuff, and it gave us some problems.'

The riders had mixed feelings about Capper's disappearance. Timmis says: 'Capper had the foresight to aim for the Tour and get us in the Tour, and I can't knock that. We were the first British team for 19 years to ride it, the first since the Tour was done by national teams. I didn't get the chance to ride the Tour again. I didn't know what was going on behind the scenes and I didn't know anything about late money. I didn't know how much it cost to get in. I was just a young lad riding my bike and that didn't bother me.

'I can't criticise him for his foresight in getting us in the race, but maybe I can criticise him for disappearing a few days from the end. I never saw him again. It really was like that. One day we came down to breakfast and he wasn't there. One minute, he had his wife and kids with him, and then suddenly he was gone. He took a team car with him and from then on it was up to Phil to get us to Paris, and there were only four of us left by then. Guy was going to get to Paris whatever way he could. It was his only chance and he was going to do it.'

Capper had gone, taking the Citroën with him and leaving Griffiths as the surviving *directeur sportif.* Luckily for all of us, he was up to the job. He had worked out that, while it was strictly against Tour rules, Steve Snowling would take over as driver of the second Peugeot as well as fulfilling his role as a mechanic. With both cars needing a mechanic – even Snowling could not drive and fix a rider's puncture at the same time – the problem was who was going to look after the Iveco and its cargo of spare bikes, tyres and all the medicines that had once been carried in the Citroën.

'Have you driven an Iveco before?' Griffiths asked me. 'Could you manage to drive it from La Plagne to Morzine?'

Well, no, and in fact I wasn't even sure which part of France we were in by then. And I was no Matt Damon, the superman from the *Bourne* films who can read a map of Berlin or Paris within five seconds while driving a car at the same time. It would take me some time to find the right road and there was a good chance I would get lost somewhere along the 180 km from La Plagne to Morzine. Nor was I overjoyed to find that I was no longer a professional journalist and was now a professional car driver. What was more, two days previously, the Iveco's brakes had failed as Nick Rawling drove the van through Grenoble, and I faced a six-mile descent along the dizzy precipices to the valley.

'You'll get there. You'll be OK,' Griffiths said.

So I set off before the race began to take the van straight to the stage finish, as agreed. Within ten minutes from the top of La Plagne, the brakes went. Helped by the parking brake (which was still operational), a large bank, a convenient lay-by and some advice from my passenger, Des

THIS IS THE END, MY FRIEND

Cahill, I managed to wrestle the Iveco to a stop. Along with the riders' luggage and spare wheels and frames, we were seemingly stranded 100 miles from Morzine.

The Tour directors had decided that the riders would cycle down the hill from the hotel at La Plagne to the start at Aime, a daft idea totally ignored by the Système U team, who drove down in their cars. I was forced to stand by the roadside as scores of journalists, Tour riders and Tour officials drove past.

'*Regardez, l'ANC ont baisé les choses à nouveau,*' ('Look, ANC have fucked things up again') smiled the Système U *directeur sportif* Cyrille Guimard as he went past the beached Iveco, but I got a revenge of sorts when I heard that Monsieur Cyrille had been banned from the stage for breaking official rules.

'ANC, ANC, ANC,' chanted a grinning Friedhelm on his way down, and few of the ANC riders, used to daily disasters by then, said a word. Elliott shouted, 'What's up?' as he rode past, but he had disappeared before I could find an answer. Finally came the ANC team cars. Griffiths left Nick Rawling to cope with the logistics of repairs miles from anywhere. I climbed into one of the Peugeots and left him to it.

Like Capper, by then I had begun to lose interest in the Tour de France. I had been away from home for almost three weeks and ANC hadn't fulfilled the hopes of my newspaper by winning a stage. The *Star* sold a few extra copies in Ireland – it was still virtually banned in newspaper shops there in those days – and Stephen Roche's yellow jersey win gave me a couple of back-page leads. I tried to interest the *Star* in the story of a strike by the 18 accredited photographers, who had downed tools over Tour restrictions, but as the sports editor pointed out, 'If the snappers are on strike, what are we going to use for pics?'

On Stage 23, from Saint-Julien-en-Genevois to Dijon, the strikers rode abreast ahead of the *peloton*, which virtually spelled the end of the racing, but Goddet and company were used to demonstrations like this and when it was pointed out to the photographers – mainly freelance – that they were losing a day's work they soon changed their tune.

Roche did the *Star* a huge favour when he collapsed after he almost caught Delgado at La Plagne, but I wasn't interested in the life and times of Stephen Roche by then. And anyway the Tour again kicked us up the ass, happily for the last time, when we arrived in Morzine after the last Alpine stage. Every other team was staying close to the finish, but ANC were forced to drive eight miles uphill to Avoriaz, a hideous modern ski complex with high-rise blocks 12 to 14 storeys tall.

'They must have copied Townhead in Glasgow when they built that,' said ANC's resident Scot.

Avoriaz may look fine in winter, but in midsummer it was covered in muddy rain-swept sidewalks and all the windows were boarded up. Elliott complained about having to walk 300 yards from the apartment through the rain to the dining room, where another Madame Angry – pulled in halfway through her summer break, much to her annoyance – waited to serve us. The mechanics had to wash the bikes in the open and, for staff, riders and journalist, morale was at its lowest. After I rang the office and found out that Nick Faldo had won the Open, I tried to cheer everyone up with the news, although most of them had never even heard of Nick Faldo.

But the Tour de France was almost over for all of us. Only the various inquests were left.

'The closer Paris got, the more my morale got better,' says Elliott. 'The scenery started looking better. All the big clouds of the last three weeks were drifting away. I had a good time trial in Dijon, which could have been even better except a gendarme sent me down the deviation for the team cars and I lost 20 seconds or so. I didn't really mind. We were home and dry.'

As had been expected, Roche won his specialist time trial in Dijon to leave Delgado to wait another year for his own yellow jersey, and the Irish arrived in force for the last two stages.

'Until he won in Dijon, people back home had no idea about the Tour de France,' says Lucky Des Cahill. 'I celebrated in a posh restaurant in Dijon and I had a fantastic night in Paris at Kitty O'Shea's, and when I was walking down the Champs-Elysées I even caught myself claiming credit. I was having a beer or two in celebration and finished up staying an extra day.'

Guinness or no, there was no way I was going to stay an extra day.

Dijon was awash with tricolours and Irish accents. The city might have been famous for mustard and the Dukes of Burgundy, but after that night it will be remembered for Guinness. Most of the Irish fans had arrived without accommodation. A crowd I met solved that problem by drinking all night in the bar of the ANC hotel. By daylight, a group of baffled and unsmiling French skinheads had arrived as the Irish belted out 'The Wild Rover' and 'Molly Malone'.

'I don't think those skinheads are too happy about this,' I told one of the Irish fans. 'There could be some trouble here.'

'There will be no trouble here,' said one of my new friends. 'But if there is, Brennan will look after them. Brennan is a hard man.'

'You mean a hard man as in a *hard man*?'

'Exactly.'

Brennan, who, with a mate of his, spoke only in Gaelic, was halfway through 'Amhrán na bhFiann' when I got the message. By 5 a.m., the skinheads were happily joining in with 'The Irish Rover' and Brennan, or whatever his real name was, was still leading the way.

Most of the Irish arrivals hadn't a clue about cycling and

I had suddenly become an expert: 'Roche has always been a good time trialist' and rubbish like that. I was happy to join in in Dijon and to announce some Irish fealty, but I had already decided that I would not be travelling with ANC to Paris by car and that I would make my own way there. I managed an hour's sleep. When Griffiths knocked on my hotel door and then walked in to announce that 'the cars are ready to go', I was hiding under the bed. I'd had enough.

I caught the train from Dijon and six hours later, and a few seconds behind stage winner Jeff Pierce, Roche and his yellow jersey crossed the finishing line on the Champs-Elysées.

Even the last stage had had a sting in the tail for ANC.

'The stage to Paris was not what I'd heard about,' says Timmis. 'They all said it was a nice piano ride to the city and the race didn't start until you could see the Eiffel Tower. Roche was in the yellow jersey, he'd won the Tour, but he also had the green jersey, which is traditionally for the sprinters. He was only a couple of points ahead of van Poppel, the Dutch sprinter with the Superconfex team. Well, Superconfex had this massive rivalry with Panasonic, the other Dutch team. It was Jan Raas against Peter Post. They hated it when the other team won anything.

'Superconfex had heard that Panasonic were going to go for the intermediate sprints to try to take the points away from van Poppel. Panasonic couldn't win the green jersey themselves, but they'd rather Roche had it than van Poppel be on the podium in Paris. That's how these things work. Panasonic knew Roche wasn't going to contest the sprints because he already had the yellow jersey and he didn't want to get involved in racing for the green jersey. So Panasonic attacked from the gun and it was absolutely crazy. Even Robert Millar said, "I don't know why we're bothering with this, but we've been told to attack." Two teams who were enemies, but we all had to go along with it.

208

'But it was a big high racing round Paris, knowing you'd finished the Tour. It did ease up a bit before we got to the Champs-Elysées. I got over the last hill and saw the Eiffel Tower, and I knew I'd achieved something.'

At least Timmis, Elliott, Palov (smiling for the first time in three weeks) and Gallopin could do their long-awaited lap of honour, climbing on top of the ANC team cars and riding slowly along the Champs-Elysées. For the first time on the Tour, *all* were smiling at once.

As most of us had expected, Capper did not reappear for the Paris banquet, leaving Donald Fisher, there with his wife, to perform a farewell speech. It was 23 days after Capper's first little greeting speech in Berlin, and for the remains of ANC the banquet was more like a funeral than a celebration.

'Tony could not make it, but he sends his congratulations,' said Fisher.

'Congratulations? What for?' asked Palov. 'We have done nothing.'

'But you've finished the greatest bike race in the world!'

'We have done nothing,' repeated Palov.

Too tired to celebrate, the party broke up almost on the sweet course and Griffiths rose to carry out his last duty as team director in France.

'Don't forget, Omar, Malcolm, Adrian, off at seven in the morning.'

'But will someone wake us up?' asked Palov.

'I will never forget the drive back from Paris to Calais the Monday after it was all over,' says Griffiths. 'No one spoke. It was silence all the way. It was like they were thinking, "What on earth was that?"'

Timmis says: 'We went to the Tour organisers' party in Paris and it was a bit of an anticlimax. We got up the Monday morning and it was very strange. What do we do now? There weren't any post-Tour criteriums for us when we went home. I think we rode a race in York a couple of nights later. On that Monday morning, I woke up and knew I didn't have to race. It was nice to have a normal bowl of cereal instead of having to cram down this huge breakfast.'

'Usual spelling of Iveco?' asked Tommy.

'Do you know what an Iveco is?' I demanded of my personal copy-taker.

'Yeah, I've got one at home,' he said.

I had no answer to that, but by the end I had to say I had fulfilled most of the demands of the *Daily Star*. I had worked out all the necessities for being a reporter, and I even got a hero-gram from the sports editor and the editor a few days after I got back to work. I had learned how not to say to someone like Elliott, 'You had a hard race today, didn't you?', to which there was only one response, if you got a response at all. I had ridden a bike for 100 miles from one French city to another. I had managed my own little Around the World in 23 Days. It had been unforgettable but not something I would want to repeat.

If the end was nigh for ANC, its staff and its riders, by the time I got back to Manchester the best days were over for the *Daily Star*, too. The editor, Lloyd Turner, had famously founded the 84 Club, a drinking club in Fleet Street, with Peter Tory of the *Daily Express*, but during his days at the *Star* Turner, unlike most of his staff, was teetotal. When I got back to Ancoats, it was to hear rumours that Lloyd had taken up drinking again – and he'd told me that at one time he used to go through three bottles of champagne a session – just before he and the *Star* were taken to court and sued for libel by Jeffrey Archer over claims that he had had sex with a prostitute.

Archer was awarded a then-record £500,000 in damages, which was an awful lot of money for a tabloid in those days, and Turner had to pay some of the price with his sacking. In 2001, Archer was convicted of perjury and perverting the course of justice at the 1987 trial and was imprisoned.

'Gotcha,' said Turner's widow, Jill, according to the *Daily Telegraph*. But Turner was dead by then, as was poor Monica Coghlan, the prostitute at the centre of the scandal.

Within a year of my return from Paris, the *Star* had a new, seedy editor and new, seedy owners and was a new, seedy newspaper. Turner's replacement was Mike Gabbert, who as a *Sunday People* reporter had uncovered the 1964 football betting scandal, and he had been brought in by our new owner, the pornographer and *Sunday Sport* owner David Sullivan. It was plain in which direction Gabbert and Sullivan were taking the *Star* from the start.

On their first day, I can recall staring down at a sports headline like a witness at a fatal road accident. It was around 144 point in size, two inches deep, and ran right across the gutter that divides the inside pages of every newspaper. In the trade, this is known as a spread-over, a common tabloid device for a particularly meaningful story, in this case a midweek game between Liverpool and Manchester United. The headline had been sketched on the full-size columnar pads on which the *Daily Star* back bench designed page layouts. It read: 'PETER THE PLONKER'.

The plonker in question was Peter Beardsley, the Liverpool and England midfielder. Liverpool were the dominant force in British football at the time but had suffered a rare defeat at home, and Beardsley had endured what we now know colloquially as a mare. In 1988, the presentation of sporting events had not reached the excesses of today, although the dumbing down had certainly begun. It seems laughable now to recall the breast-beating over the use of the word 'plonker', applied as it was to a sports personality. Key the word 'plonker' into, say, the *Guardian*'s search engine today and you will get a dozen pages of hits with the description applied to everyone from David Cameron to Peter Andre. But the notion that a sportsman could be held to account in such lurid fashion was unknown at the time.

It was a sign that in future there would be no such thing as the reporting of facts innocent of interpretation. Behind every fact presented to the reader from now on would be a judgement. And the judgement here was that Peter was a plonker and single-handedly responsible for defeat – ignoring the fact that the Liverpool defence had also had an off-day.

Most of us thought the headline totally out of order and said so. Others thought differently.

'Now that's what I call a real *Daily Star* headline,' said Gabbert, our new editor, plonking down a tea mug emblazoned with a woman's jiggling tits. 'Just a pity that "Peter's a Proper Plonker" won't fit.'

Gabbert was the archetypal rain-coater, a man who effortlessly and unashamedly oozed sleaze. He had – or so it was said – lost jobs in the past because of sexual and financial malpractice, and he always looked on death's door (he was, as it turned out).

His arrival in the wake of the sacking of Turner had been poorly received. Gabbert's vow to take the *Daily Star* down to the market in which his last newspaper, the *Sunday Sport*, swam sparked a string of resignations.

His world contained women with 48DD breasts, buses on the moon and the news that the body of the world hide-and-seek champion had been found in his closet after 20 years.

No one had the slightest respect for Gabbert, but he was right about one thing. From that day on, 'Peter the Plonker' became a typical headline, not just in the *Daily Star* but in every other red-top's sports pages. The tabloids were suddenly in competition to be rude to people. Gabbert, by default or accident, was an unlikely visionary, Nostradamus with boobs on his cheap Woolworths mug. 'Peter the Plonker' all too soon begot the head of Graham Taylor grafted onto a turnip, David Beckham's effigy in a codded-up archery target, polls in which readers were asked to name the worst footballer in the UK and columns by someone called Hatchet Man in the *Daily Mail*.

It was time to move on.

10

WHAT DID YOU DO IN THE TOUR, DADDY?

Someday this war's gonna end.
Lt Colonel Kilgore, *Apocalypse Now*

ANC-HALFORDS WERE FINISHED as a cycling team. ANC were known as ANC until they were re-branded as part of FedEx after its £120-million sell-out in 2006, and Halfords remains Halfords, still the biggest bicycle retailer in the country. The name of ANC-Halfords is mainly remembered now as that British cycling team that crashed and burned in the 1987 Tour de France, and I can hold a small measure of responsibility for this.

Tony Capper apart, however, it hasn't done anyone much real damage, and most of the staff and riders still regard the ANC-Halfords Tour with great fondness.

Last time I spoke to Griffiths, in 2011, this clever man had announced that he was going to bring out a limited number of ANC-Halfords jerseys for 2012. He insists: 'It hurts me now when ANC is associated with other failures, like McCartney. There was nothing of McCartney about ANC. ANC was a success and a lot of good things have come of it.'

Life had to go on for the riders and staff who survived those memorable weeks in 1987. Steve Taylor, Geoff

Shergold and Nick Rawling returned to their day jobs, while, in the case of the lead mechanic, Steve Snowling, I hadn't been the only man working on a night job during the Tour. He had long been embedded in work on a book on bicycle mechanics that became a great success. He now works in Belgium. Angus Fraser never got his job back from Edinburgh council and headed for the United States to be implicated in another alleged doping scandal, notably, according to documents, with USA Cycling coach René Wenzel and fellow coach Chris Carmichael (the author of *Food for Fitness: Eat Right to Train Right*). No charges were ever brought against him and the claims against Wenzel and Carmichael settled out of court.

When Griffiths met Micky Morrison in Stoke ahead of the official liquidation meeting, both had already moved on to better things, although it did take some time in the case of Morrison.

Capper appeared at the first credit meeting in February 1988, and arrived with a claim for £30,000, which took few people by surprise.

Morrison says: 'We went to the receivers' meeting and Tony was there and that was the last day I ever saw him. I'd never had a cross word with him in my life, but the atmosphere was not great. Griffo had even been saying that he was going to give Capper what for, but when we were there it wasn't war. It wasn't particularly friendly, but the outcome was that there was no money. I don't know how much was owed because I didn't have access to the budget. Tony ran all that. I know we owed tax, VAT, PAYE and creditors, and there was about three pence in the bank at the end. Tony lived life on a wing and a prayer, but he just pushed the boat out a bit too far.'

Morrison carried on in cycling, found some work with Ambrosio (an Italian cycling design company), but in the late 1990s he split amicably from his wife, the couple dividing everything. 'I moved to Spain and bought a little place, and I was doing a bit of real estate. There was a new urbanisation and I bought one off the plan, but by the time they were nearly completing it, my second wife and I realised we didn't like the area. I said, if someone comes along who's interested, we'll sell it. I made about 50,000 euros and I hadn't even opened the front door. All that pedalling around city centres!

'We bought a sensibly priced house in Torreveca, near Alicante, and with the spare money bought a second place. We were there about nine years and in all we had seven houses that we bought and sold, making a bit each time. Then a friend of mine, who worked in the mobile phone industry, invited us to Turkey. We loved the place and we sold up in Spain.

'We were going to run a dog kennel, but it's difficult in Turkey, even getting a work permit is complicated. You can't get one if there's a Turk who can do the same job, which makes it very hard. We came here six years ago and now we live in Kusadasi on the Aegean coast. Before that, we had a farm, about 20 acres, and what money I made in Spain, I virtually lost. The farm was predominantly olive trees, about a hundred and sixty trees, and we'd get five tonnes of olive oil every two years. We had ducks, geese, turkeys and a mad donkey that thought it was a kick-boxer. We bought some land adjacent that we had been renting from the government. I bought it having been told that we'd be able to build on it, but the restrictions are so tight, we can't build a thing there. It's only allowed to be used for grazing sheep and it must be the dearest field for grazing sheep in the world!

'I'm a magician now. We've also got a little house in Thailand and we go there for winter. About four years ago, I was in the market in Bangkok and I saw this chap do a trick with a cigarette. He made it disappear and I was stood there for about an hour in 90-degree heat trying to work out how he did it. I bought this little trick from him for about two euros and back in Turkey I'd do it for friends after dinner, and they loved it. It made people laugh.

'Each time I was in Thailand, I bought more tricks. Then I took lessons and finally I joined the International Brotherhood of Magicians in America, which is like the Magic Circle but bigger. To get in, you have to be endorsed by two other members, and they've got branches all over the world, including one in Istanbul and one in Izmir near where I live. I did my audition and got in. I've spent a lot of money and watched a lot of DVDs, but I love it. The ethics and code is that you guard your secrets. Magic doesn't really exist; it's a lot of props to make it appear like magic. We get a lot of British and Irish coming over because we're in a seaside resort, and I get a few gigs in the hotels and bars. I'm not going to be Bill Gates or Abramovich, but I can go out, have a free meal, a bottle of wine, entertain people and come home with £50 in my pocket. Each time you do it, you're learning something. I really enjoy making people laugh and it keeps me entertained.

'I've got two children from my first marriage, both girls, twenty-two and twenty, both at university, and I always follow the cycling these days. Me and that sofa don't part when the Tour is on.'

Like Morrison, Griffiths was to see Tony Capper for the last time at the creditors' meeting in his home city. 'We were both at the liquidators meeting in Stoke,' he says. 'Obviously, it was a bit of a surprise when he turned up with a counter-claim, which only Tony could do. I got my money eventually. I was sorted out by ANC and was not out of pocket.

'I am very, very happy that our lives crossed. He taught me an awful lot and he gave me a lot of vision. He taught me to look at people's strengths, not to put them under the magnifying glass and pick at the faults. The day I got home from the Tour in 1987, I picked up the phone and did the Assos sales myself. What I realised was that Assos was a small family business, and it helped me to move on. I've since headhunted other family businesses. Rudy Project [sunglasses] is a family business, so is Pinarello [bikes] and Corima Wheels. I've always gone for family businesses rather than multinational companies. Yellow Limited is my own family business, and some of my family work here now. It started off as a one-man operation in 1984 and now I have a number of staff at the unit in Stone in Staffordshire.

'I learned a lot from Capper, but I learned from other companies, too. One day Rudy Barbazza, who is the founder and guru of Rudy Project, invited me down to Italy and told me to come down on the Sunday for a meal. I did notice that there was a lot of his family there and not many other business-type contacts, but I didn't think much of it.

'I stayed overnight in the hotel near the office and went in the next morning and was told Rudy wasn't in. I said, "Well, he's asked me to come down." They said, "You saw him yesterday, he took you for a meal." I said, "Well, yeah, but I thought he wanted to talk business," and the reply was: "Yesterday was the first day of the asparagus season and he wanted to invite you to eat with him and his family. That was what the invitation was for."

'It was his pleasure to have me with him and his family in Treviso and take dinner. I got on the plane scratching my head. It's only really today that I understand and appreciate the gesture and how special that was. I didn't get that at the time at all. But I do now.'

What did happen to the boys of '87?

Chesneau, Gallopin and Jones retired within a year, while Elliott, Timmis, Swart, Watson, Sutton and Palov all found cycling teams, with varying degrees of success.

Two years after *Wide-Eyed and Legless* was published, I had a letter from the wife of Kvetoslav Palov in Australia, who informed me that Palov had been 'quite happy with his role in the book', which quite surprised me. She also

219

asked me for advice about finding a publisher, as she wanted to write the story of a Czech escapee from the Communist East who turned up for the 1987 Tour de France and then married a girl from Australia. It sounded like a good story, and I did my best with as many publishers as I could find, but I never heard from her again.

After Palov left the Belgian team of Ward Woutters, he had a year with an Australian outfit, Repco Cycling, before two years as an individual in Australian road races. Last heard of he was working as a system data expert in the Northern Territory.

Adrian Timmis, a man who has dedicated his life to cycling, signed a contract with Z-Peugeot a year after the ANC Tour, riding for the same *directeur sportif* who had done door-to-door battle with Capper and his team car on Stage 17 from Millau to Avignon. He was released after a year, turned to mountain-bike racing and after retirement became a *soigneur* with the Linda McCartney team, a group as chaotic as ANC. At least ANC lasted for three years – the Linda McCartney team was disbanded on the day of its launch.

Timmis was married to another cyclist, Sally Dawes, who rode for the Raleigh mountain-bike team, but that didn't work out and his remarriage was to Nicola, sister of Victor Slinn, the former Peter Buckley Junior Road Race Series winner. They have a daughter, Mollie, who was six in August 2011. Timmis is now the owner of Cadence Sport and specialises in bike fitting and coaching, based in Barton-under-Needwood, Staffordshire. As one would expect, he is an expert at looking at a rider and seeing that their saddle is too low or the handlebars are in the wrong position. Maybe he was making mental notes about the height of his own saddle when Griffiths and Snowling were arguing the toss in the Alps.

'Mollie knows that I was a cyclist,' he says. 'She's got a bike and we've not pushed her to do it, but she's been asking to do the Under-8 Go-Ride races at the mountain-bike races. Yesterday, she got a bronze medal and a certificate, so she's hooked, and now, believe it or not, she wants to go to the Tour de France next year. My nieces are six and twelve, and they're in mountain-bike races, too. If Mollie gets to the stage where she wants to take it seriously, I'll not be the one to push her. If she gets good at it, I'll get her a coach she can argue with! At least she can't say, "You don't know what you're talking about."

'I'll teach her to mend her bike and she'll not be like her mum, who seems to have a magic fairy who cleans and mends her bike! My wife is from a cycling family. I met her in Sheffield after we got set up by Chris Walker and his wife Lynn. We had both been married before.

'When I rode the Tour, I was young, free and single. I had no commitments, no mortgage. That's probably why the money didn't bother me as much and maybe that's why Shane was more worried about it. He had a family. I was on £6,000 in 1987 and I only got paid half of it. For years, whenever I saw an ANC van I thought, "Where's my money?"

'I've not seen the Tour outside this country. I went in 1994 and I was in London in 2007. It was nice to be there with my family, so they could see how big it was. To have my mum and my sister and her family there was amazing. I had passes for the Saturday, and I took my brother-in-law and my niece to the area where the buses were parked and got some photos with Robbie McEwen and Yaroslav Popovych. They took time out for us, although they didn't know me.

'My mum, it's a bit of a regret that she didn't come to Paris to see me. It's a bit sad she didn't get to go there. My dad died when I was seven and Mum is not a big traveller. It would have been nice for them to have been there. These days, everyone's family goes, but travel is a lot easier and cheaper now than it was in 1987.'

The general opinion among the cycling press, and many of his teammates, is that Timmis's career was destroyed by the '87 Tour, and to some extent he agrees. 'When I joined Z-Peugeot, it was a much bigger team. It had a long history, and I'd been to the service course in Paris. We had an early training camp and get-together, and it was bigger than ANC. There were more riders, more staff. It was more clearly defined. It was what I'd dreamed of – well, at the start, anyway. I had a two-year deal, but, being young and naive, I didn't look at the contract, which was in French. I didn't have a good year, and at the Nissan they told me they didn't want to keep me for the following year, which was a blow, big time.

'In 1987, I finished my season after the Tour of Britain. I was on my last legs there. I didn't talk to anyone about it and I didn't get any advice. Sean Yates and Graham Jones said the Tour de France was too much for me at the time and I wasn't ready for it. Hindsight's a great thing, but in 1988 there weren't really many days when I got going at all. I had flashes, but I didn't build up enough of a back-up team, or people who could advise me. I should have had a coach, just someone to talk to, and that's my fault. I always listened to people, but I didn't get any support behind me.

'I used to go training with John Herety, Paul Sherwen, Graham Jones. I'd pick their brains and ask for advice, but I didn't have someone I could go to and talk about planning my training or my racing. My way of dealing with a setback was to train more and more. Maybe I needed a bit more rest. I should have had blood tests to find out what was up with me.

'If something was wrong with you, you went to your GP, who would ask what you were doing, and as soon as you told them you were riding hundreds of miles a week, they'd decide that was the problem. I know I've got low haemoglobin. It's very rarely gone above 12. I have a haematocrit of 37. I didn't know that then. I knew I was borderline anaemic. I was tested at 16, but even with iron tablets I never got any better. I was so tired, and I was up and down all the time. I was mentally tired because I would do a consistent training effort but it never translated into form. I'd have really good days and really bad days. In the races in 1988, one day I'd be towing the bunch for ten miles, the next I'd do nothing. It took me a few years to get over that.

'I've been over the mountains since, working for teams. I was the manager for Great Britain at the Tour de l'Avenir in 1999, when Russell Downing and Charly Wegelius rode. I drove the team car over the Col de la Madeleine and a few others, but three years ago was the first time I had ridden there again. I wasn't as fit as I was in 1987, but it made me appreciate a bit more what I had achieved in finishing the Tour. It was quite emotional.

'I knew the Tour was hard, but it was a bit of a blur. I was getting up and doing my job and surviving each day, but going back to ride the hills made me realise what I had done and realise how I wasn't prepared enough for it. I was supposed to be a climber but that was because I was light. Being light doesn't make you a climber. I needed to base myself in the mountains and train in the mountains. I needed to increase my strength.

'When I rode the Tour, I was 64 kg. Because I was small, I thought that was my ideal weight, and no one said any different. But in 1995, when I won a couple of national points series mountain-bike races and Rochester crit, I changed my diet. I cut out wheat and I got down to 61.5 kg. I was stronger than I'd ever been. Looking back, that should have been my climbing weight – that should have been my Tour weight, because you can't maintain that all year.

'The Tour was a big thing. It was what I'd dreamed of as a kid. It was a strange way to get into it, with ANC. We weren't a big Continental team, and it was a little bit scary stepping into the unknown. Graham Jones knew what it was about, as he'd done it before. We all went there to do the best we could, but it was a lot tougher than some of us had imagined. You dream of getting up there on a stage and I did have that in the back of my mind, but then you realise there are 200 riders trying to do the same thing. My best was to Bordeaux. I was away with Allan Peiper and Phil Anderson, and I was having a really good day, and then I led Malc out for the sprint and I stayed up there.

'Thinking of Capper and ANC, I think if it had just been Phil Griffiths we'd have been fine. But we had Tony there trying to be a DS. He gave us a bollocking for not getting in what he called a "soft break". But the break went at 35 or 40 miles an hour, and I don't call that soft. Tony wasn't a rider so it was hard to take that kind of thing from him at times. Even Phil didn't like that. We were all nailed, absolutely knackered.

'People have said I was quiet and kept myself to myself, but that's just me. One of the reasons I enjoyed cycling was because I could express myself with the way I was riding. I wasn't one to get into arguments. I just wanted to ride my bike. I don't like conflict like that, whereas Malc doesn't mind a bit of conflict. I think I change a bit in a race, but off the bike my way is to be quiet and take a back seat, keep myself to myself. It's the way I've always been. It was nothing to do with the team.'

When Paul Watson joined Hitachi in 1988 it didn't take him long, like Timmis, to start missing the good old days at ANC. He says: 'When we went training with Hitachi, we were doing a six-hour ride, and I thought we might pull over and go for a coffee or something, but we just pulled over in a lay-by and there were juggernauts going by. It was raining, so we sheltered under the car's tailgate, taking on a drink and some muesli bars, and I was thinking, "This is not what I like doing."

'I should have toughed it out a bit, but I couldn't

understand why we couldn't have a giggle for half an hour in a coffee shop. Then they found me a hotel and I decided I would only train an hour a day. The team manager, Jef Braeckevelt, was friendly with the hotel owner, who knew I wasn't training, so I had to be clever. I'd ride out to the canal, have a sleep on a bench, go and get a coffee and a cake and put a spurt on so I was sweating when I got back to the hotel. A couple of weeks later, Braeckevelt said to me, "Good boy, now the form will come."

'On one Hitachi team training camp in the south of France, we'd been there five or six days training and we had an easier day and we were just expected to sit around in the hotel, resting. We did these monster rides and we'd come back to our rooms and watch some 1940s black-and-white French movie on TV. You didn't have the Internet. You couldn't watch British TV. You couldn't even phone home. I used to be pulling my hair out thinking, "Come on, we've got to get out of here." I wanted to scream, "Will someone please come into town with me?" I'd get one of the guys to put his shoes on, then go and get another, and by the time he was ready the first guy would be back in bed. In the end, what happened quite a bit was that the manager drove us into town, past all the bars and cafés, so we could walk around a hypermarket. I was almost in tears.

'I wanted to do as well as I could, but you get to a point where you realise, "Hold on a minute, I can't do anything else."'

Hitachi, says Watson, was the end of what he calls the old guard – the cigar-smoking Mafia-type team manager. 'Jef Braeckevelt was a nice guy, but Albert De Kimpe, who died in the '90s, was a gangster. There's no other word for it. He ran the team. He was a big, big guy, big cigar and braces. The Belgian Mafia, basically.'

Watson refused the chance to 'improve your career' as he'd been told he could when he had first joined Hitachi. 'I had another good ride in the Flèche Wallonne, and I was starting to get some flashes and feel some sparks. But I got the feeling there were drugs . . . I didn't feel comfortable about the whole thing. Before a race, I would empty my water bottles and refill them, because I started not to trust what was in them. Some of them couldn't seem to get their heads around the fact that I was on multivitamins and nothing else, and they wanted me on a programme. That was starting to get to me, because I didn't want to go that far.

'I think every rider comes to the point where they have to make a choice to go with it or not, and I didn't want to. Looking back, I wish I had, but I just didn't. It seemed like every rider looked after themselves. It was "whack a bit of this in, have some of that for this race, if you're tired have this". That wasn't for me.

'There were a few times when I felt amazing and the legs weren't hurting. Rather than put it down to the fact I had some form coming, I started to wonder if they were putting something in my bottles. I really don't think they would have done that, but I did empty my bottles a few times.' (It should be said that Jef Braeckevelt has never been accused of doping his riders and, in fact, when he was *directeur sportif* with Katusha Cycling in 2009, he terminated the contract of a rider who refused to sign the team's anti-doping charter.)

Watson adds: 'I don't think about my time as a pro. As time goes on, reading about all the doping going on, you realise we were so underprepared. It was like going to war with no bullets. I'm not saying it's completely clean now, but the playing field is levelling off a bit.

'Even in my amateur days, my heart wasn't in it. Most of the other riders were trying their best and were determined to succeed. I once lived with Brian Holm, a Danish rider, and we'd go out. I'd do an hour and a half, then go home and get the pot of tea on. He'd come back five hours later. That's the difference. I should have been a 1,500-metre runner or something.

'Looking back, knowing how I am physically and genetically, I am not cut out for Tour riding. I was more for the classics. I could empty it out on one day, maybe two, but don't ask much more after that. It's not so much physically, it's mentally. I just crack, and I haven't got the attention span. I keep thinking, "I'd rather be doing something else." I'm the same now. I should have done the spring classics, taken a break in the summer and then come back and done the autumn classics, but, as it was, I was totally burned out in 1987.'

The Tour de France of '87 ended Watson's season, but before he headed for Hitachi he had the grace to write to Capper. 'After it was all over, I wrote him a letter to thank him. Maybe he could have done something different, but at the end of the day he probably lost a lot of money. He tried, and his heart was in the right place. Hopefully I'm not wrong, but I don't think he was trying to rip us off. I think it all went horribly wrong and there was no way out. But I don't think he set out to do that at all.'

Watson will be among the first to admit that his candour has got him into trouble down the years. Late in 1988, Geoffrey Beattie, a journalist at the time but later better known as the psychologist on the *Big Brother* TV show, took 'a relaxed' Watson out for a drink to talk about cycling, particularly his time with Hitachi. The interview, and a subsequent article in *The Guardian*, got Watson banned from cycling.

'I don't regret having said anything, but I regret the way I said it. If I'd intended to say something, I'd have said it totally differently. But it came out so poorly. Beattie was at the University of Sheffield and I met him socially in a Sheffield bar and we got chatting. It was Christmastime. We were talking about cycling and he was telling me all about what they took in weightlifting. I was naive. I knew he was a journalist, but I thought he was going to do the story in a certain way, but it ended up being a big piece in

The Guardian. It was embarrassing. The stories I told him were really clichéd ones and it was all a bit naff.

'The British Cycling Federation, I'd like to know where they were coming from. I hadn't taken drugs. I wasn't saying I was taking drugs. But they said I was bringing the sport into disrepute by saying that drugs may be being taken. Instead of investigating it, their answer was "Ban him". I applied for a licence and they wrote back and said it was refused. I'd mentioned something they'd rather sweep under the carpet, so I was the baddy.

'I was 27, and I'd recovered from my illness and I was absolutely flying, but I had nowhere to let it out. I was running. I was doing 31-minute 10 kms, I won the British duathlon championships. I was going really well, but I couldn't ride anything, and I couldn't be amateur because I'd been professional. The only option was to go to America and do mountain biking. The North American Mountain Biking Association wasn't part of the Union Cycliste Internationale.

'I had a friend in San Francisco who was a junior road champion, Daniel Westbury. He was the son of Phil Corley's ex-wife, and I went and stayed at his. I didn't have a mountain bike, but I was really fit. We went to a local Bay Area bike shop and they lent me one. I went to the first race and I was leading it by about a minute when I punctured. I got off and put my hand up. Everyone just waved back!

'I'd rather have had another couple of years on the road, but I did love the mountain biking. The Bay Area is one of the most beautiful places in the world and the money was good, too. You'd fly out to a race and they'd have a party before the race, then you'd race and there'd be a party afterwards. It was great, much friendlier, much more relaxed.'

Watson had had a year as a professional mountain biker when he broke his arm while trying out some new clipless pedals that had been sent to him to test. The accident ended his career as a cyclist. 'At the time, they sent them out with the tension wound up tight and if you wanted them looser you wound them out. So I went out training on Mount Tam and I was coming down this little descent. I wasn't going fast, but I slipped and needed to get my foot out, but my foot was stuck. It was such a lame little crash, but I hit a tree on the way down. They had to put a plate in my arm, but there were some complications and the plate trapped my radial nerve, so I lost the use of my right arm. They took 18 cm of sensory nerve out of my leg to replace the radial nerve in my arm. At the time, it was cutting-edge surgery.

'That put an end to my mountain biking and I spent a year trying to sort out my arm. At the time, I was riding for Marin Bikes and I felt bad because there was nothing in the contract to say they could stop paying me if I got injured, so they had to keep paying me. So I said I'd come into the office and manage the rest of the team and try to get some sponsors in and generally just do whatever I could. I didn't want to be bored at home. I was quite good at it, and I managed the team and went on the circuit with them.

'I did get a pay-out. They settled out of court for a pretty big six figures, and that was helpful. I'd rather have had my arm fixed properly. The maddest thing is, I couldn't do press-ups properly until a few weeks ago.

'I came back to England in about '95 or '96 and started buying houses. I couldn't have picked a better time. Back then, you could buy houses really cheap. Lucky, really. I was looking for flats and houses in Milton Keynes and Sheffield to rent out or turn over. I managed to sell quite a bit before the crash. At the peak, I had 32 houses, and I sold almost all of them before the prices crashed.

'Some others I've turned into single-night lets now and we've got 52 rooms. It's for people who are on short contracts – construction or IT. They stay with us Monday to Thursday and then go home at the weekend. Little teams with a van and a week's work in the area use them. They were mortgaged but with the view to get out at the right time, which I did. I understood how the financial system is set up. They whip up credit and then it collapses. Boom and bust is part of the system.

'I feel really lucky. I have always been into photography and film, and I've been doing some filming. Last year I spent with the HTC-Columbia team [world champion Mark Cavendish's team at the time]. This year I've been filming GT2 motor racing. I enjoyed being with HTC-Columbia, and I do thank the guys, because they were really accommodating.

'It was great being with them, but I did see part of why cycling wasn't for me. It just doesn't let up. On one side, they have the Internet and TV and stuff to divert their minds, and they have so many staff and support that we didn't have, but they have even more cameras and tape recorders shoved in their faces, so it's not easy. The distances aren't as far as we did, but then again it's faster than we went. It's got to be the hardest sport out there.

'I got married in America and that never really worked out. Then a number of girlfriends, one big one that slipped away, and my girlfriend now. No kids. Too much flitting about and I never stayed in one spot long enough.

'I was thinking the other day, there's not one picture in my house of me cycling. I have kind of got this love–hate thing with the sport, and I think that happens to a lot of people. They get burned and they start to hate it and then they come back to it. Malcolm was very reserved and quiet and does his own thing. Adrian is exactly the same. I got on all right with everyone. I lost touch for 15 years and I didn't speak to anyone. Then Brian Holm, who's now manager of the HTC team, invited me to the Tour of Britain when he was with T-Mobile, to spend the week in the team car with him. That kind of got me back involved a bit.

'Look, 1987 was a golden moment . . . well, not a golden

moment, but a big moment in British cycling. And it was nice to be part of it, even if it didn't turn out the way I wanted. If you're a boxer, what do you do? Take more punches or throw the towel in? I'd taken way too many punches as it was.

'The article in *The Guardian* followed me for a long time. It upset a lot of people, a lot of people were pissed off by it, and it made me feel I'd let them all down. Kimmage and Festina came later . . . but I was there first and too early.'

Unlike Watson, Graham Jones found it difficult to leave cycling alone, even when approaching retirement. At the end of the '87 Tour, he went out to Australia for the Sun Tour with Malcolm Elliott, who had ridden it for a number of years. Past winners included Elliott himself, Shane Sutton and his brother Gary. In those days, there were two stages a day, with riders staying in people's houses, rather than in hotels, and, after his trials in Europe, it couldn't have been better for Jones. The six-day race was won by the Italian Stefano Tomasini, but Jones wasn't there to win, or even to compete at a significant level. He had gone for a week of rejuvenation. He ended up staying for four months.

He says: 'You'd do the afternoon stage and then a couple of you would meet someone and they'd drive you back to their house, give you a meal and a bed for the night, and then drive you to the start the next day. It was great and there was good money in it. I had no idea what I was going to be doing the following year. My girlfriend at the time, her dad had put this team together. He had been involved with the Viking pro team that Pat McQuaid had ridden for in the past. Even that year, when it came to road races, I showed I could do it. I could still perform at that level. But I think at that time the crit series was on the wane a bit, and the high point had gone a bit for the British pro scene.

'I stopped racing and went to work for the company I'd been riding for, putting bikes together and eventually becoming their procurement manager. The mountain-bike boom was happening at the time. Then I was doing quality control, going out to the factories in the Far East, in Malaysia and Taiwan, and I spent four months of the year out there.

'I went out to watch the Tour of Lancashire, the Nick O Pendle climb, and I bumped into Keith Bingham of *Cycling Weekly*. He said, "Do you fancy coming out to be a driver on the '89 Tour de France?" It was Keith, Geoffrey Nicholson and Sam Abt, and they'd had a driver lined up but he'd broken his leg, or maybe his arm, so they asked me. There was no money in it, but it would be all expenses paid. So it was back to the Tour.

'That was the LeMond against Fignon Tour, won by eight seconds by LeMond, and I enjoyed it so much I did that for a few years. Then in 1993, that was the year before the Tour de France was coming to England, they had a couple of VIP cars for guests, journalists or council people or sponsors, and I drove one of those. There used to be a thing in the Tour called "Kilometre 92", which was a buffet on the route, roughly 92 kilometres through each stage. So we used to go to the start and then we'd drive the route, stop for lunch at the buffet and then get to the finish and go to the press room. There was one of those at Saon, and I got introduced to Simon Brotherton, who had been invited down to see the 1993 Tour for a couple of days, and he was the one who beat down the doors at the BBC to say they should cover the Tour.

'He did it for BBC radio in 1994, but he ended up travelling with William and Alasdair Fotheringham, the journalists for *Cycling Weekly*, and they obviously had different agendas. It's hard work on the Tour and you can't share jobs like that. He ended up travelling with them to cut costs, but Will's idea was to go to the start, do the interviews, drive down the route at speed, stop for an hour-and-a-half lunch, then whizz to the finish. Simon was dumped out in the finish straight half an hour before the race was due to arrive and he hadn't seen anything! He had to do his report for the radio having seen none of it, and then he had to wait around while Will and Al filed their stories. So he persuaded the BBC that he needed a proper set-up with a producer and a driver/co-commentator. And they contacted me.

'I did my first one in 1995 and I've been doing it ever since. It pays reasonably well and I enjoy it. I'm not a big cycling fan these days, although I keep up with what's going on. But the one event I wouldn't miss is the Tour de France. It's something special, and I find it hard to imagine what it would be like to miss it.

'I met [race promoters and organisers] Alan Rushton and Mick Bennett, and I ended up doing team liaison at the Tour of Langkawi in 1998. Then they asked if I'd do the Radio Tour at the Tour of the Philippines. It was an amateur race, but it was 18 days. Then they said they'd be in touch before the PruTour, the Tour of Britain that was sponsored by Prudential. I did that in 1998 and 1999, but then the sponsor pulled the plug and it was back to zero again, picking up bits and bobs. I got some work with the American broadcaster OLN in the 2000s, working with Sherwen and Liggett. I did the Giro, Vuelta and Tou, and in early 2004 I got a call from Mick Bennett asking if I would help with the Tour of Britain. I didn't think it would take off, but that year I did virtually everything, from driving to commentating. It's gone from strength to strength.

'People knock us sometimes, but it's hard in this country to make a bike race happen. It's the most congested country in Europe and we have a public that doesn't appreciate bike racing the way they do in Europe. We go from the middle of Wales to the south of Wales on a weekday without proper road closures and without a public who are expecting it or understanding it. But we are making massive progress.

'I don't like blowing my own trumpet, but I have seen cycling from so many different sides. There's not many people who have the experience I've got – as a rider, working for the media and as a race organiser. There's pretty much nothing I haven't had a go at.'

Like Lord Lucan, Tony Capper first vanished, was spotted several times in several places all over Britain, and then disappeared again. So far, no one has managed to pin him down, which is, perhaps, what he wants.

'I heard he tried to set up another business, another franchise thing, but it didn't work,' says Micky Morrison. 'His stepbrother, Rod, had an ANC franchise in Bristol and I did hear he was a driver for Rod at one stage.'

Phil Griffiths says: 'Capper's down in the West Country, and I gather that in the end it didn't go so well for him. Amazingly, on the Tour of Britain last year, a guy came up to me and said, "Do you know who I am?" And I said, "Not a clue." He said, "I'm Grant Capper." It was Tony's son, one of the lads who had upset us so much on the Tour. I said, "You're not going to believe this," and I opened the team car door and Malcolm Elliott was there, still racing. He was just as surprised as I was.'

Of all the ANC staff and riders of '87, only Shane Sutton can claim that he has spotted the real Tony Capper. When Sutton was riding for his last team, Banana-Falcon, in Spain's Tour of Murcia in 1991, a familiar figure drove up alongside. Capper was prepared to chat about old times; Sutton was not.

He says: 'We were driving to Benidorm to do a training camp when he pulled up alongside us at the lights. I tell you, the guys had to hold me down to keep me in the van. I wanted to punch him in the guts. That was the last time I saw him, too.'

In the summer of 2011, I found the courage to take a train from Barrow-in-Furness to Sheffield to interview Malcolm

Elliott for this book. It was my first job of work in three years and, as I had feared, I made a few mistakes along the way. I waited for half an hour on the wrong platform in Barrow before being told that the train to Sheffield, via Preston and Manchester Piccadilly, was leaving from the opposite side. I had to ask guards at all three stations to tell me when to get off. But at least by then I knew who Malcolm Elliott was; three years previously, I couldn't even remember the name of my mother.

Like many writers, I thought I could carry on for ever. Writers don't have to retire at the age of 65, as long as they remain reasonably healthy. But of course nothing is written in stone.

In April 2008, I was woken in the middle of the night by a savage pain close to my left eye. When I looked in the bathroom mirror, one eye was looking in one direction and the other eye in another. I was single by then, and I found myself unable to work out how to use my mobile, or any telephone. After four hours of frustrating effort, I managed to get a suitcase and some clothing together and set off to Furness General Hospital. On the way to the nearest taxi rank, I walked straight into a little girl wandering in the opposite direction with her family. I hadn't seen her at all. The taxi drivers thought I was drunk and took the mickey out of me for about 20 minutes, but finally worked out where I was heading. The driver, a female, charged me £11 for a journey of less than a mile. That much I do recall.

It was an aphasia/stroke, and after three days in intensive care I had discovered I had lost the power of most of my speech and vision and could not read or write. In other words, I had become a two-year-old child overnight. Like most children of that age, I could not retrieve the names of objects and couldn't put words together into correct sentences.

'You sound like that guy who used to be on TV with all those nonsense words,' said a friend the day I went home after three months in hospital. He meant Stanley Unwin, the comic who invented his own words in classic lines like: 'If you've done an overstuffy in the tumloader, finish the job with a ladleho of brandy butter, then pukeit all the way to the toileybox.'

My friend wasn't far wrong. I still have a copy of my first attempt at an email, in July 2008, to another friend, a movie fan. It was worth keeping:

> Deer Steff,
>
> I was titillated by Tony Montana's assent threw the Cokaine cartels of Florida and South America in the mewvie Scarface: first he's hanging out with street dealers, then local Mister Big-tipe characters, before climbing to the top of the power pyramid where corrupt politicians teeter. Me own experiences at Upton Park parrallell that exactly.

Precisely.

The staff at Furness General Hospital were marvellous, but obviously I wanted to get out as soon as possible. Equally obviously, under the circumstances, they wanted me to stay as long as possible.

'Come on, Mr Connor, time for today's test. Let's see if you can make us a cup of tea and if you get it right this time we might ask the doctor if we can let you go. That's right, find the kettle. No, the kettle, Mr Connor, not the toaster. That's right, now a bottle of milk. *Milk*, Mr Connor, not the bleach.'

And so it went on, until finally I managed to make a cup of tea for the nurses, I could walk up and down stairs without falling and, having lost two stone in weight, I could start eating properly again.

Aphasia, however, takes a lot of beating. A year later, finally able to watch TV, my favourite programmes were *Copycats* and *Fab Lab*. *Blue Peter* was beyond me and it took me ages to correctly answer one of the opening questions in *The Weakest Link*. The speech and language therapist at Furness General Hospital can laugh with me now when she recalls my score of one out of twelve in her animal-naming test. I got 'dog' right, but that was it.

My writing career seemed to be over – until Google came to the rescue. It was ludicrously difficult, and took a long time, but I managed to work out some sort of writing method. Composing a short text about Lourdes, the famous Hollywood movie closely connected with the city and the star of a film I have seen dozens of times should have been easy. But I couldn't remember any of the details, except that the woman had once been married to a famous Hollywood producer who had produced a famous film that had starred a famous actor known as 'the King of Hollywood', the only helpful words that came to mind. Simple after that: look up 'the King of Hollywood' on Google; follow that to Clark Gable on IMDb; go from there to *Gone with the Wind* on IMDb; find the name of the producer of *Gone with the Wind*; look up David O. Selznick; find the details of his career and his marriages; click on the name of Jennifer Jones; discover that she starred in *The Song of Bernadette* and that should bring you back to Lourdes. I also found it wise to write down her name and the other details I needed immediately . . . because everything would have been forgotten within a few seconds.

With little else to do, it was the sort of challenge I began to relish, and it could have been a lot worse. I wasn't going to drive again, but aphasia has far worse ways of badly damaging its victims, notably their efforts at normal conversation. There was always the fear that people (in particular taxi drivers) would be convinced that you were either drunk or senile, someone who had been let out for the day. For two years, close friends and family apart, I didn't want to talk to anyone – until I climbed on the train to Sheffield to see Malcolm Elliott, his wife and their two young children. It was an ordeal for me (probably for them, too), but at least I had warned them in advance. It did me an immense amount of good in the end.

Apart from his large house, a beautiful family and the fact that he seemed to have gone off fast cars some time in the past ten years, nothing much had changed with Elliott. He had the suntan, the same long bleached blond hair, the same weight (around 12 stone), and the same slow, flat-footed, energy-saving shuffle I had come to associate with pro cyclists in 1987. I recalled that of the 2,629 miles and 25 stages of the '87 Tour, winner Stephen Roche probably walked less than 800 yards. Pro cyclists do not like walking – and Elliott, close to his 50th birthday, was still a pro cyclist.

'You got our Malcolm off to a tee,' his mother had said when I met her in the Elliott family home in Sheffield two years after the '87 Tour. And if a mum says that of a book, you must have got something right. Like Paul Watson and Phil Griffiths, Elliott has always been quite canny with money, despite the problems he has had down the years with teams that have gone bust or simply refused to pay him. When I first persuaded him in 1989 to travel to London by train with me to see the publishers of his autobiography, Pelham Books, Elliott was appalled when I insisted on paying for first class. At the time, I thought of him as a typical tight Yorkshireman, but in fact he is just a shrewd Yorkshireman.

His good friend Phil Griffiths agrees: 'At the end of 1985, ANC were getting ganged up on quite a lot by other pro teams, which is a natural process in races. Capper said, "What are we going to do about this?"

'I said: "Well, there's one rider, a young rider, in the UK, who I'd like to sign."

'Capper did listen, he did take on board what I knew about cycling, at this point anyway. So I invited Malcolm down to meet us after a crit in Hanley.

'Before the meeting, Capper had a piece of paper and he put it face down on the table. He said to me, "This Elliott guy, what are we paying him?"

'And I said, "Whatever he asks for."

'Capper was amazed at that statement, but I told him, "Well, if Malc is on £12,000 at Raleigh, he'll ask for £14,000. If he's on £13K he'll ask for £15K. He's going to ask for more than he's on now, but he's not going to be thinking too far out of the box."

'Malcolm came down and asked for £14,000 plus bonuses, plus the insurance on his Porsche. Capper immediately agreed and said, "Fine."

'Malcolm then hesitated and said, "Er, well, I need time to think about it."

'Capper tore up his piece of paper. It was only a symbolic thing, but he ripped it up and said, "Let's start this conversation again. How much would you like to ride for ANC in 1986, to sign today?"

'Malcolm put another £2,000 on the bill and signed it away. Capper was laughing at Malcolm's approach and attitude. He loved that kind of thing. His thing was that you should ask for what you were worth.'

Unlike many sportsmen who find it difficult to cope with life outside of sport and its rules, Elliott managed to retire and spend several years 'off the rails' before starting to race at a high level again.

In 2004, he was still good enough to beat a young Mark Cavendish, the world road race champion in 2011, to the first stage in Ireland's Rás, and the picture of that has pride of place in his Sheffield study. He and his wife Clare have a large house atop one of the city's many hills, and plainly Elliott has put some thought into this. His two girls go to local schools – one of them at the bottom of his garden – and his mother lives close by. His current team, Motorpoint, supply him with a car and, after a cycling career that has lasted more than 20 years, life could hardly be better.

'Until I got married and had the first child in 2002 I had been really off the rails for a few years and the family really gave me a new purpose,' he says. 'Life evolves, you know, and anyway you can only do that for so long. You get bored in the end. The girls watch the Tour now and they ask, "Are you in this, Daddy?" I tell them I have ridden it – about twenty-five years ago – and at six and nine they can't really grasp that. They see photos on the wall of me in the Tour of Britain throwing champagne at everyone and they say, "Daddy, you're making a real mess of that!" And, worst of all, "Why doesn't Daddy bring trophies home now?"

'Phil Griffiths had gone on the Étape du Tour early in 2003 and persuaded me to have a go, and I finished 100th on a few weeks' training. I had had five and a half years out, but I went out on a couple of Sundays, then started training to enter a few masters races, then I took it from there. I was 36 when I finished the first time, and I doubt if I would have been as good now if I hadn't dropped out.'

Elliott was 15 when he first discovered cycling, using his sister's bike – until he managed to break it. 'Dad started pushing me to join a cycling touring club and, like a lot of cyclists, they were an odd bunch, but when I met up with the Rutland Club they decided I had some talent. But there was no agenda of becoming a pro. My parents separated when I was seven, but they stayed close. The best thing about the '87 and '88 Tours was they got back together – after 20 years apart. The Tour had everything to do with that, as they came over to see me in France. Dad died in 2002, aged 74, but Mum is still close by.

'Most of my mates are around here. Do you remember in the book when you wrote that I said, "Pass us my helmet, I feel aggressive today." When I meet my mates now, they always say, "Are you feeling aggressive today, Malc?" It's a standard joke for them now.'

It was at Troyes during the '87 Tour that I realised Elliott might be Britain's best sprinter, but he was poles apart from dedicated professionals like a Kelly or a Millar. While the rest of the ANC team took off for shower, massage and food, Elliott persuaded Griffiths to drive him to see a mate who ran a garage in the town.

He also saved the life of an Italian – Griffiths had wanted to throw him out of the car door window – who was working for the Del Tongo team and had asked for a lift to his hotel in Troyes. ANC's hotel was in Romilly, several miles away, and the Italian eventually said, 'You go wrong way.'

'What do you mean, wrong way?' asked Griffiths.

'I go to station hotel,' said the Italian. 'You go there too.'

'No, Romilly, Romilly,' roared Griffiths. 'We go to Romilly.'

'No, my hotel in Troyes,' said our frightened passenger.

'You mean you wanted me to drive you 200 yards from the finish to your poxy hotel?'

'Throw him out here,' demanded Elliott. 'What a wanker.'

As so often, Elliott could not stay angry for long, and he persuaded a reluctant Griffiths to take the Italian back to town.

'Nexta time . . . you walka,' said Elliott in his best Italian.

He could be tough at times, particularly to a 'civilian'. After his near miss in the sprint into Avignon, I, mistakenly, asked him, 'Did van Poppel go past you and the rest?', meaning, did he come from behind or did he lead the sprint out?

Elliott replied, with heavy sarcasm, 'Of course he came past, he finished first, didn't he?'

I gave back as good as I had got, after that we got on fine, and suddenly we discovered we were friends.

He still regards the Tour of '87 as the most memorable few days of his cycling career: 'On the first day in the Alps, Steve Swart had gone, leaving just four ANC survivors, and it had become a matter of honour for everyone to finish.

Having got that far, we were close to being able to say, "Yes, I finished the Tour de France," rather than, "Yes, I rode it, but I didn't finish it."

'In the last week, when you try and think back to the start, it seems a lifetime ago. So much happens in those three weeks, every day is a whole story, twenty-one chapters in your life in as many days. After the first day, I was too smashed to form an opinion about the way things were being done by Capper and the staff. Being dissatisfied with something takes away your energy and you can't afford that. Personally, I think they did an admirable job, given what they had to put up with, and ANC were no worse than a lot of Spanish teams I joined later.

'Capper? Well, I saw him around at various races in '85 before I joined ANC, and I got into talks with Griffo about the possibility of joining ANC the year after. There were no issues with late payments for me in '87 because my contract was with ANC. Guys like Shane were contracted to Action Sports and they didn't get anything.

'Capper was a bit of a slob, but he meant business. His personal habits left a lot to be desired, but he had an endearing quality and he got the best out of people. Over the years, I have never had a beef with him. I mellowed a long time ago and I would be happy to meet him again.

'After the Tour of '87, my head had gone. I was supposed to take part in the Kellogg's Tour of Britain ten days after I came back from France, but I borrowed an ANC car and went to Biarritz with some mates. I did some sunbathing and had late nights and bingeing. Back home, during the Kellogg's, two suits approached me in the Holiday Inn in Birmingham and announced themselves as agents for ANC. Mr Capper had nothing to do with ANC any more, they said, and offered me £350 to carry on. Halfords said they were keen to run a new team, but I found them hard to pin down.

'However, most cyclists will tell you you can't just down

tools, because it could affect your career – and most team owners know that. I went on the Nissan Tour of Ireland and I was back in the old habit of staying up until 5 a.m. and then racing a few hours later. Amazingly, I felt like shit when the first stage started but then somehow managed to win it. I found myself a wanted man again all of a sudden, and Z-Peugeot, Hitachi and Système U all made approaches.

'It was usual in cycling then to do all your business deals on the roadside during a race. Eventually, I went for Fagor and Roche, or rather Roche and Fagor. When I saw Stephen after the Nissan in Dublin, he said, "You'll be riding with Fagor, so don't sign for anyone else."

'When I went to the Fagor press conference in San Sebastián in January '88, within a couple of hours I was wishing I was back with Capper and ANC. The Fagor owners wanted Roche's mates, Patrick Valcke and Phillipe Crépel, out as *directeur sportif* and team manager. From then on, it was a war between Roche and Miguel Gomez, the commercial director of Fagor. Roche had had a recurrence of a knee injury and, once the doctors had been into his knee again, Gomez and his gang got rid of Valcke. With all this bedlam going on, the Fagor management said I was going to ride the Tour de France again.

'I didn't get a stage win, as van Poppel was in his prime, with four wins, and things didn't go too well for Fagor. Sean Yates slaughtered everyone in the individual time trial at Lieven, but Bob Millar was on his way to a win in the Blagnac–Guzet-Neige stage in the Pyrenees when a gendarme sent him up the *déviation* for the team cars. Three days later, Millar climbed off and, just like ANC a year earlier, we finished with four riders in Paris. At least I could say I had finished two Tours.'

Elliott has never been lucky with cycling management down the years. After ANC failed in 1987, Fagor fell apart on the back of Roche's inability to race through injury. He won the Vuelta a España points classification with another

Spanish team, Teka, in 1989, but he was soon on the move again, this time to the United States. The way things are going, he will soon have had more cycling team managers than Ernest Borgnine has had film directors – and Ernest Borgnine is still working at the age of 95.

'I had some good times in the States with Chevrolet in 1997, but then it became a repeat of ANC ten years earlier. I was paid for the first three months then the money dried up. "Can you race for nothing?" they asked me. It was a shambles and it was run by a bit of a dick. A temporary situation became permanent. Something similar happened when I joined Comptel–Colorado Cyclist and they had financial trouble. I decided to retire at the end of '97 when I was 36.

'For the next five years, I bought a few properties with a mate in the building business and my father-in-law. I do some cycling now for Griffo and Motorpoint. I had intended to retire when I was 50, but I guess I can't beat the bug.

'I'll never forget the Tour of '87, and it played a huge part in my life, along with those of all the riders and probably the staff, too. Do you recall Swart's last night in Morzine after the last Alpine stage? The Tour was over for him and I went over to console him. I was going to miss him. Apart from anything else we were moving from a majority of riders to a minority. By then, we were outnumbered by staff three to one. Swart, though, was as cool as ever.

'"It's no big deal," he said. "In 25 years' time, it won't matter to anyone. No one will remember it." Maybe he was wrong about that one.'

APPENDICES

OVERALL

1. Stephen Roche (IRE), Carrera, 115 hours, 27 mins, 42 secs (4,231 kilometres at 36.645 kph)
2. Pedro Delgado (SPA), PDM, at 40 secs
3. Jean-François Bernard (FRA), Toshiba-Look, at 2 mins, 13 secs
4. Charly Mottet (FRA), Système U, at 6 mins, 40 secs
5. Luis Herrera (COL), Café de Colombia, at 9 mins, 32 secs
6. Fabio Parra (COL), Café de Colombia, at 16 mins, 53 secs
7. Laurent Fignon (FRA), Système U, at 18 mins, 24 secs
8. Anselmo Fuerte (SPA), BH, at 18 mins, 33 secs
9. Raul Alcala (MEX), 7-Eleven, at 21 mins, 49 secs
10. Marino Lejarreta (SPA), Caja-Rural, at 26 mins, 13 secs
70. Adrian Timmis (GB), ANC-Halfords, at 2 hours, 19 mins, 21 secs
94. Malcolm Elliott (GB), ANC-Halfords at 2 hours, 48 mins, 39 secs
103. Kvetoslav Palov (CZE), ANC-Halfords, at 2 hours, 59 mins, 4 secs
133. Guy Gallopin (FRA), ANC-Halfords, at 3 hours, 49 mins, 48 secs
Started: 207
Finished: 135

STAGE WINNERS AND LOSERS

A total of 23 teams and 207 riders from 22 different nations began the Tour de France of 1987. After 25 stages and 2,629 miles, 135 finally arrived in Paris. In terms of survival rate, the most successful teams were Système U of France and Café de Colombia, which both finished with their full complement of nine. The least successful were the Italian Supermercati and the Colombian Ryalco squads, which finished with two riders each.

Prologue: 1 July, West Berlin, time trial, 6.1 km
Winner: Jelle Nijdam
Yellow jersey: Jelle Nijdam

Stage 1: 2 July, West Berlin, circuit race, 105.5 km
Winner: Nico Verhoeven
Yellow jersey: Lech Piasecki

Stage 2: 2 July, West Berlin, team time trial, 40.5 km
Winners: Carrera
Yellow jersey: Lech Piasecki

Stage 3: 4 July, Karlsruhe–Stuttgart, 219 km
Winner: Acacio da Silva
Yellow jersey: Erich Maechler

Stage 4: 5 July, Stuttgart–Pforzheim, 79 km
Winner: Herman Frison
Yellow jersey: Erich Maechler

Stage 5: 5 July, Pforzheim–Strasbourg, 112.5 km
Winner: Marc Sergeant
Yellow jersey: Erich Maechler

Stage 6: 6 July, Strasbourg–Épinal, 169 km
Winner: Christophe Lavainne
Yellow jersey: Erich Maechler

Stage 7: 7 July, Épinal–Troyes, 211 km
Winner: Manuel-Jorge Dominguez
Yellow jersey: Erich Maechler

Stage 8: 8 July, Troyes–Épinay-sous-Senart, 205.5 km
Winner: Jean-Paul van Poppel
Yellow jersey: Erich Maechler

Stage 9: 9 July, Orléans–Renaze, 260 km
Winner: Adri Van der Poel
Yellow jersey: Erich Maechler

Stage 10: 10 July, Saumur–Futuroscope, time trial, 87.5 km
Winner: Stephen Roche
Yellow jersey: Charly Mottet

Stage 11: 11 July, Poitiers–Chaumeil, 255 km
Winner: Martial Gayant
Yellow jersey: Martial Gayant

Stage 12: 12 July, Brive La Gaillarde–Bourdeaux, 228 km
Winner: Davis Phinney
Yellow jersey: Martial Gayant

Stage 13: 13 July, Bayonne–Pau, 219 km
Winner: Erik Breukink
Yellow jersey: Charly Mottet

Stage 14: 14 July, Pau–Luz Ardiden, 166 km
Winner: Dag Otto Lauritzen
Yellow jersey: Charly Mottet

Stage 15: 15 July, Tarbes–Blagnac, 164 km
Winner: Rolf Golz
Yellow jersey: Charly Mottet

Stage 16: 16 July, Blagnac–Millau, 216.5 km
Winner: Régis Clère
Yellow jersey: Charly Mottet

Stage 17: 17 July, Millau–Avignon, 239 km
Winner: Jean-Paul van Poppel
Yellow jersey: Charly Mottet

Stage 18: 19 July, Carpentras–Le Ventoux, time trial, 36.5 km
Winner: Jean-François Bernard
Yellow jersey: Jean-François Bernard

Stage 19: 20 July, Villard-de-Lans–Aix-les-Bains, 185 km
Winner: Pedro Delgado
Yellow jersey: Stephen Roche

Stage 20: 21 July, Villard-de-Lans–L'Alpe d'Huez, 201 km
Winner: Federico Echave
Yellow jersey: Pedro Delgado

Stage 21: 22 July, Bourg d'Oisans–La Plagne, 185.5 km
Winner: Laurent Fignon
Yellow jersey: Pedro Delgado

Stage 22: 23 July, La Plagne–Morzine, 186 km
Winner: Eduardo Chozas
Yellow jersey: Pedro Delgado

Stage 23: 24 July, St-Julien-en-Genevois–Dijon, 224.5 km
Winner: Régis Clère
Yellow jersey: Pedro Delgado

Stage 24: 25 July, Dijon, time trial, 38 km
Winner: Jean-François Bernard
Yellow jersey: Stephen Roche

Stage 25: 26 July, Creteil–Paris, 192 km
Winner: Jeff Pierce
Yellow jersey: Stephen Roche

PRIZES

Total prize money in the Tour amounted to about £630,000 (Lance Armstrong's yearly tax bills these days) split into 21 different categories. The main winners were:

Overall winner (yellow jersey): Stephen Roche (Ireland), £18,000 and a holiday flat in the Pyrenees worth £12,000, plus a Peugeot 405 SR Injection worth £11,500

Points classification for the number of highest finishes (green jersey): Jean-Paul van Poppel (Holland), £3,200

Best climber (polka-dot jersey): Luis Herrera (Colombia), £1,800

Best young rider under 24 (white jersey): Raul Alcala (Mexico), £1,500

Intermediate Catch sprints (red jersey): Gilbert Duclos-Lasalle (France), £1,000

Performance classification (multicoloured jersey): Jean-François Bernard (France), £2,000

Best time triallist: Jean-François Bernard, £1,800

Overall team winners: Système U (France), £4,000

Overall team points winners: Système U (France), £1,300

Each stage winner won a cash prize of £1,800, a diamond-studded map of France worth £2,000, plus a Peugeot Junior car worth £4,500. French bank Credit Lyonnais gave an extra £5,000 to the overall winner and £3,000 to the best young rider.

In addition there were:

A prize of £1,500, the Henri Desgrange Prize, for the first rider across the Col du Galibier on Stage 21

A prize of £1,000, the Charles de Gaulle Prize, for the first rider to reach de Gaulle's birthplace at Colombey-les-Deux-Églises on Stage 7

A prize of £150 for the sprint winner on the Champs-Elysées on Stage 25

A prize of £350 for the rider voted the most affable on the Tour by his fellow riders

A prize of £800 for the rider considered the most combative

FINES

The *commissaires* handed out fines on a daily basis. The most numerous, along with typical penalties, were:

Dangerous driving by a *directeur sportif*: £75
Pushing a rider: £11 for the rider and £80 for the *directeur sportif*
Pacing a rider with the team car: £19 for the rider and £80 for the *directeur sportif*
Opening a team car door on the left: £37
Not displaying a competitor's number: £19
Not signing on before a stage: £11
Having two team cars in the first rank of the race convoy: £10
Throwing rubbish out of the car window close to the *peloton*: £10
Feeding from the team car in the *peloton*: £10

Three riders – Guido Bontempi, Dietrich Thurau and Silvano Contini – were found guilty of doping. As first offenders, they were each fined £500, given a ten-minute time penalty, placed last in the relevant stage and handed a one-month suspended ban from the sport.

The *directeur sportif* of Système U, Cyrille Guimard, was thrown out of Stage 23 because his team descended from La Plagne in their vehicles instead of on their bikes.

THE TEAMS

The teams that competed in the 1987 Tour de France, in order of success that season.

Toshiba-Look-La Vie Claire (France)
Carrera Jeans (Italy)
Hitachi-Marc-Rossin (Belgium)
Z-Peugeot (France)
BH (Spain)
PDM (Holland)
Système U (France)
Reynolds-Seur-Sada (Spain)
Teka (Spain)
Ryalco-Manzana-Postobon (Colombia)
RMO-Meral-Mavic (France)
Caja-Rural-Orbea (Spain)
Fagor (France)
Café de Colombia (Colombia)
Superconfex-Kwantum-Yoko (Holland)
Panasonic-Isostar (Holland)
Del Tongo-Colnago (Italy)
Kas-Miko-Mavic (Spain)
Joker-Emerxil-Eddy Merckx (Belgium)
7-Eleven-Hoonved (US)
Roland-Skala-Chiori (Belgium)
Supermercati Brianzoli-Chateau d'Ax (Italy)

ANC-Halfords-Lycra (Great Britain)
Directeurs sportifs: Ward Woutters and Phil Griffiths
221 Malcolm Elliott
*222 Bernard Chesneau
223 Guy Gallopin
*224 Graham Jones
225 Kvetoslav Palov
*226 Shane Sutton
*227 Steve Swart
228 Adrian Timmis
*229 Paul Watson

*Abandoned